Custodians of Conscience

Custodians of Conscience

Investigative Journalism and Public Virtue

James S. Ettema and Theodore L. Glasser

Columbia University Press
New York

330000000 661
070.4
ETT   '03

Columbia University Press
Publishers Since 1893
New York   Chichester, West Sussex
Copyright © 1998 Columbia University Press
All rights reserved

Library of Congress Cataloging-in-Publication Data
Ettema, James S.
   Custodians of conscience : investigative journalism and public
virtue / James S. Ettema and Theodore L. Glasser.
      p. cm.
   Includes bibliographical references and index.
   ISBN 0–231–10674–2 (cloth). — ISBN 0–231–10675–0 (pbk.)
   1. Investigative reporting.   2. Journalism—Objectivity.
   3. Journalists—Interviews.   I. Glasser, Theodore Lewis.   II. Title.
PN4781.E88   1998
070.4'3—dc21   97–39066

∞

Printed in the United States of America

c 10 9 8 7 6 5 4 3 2 1
p 10 9 8 7 6 5 4 3 2 1

For our parents
Marilyn and John Ettema
Adele and Philip Sokolowsky
and in memory of
Alfred Glasser

Contents

Preface

This book is the result of a scholarly and friendly collaboration that has spanned more than a decade—a collaboration between us, the authors, of course, but also with the journalists whose thoughtful commentary and distinguished reporting are recorded here. Our project began in the 1980s at the University of Minnesota, where we both had faculty appointments in the School of Journalism and Mass Communication. Specifically, it began as a pilot study, funded by the University of Minnesota Graduate School, of WCCO Television's "I-Team," an investigative reporting unit at the CBS affiliate in Minneapolis. With this case study we gained additional funding from what was then the Gannett Foundation, now the Freedom Forum, that we used to interview award-winning investigative reporters across the United States. Those interviews continued through the mid-1990s.

For whatever it's worth, ours is a study of journalists designated by other journalists as among the best reporters doing the best reporting. For our interviews we sought out newspaper and television reporters whose investigations had won national recognition from their peers: a Pulitzer Prize, an Investigative Reporters and Editors (IRE) award, or an Alfred I. duPont–Columbia University Award in Television and Radio Journalism. And among those, we sought out reporters recommended by other reporters. Not everyone recommended could be interviewed, of course, but everyone we interviewed had earned the respect of others who practice the craft.

In the interviews we focused extensively on the reporting of the award-winning stories. Our intention was to ground our discussions in the actual experiences of journalists rather than (or, at least, in addition to) the conventional wisdom of journalism. As it turned out, the interviews were extended, often rambling conversations with likable people who, though typically modest about their accomplishments, had interesting things to say about them. Most interviews lasted the better part of a day, and a few continued beyond that. We taped and transcribed all the interviews, creating a useful if unwieldy archive of quotes, anecdotes, lists, metaphors, examples, explanations, illustrations, and pontifications—theirs and ours.

We approached each interview with the conviction of ethnographers committed to sorting out journalists' "structures of signification," to borrow from Clifford Geertz's description of social anthropology. We did our best to let our "informants" say what they wanted to say and to say it in their own words; it wasn't so much a question-and-answer format (though we asked questions and they provided answers) as it was an elaborate, open-ended conversation that we tried to steer in directions we found interesting. These conversations in turn became the basis for our "data," which are, to turn to Geertz again, "really our own constructions of other people's constructions of what they and their compatriots are up to."[1]

It's difficult to reconstruct the evolution of this project with any precision, except to say that where we ended up is a considerable distance from where we began. From time to time we changed our minds, shifted our thinking, disagreed, argued, and generally pursued this work without really knowing, though always wondering, where exactly it would go and what in the end we would agree to say about it. As we continued to read related and unrelated work, we saw new opportunities for analysis and interpretation and new possibilities for saying something interesting—maybe even important—about press practices and performance. To be sure, serendipity played an incalculably exciting role in the development of our work; we did not know when we began that Paul Fussell's analysis of literary irony in *The Great War and Modern Memory*, to take but one prominent example, would aid our study of investigative reporting.

Although we have reported on this research over the years here in the United States and abroad, through lectures, symposia, convention papers, and journal articles, we never intended to publish this work serially and then reconstitute it in book form. From the beginning we imagined a book-length treatment of this project, something that would give us the space and place to bring it all together within whatever framework we thought we could provide. At the same time we were eager to see what made sense to others; we wanted to know which claims seemed strong and which ones seemed weak, which interpretations seemed compelling and which ones seemed lame, which arguments made a difference and which ones didn't. These were judgments we didn't want to make entirely on our own. This book, then, benefits from our previously published work but extends it considerably. It is not a map to our thinking over the years but rather an occasion to share our current thinking. Most material in most chapters appears here for the first time. Even in the three chapters for which we draw extensively from material that first appeared else-where,[2] the analysis we offer here, thanks in part to what others have been able to do (or not do) with our work, is substantially revised and expanded.

Our project has been truly a collaborative effort—not in the simple sense of something we worked on together but in the deeper sense of having produced something together that neither of us could have produced alone. It has benefited from a distinctive combination of interests and insights, preferences and proclivities. If we were conglomerates explaining the benefits of a merger, we'd say something about synergy, but we're not, so we won't. But we would like to say that we had fun, and learned a lot, working with each other. We also would like to say that we learned a lot from our students and from many colleagues who shared insights and ideas with us. We have acknowledged—though hardly repaid—our intellectual debt to some of them, at least, by citing their work in the chapters that follow. To all of them, and to the reporters who were extraordinarily generous with their thoughts as well as their time, we offer our thanks.

JAMES S. ETTEMA
Northwestern University

THEODORE L. GLASSER
Stanford University

Custodians of Conscience

1

Introduction:
The Reporter's Craft as
Moral Discourse

Nightmares come to us now as the news: a woman is riding alone in the elevator of a Chicago Housing Authority apartment building when the elevator stops abruptly. From the trapdoor in the ceiling, two men point a gun and order her to undress. "I tripped across the elevator floor to the buttons to get the elevator to move or alarm to go off, and no button, no alarm, nothing worked," she later tells a television reporter. "I stood there on the elevator, naked, in the dark, and it's almost like waiting on Judgment Day because you know somebody's going to come in there after you when there's nothing you can do." The men rape her.

Also in Chicago two men grab a teenager on the way home. She too is raped. "The taller guy, the bigger one with the blond hair, he raped me first," she recalls for the reporter. "I said, 'I'm not fighting you back. Just don't kill me and don't hurt me.'" She also recalls that the attackers laughed at her as she bled and cried.

These are nightmares-become-real for the victims, but only mass-mediated bad dreams for the rest of us. Many such images of savagery and suffering race through the fevered public consciousness of television news before slipping away into the institutional memory of police reports and crime statistics. However, these images of crime became more than computerized memory traces when they were recorded by a journalist, Pam Zekman, widely regarded by her peers as one of the best investigative reporters in broadcast journalism.

In a distinguished career that took her from newspapers to television in a great town for news, Zekman has demonstrated mastery of a journalistic genre that invests such images not only with human interest but with public significance. She gave public moral meaning to the experience of the woman on the Chicago Housing Authority (CHA) elevator, for example, by juxtaposing it with accounts of men who should have repaired and maintained elevators but did not. In a series of reports entitled "Elevator Rip-off: An Open and Shut Case" Zekman introduced her viewers to a number of these men:

> This is George McNamara. He's a Westinghouse elevator mechanic assigned to work on CHA elevators; paid nearly $19 an hour.
>
> McNamara claims he was hard at work on the day we took these pictures. His time sheet says he spent the entire 8-hour day working on elevators in seven CHA buildings. But for 4 1/2 hours that day he was nowhere near an elevator. He spent most of that time at a sandwich shop he owns with his wife.
>
> McNamara is not an isolated example of a payroll cheat. Our investigation found that at least 25 men—nearly half the Westinghouse mechanics and supervisors assigned to the projects—are ripping off the CHA.[1]

As the story unfolded, viewers saw videotape of one worker after another entering a bar or just sitting in the car during the workday. In interviews several workers said they sometimes took the afternoon off just to get away from the housing projects. Others said they went to bars to consult with their supervisors. Meanwhile, a newly appointed CHA official blamed both the labor union and the Westinghouse company for the four hundred injuries and twenty deaths during the the previous fifteen years. He vowed to take quick action. A union official, however, maintained that the workers were doing their job—until he was confronted with the videotaped evidence. Company officials had no comment. And in the midst of all this official evasion and obfuscation, viewers heard a mother say of her young son, who fell thirteen stories to his death when an elevator door swung open at the bottom, "The way my baby went, I don't feel that it should have ever happened."

Another synthesis of hard facts and righteous indignation was Zekman's account of the rape of the homeward-bound teenager. In the series entitled "Killing Crime: A Police Cop-Out," the reporter found the public moral meaning of that case, along with more than a thousand other rape cases from the previous year, in the fact that the cases, at first, were denied any meaning at all:

In police jargon, the complaints were "unfounded"—as if to tell nearly half the women who reported rapes that the rapes never happened. Chicago's unfounding rate is six times higher than other major cities we studied. To find out why, we obtained confidential police reports. The reports show how the police cover up the true number of rapes. They do it by discounting medical evidence, eyewitness accounts and, worst of all, the victim's own story.[2]

As this story unfolded, viewers learned that the teenager was treated at a hospital for bruises, bleeding, and vaginal lacerations serious enough to require surgery, yet detectives reported that her story was a fabrication. And in another case detectives ignored the report of a witness who came to the aid of a rape victim who ran naked from an alley screaming for help. Viewers heard police officers say that "killing" the reports of difficult-to-solve rapes, robberies, and burglaries is standard operating procedure for keeping the crime rate down. Next, they heard the superintendent of police boast of Chicago's success in controlling crime. And finally, they heard the voice of the victim: "They just let it go. They didn't care. So a rapist is loose on the street, doing more harm. Right?"

A Morally Engaged Voice

Investigative journalists, as Zekman demonstrates, can issue a compelling call for public moral indignation. Their particular sort of reporting yields stories that are carefully verified and skillfully narrated accounts of specific injury and injustice but stories with a meaning that always transcends the facts of the particular case. Their stories call attention to the breakdown of social systems and the disorder within public institutions that cause injury and injustice; in turn, their stories implicitly demand the response of public officials—and the public itself—to that breakdown and disorder. Thus the work of these reporters calls us, as a society, to decide what is, and what is not, an outrage to our sense of moral order and to consider our expectations for our officials, our institutions, and ultimately ourselves.

In this way investigative journalists are custodians of public conscience.[3] To think of journalists in this way, however, is not to suppose that they can, all on their own, repair systemic breakdown or clean up institutional disorder. They are not, after all, the keepers of the legislative and legal machinery necessary to complete the task of civic reform. And neither is it to suppose that journalists are moral arbiters who can decide, all on their own, how everyone else ought to behave. They are not the guardians of some superior moral knowledge. Rather, these journalists hold the means to report and disseminate stories that can engage the public's sense of right and wrong. These journalists are, in other words, custodians of exactly what we imagine conscience to be: a morally engaged voice.

The particular voice of Pam Zekman has long been heard in Chicago on WBBM-TV. In a small office where Emmy and duPont-Columbia awards casually serve as bookends and paperweights for the directories and files that are everywhere, she talked about her kind of journalism. "I look for a subject, first of all, that is going to affect a broad spectrum of people, a subject that they can relate to," she said. "I look for something that is more than just a single individual who may be hurting a small group of people." This reporter's goal, however, is not simply audience appeal. "I look to whether or not it's an area where something needs to be done," she continued. "Is there a need for regulation? Is there a need for legislation? Is there a need for stepped-up enforcement by some governmental agency that's not doing its job?"

Zekman's criteria for a good investigative story are nowhere better exemplified than in "Killing Crime: A Police Cop-Out." With a note of pride in her work she reviewed the origin and the outcome of that story:

> The "killing" of crime reports was something that black policemen had been screaming about for years. Nobody had paid much attention to it, but I wanted to show that it affected more than just low-income residents. The story was about a pervasive problem, a scandal in the police department, that was not necessarily the doing of one individual but was systematic pressure to kill crime reports exerted from the top. . . .
>
> [Police Superintendent] Brzeczek got up at his last press conference before he resigned and announced that his audit had not only confirmed our findings but more. It was the first time in my entire career that a public official had gotten up and admitted that everything we said—and more—was true. They completely changed the whole reporting system in the police department.

Investigative journalism, in Zekman's hands, is socially concerned, but its focus is not on abstract social issues. She is concerned with the poorest of Chicago's citizens and the safety of Chicago's streets, but her stories do not analyze The Poverty Issue or The Crime Issue. Rather, her reports are accounts of people who were harmed when certain individuals and agencies failed to properly maintain public housing and of crimes covered up when the police department violated FBI reporting guidelines. "There are lots of stories about social issues that are interesting," she said, "but unless they have that investigative edge, I'm not interested." For Zekman that edge is the exact combination of public importance and individual wrongdoing exemplified by a series of reports entitled "License to Deal." Work on that series began, Zekman recalled, the way many investigations do:

> The "License to Deal" series began as a tip—a complaint by a community group about one clinic. I wouldn't be interested in doing that story if it was only one clinic, but we did some preliminary research and discovered that it wasn't just one clinic. It was a chain of clinics—and the more we got into it, the bigger it grew.
>
> And then we learned that the combination of drugs that was being given out was "loads." It was something that had been a big problem in L.A. and then in New Jersey and now it was in Chicago. So, now I had a situation where I didn't have just one community being affected by one bad clinic, I had fourteen clinics all over the city. I had a major new drug being abused in Chicago that had not been previously exposed. And then on top of that I had Medicaid fraud.

In short, "License to Deal" was not an analysis of drug trafficking but a tale of doctors and pharmacists gone bad. "Some people would argue that I pick subjects for the villains and the heroes," Zekman concluded. "One of the things that really fascinated me in 'License to Deal' was the morality of those people—doctors, pharmacists, owners—who could exploit addiction so callously." Zekman is, then, a reporter who wants to reveal significant instances of systemic breakdown and institutional disorder, but she also wants her revelations to flow from gripping stories about the machinations of villains and the plight of victims.

Investigative reporters are masters of the personal story with a public moral. "There are some investigative reporters who really love stories about a politician with his hand in the till," said Loretta Tofani, another reporter who demonstrated mastery of this journalistic genre. "I'm not so interested in that, although wrongdoing of officials ends up becoming a substantial part of my stories. I'm not interested so much in individual acts of wrongdoing as systemwide problems—how a system breaks down." Here, then, is another intellectual heir to the muckraking tradition of Progressive Era journalism. "What really interests me," Tofani added, "are the stories that everybody thinks they know about, that everybody thinks they see but don't really see."

As a young courthouse reporter for the *Washington Post,* Tofani won professional prominence—and the Pulitzer Prize—with her series of reports about sexual assaults against inmates of the Prince George's County Detention Center in Maryland. "Everybody knew that rapes happen in jail, but they didn't know who the people getting raped were and whether they were innocent or not," she said. "They didn't know who the rapists were. They didn't realize that the jails were responsible."

In the series entitled "Rape in the County Jail: Prince George's Hidden Horror," Tofani began with one victim's savagely ironic experience. Kevin Parrish, a twenty-year-old student, had been in jail on a drunk driving charge less than an hour when he was beaten and sexually assaulted. After the attack he went to the jail clinic with blood pouring from his face, chest, and arms. A medic bandaged his cuts and treated his broken nose. An hour later his mother came with the $50 necessary to bail him out. In her story Tofani next showed that what happened to Parrish was not an isolated instance of misfortune:

> In on-the-record interviews 10 guards, 60 inmates and one jail medical worker said there are approximately a dozen incidents of forced sex each week in the jail for men and women awaiting trial or sentencing.
>
> The victims of these violent crimes are, of course, in custody at the time, but most are legally innocent citizens. About 70 percent of the jail's 450 inmates are awaiting trial, some on such charges as drunken driving, shoplifting and trespassing. . . .
>
> The problem of jail rapes is so well known that judges sometimes put men they consider vulnerable on probation rather than send them to the jail after they are convicted.
>
> "This is the kind of thing that's so bad you shut your mind to it," says Prince George's County Circuit Court Judge Vincent Femia. "It's easier to blot it out than to come to grips with the fact that it's happening in our own society."[4]

"The best stories," Tofani concluded, "are when you see situations where people are being abused or their rights are really being trodden upon, and through the reporting it becomes so clear that there is the potential for bringing about results."

Jonathan Kaufman is another reporter who achieved professional prominence with stories about people whose rights were being trod upon. "I do the kind of reporting I do, in part, because I think newspapers should write for people who otherwise would have no voices," Kaufman said. "If we're not going to write about homeless people and poor people and people discriminated against, who will?" And, in a series of articles collectively entitled "The Race Factor," the *Globe* did indeed write about people discriminated against. Much of Kaufman's reporting for the series focused on the documentation of racial discrimination in hiring and promotion. In an article headlined "At Boston's Top Levels, Few of the Faces Are Black," he reported: "Boston today is the hardest metropolitan area in America for a black person to hold a job or earn a promotion. . . . While other cities may carry reputations for being more hostile to blacks, Boston has fewer blacks in corporate policy-making portions—3 out of every 100—than any other major metropolitan area in the country."[5]

"The Race Factor," which won the Pulitzer Prize for the *Boston Globe* in the category of special local reporting, might not have met Pam Zekman's criteria for a story with an investigative edge. The series did encounter many victims of discrimination and did confront a few villains, but it was far more concerned with revealing large-scale patterns of discrimination. Thus the series marks the point at which investigative reporting becomes another journalistic genre: interpretive reporting. However, this investigation of esteemed Boston-area institutions, including Harvard University, hi-tech firms, and the *Globe* itself, was more of an attempt to "take names and kick ass," as the saying goes, than most writing on The Racism Issue. "We didn't put anybody in jail, but by running those stories across the top of page one of the *Globe*, you change the way people talk about issues," said Kaufman. "That's what attracts me to it."

A Paradox

What should attract all of us, as readers and as citizens, to investigative journalism is its willingness to confront a certain sort of social reality: the reality of outrageous civic vice and, by implication, the possibility of enhanced virtue in the conduct of public affairs. And what might attract those of us specifically interested in the nature of public moral discourse to investigative journalism is its claim to confront the realities of vice and virtue without a moral sense of its own. It insists that its highly charged discourse of victims, villains, and institutions in disarray is nonetheless objective social knowledge—facts unmediated by human interests or values.

This apparent paradox creates an interesting tension, if not a contradiction, in journalists' understanding of the intellectual foundations of their craft. "I want Boston to be the best city it can be," said Kaufman. And when speaking of his work on the "The Race Factor," he seemed to revel in the power of his appeal for enhanced public virtue. "I love getting people's attention," he said. "I want them to respond, 'This is an outrage.'" When pressed on the point, however, Kaufman was uncomfortable with the idea that his work was driven by a commitment to, or even an understanding of, what was *good* for the city:

> I think it was driven by a sense that it was *important* to the city. The *Globe* has been accused of being above the city and pointing down and saying, "You people should act better. You people should act like good, well-to-do liberals." My feeling here—and the way we wrote about institutions—was that this was crucial for the city to face. It wasn't something we wanted to impose on people, but the city was being torn apart. Newspapers are not just repositories of what happened yesterday. This was a very activist piece. It tried to say, "There's something important going on here that we must think about and think about hard."

Though justifiably proud of his "activist piece," this reporter wanted to discuss his work in terms of news judgments (what's important) rather than moral judgments (what's right). To be sure, Kaufman was not the only reporter who wanted to do so. "I do think that journalists and editors act as judges and juries about what's newsworthy, but it stems not so much from right and wrong as important or unimportant," said Bill Marimow, a winner of the Pulitzer Prize for his investigative reporting at the *Philadelphia Inquirer*. "I don't pretend to be omniscient, but what I am is someone who's been a reporter at the *Inquirer* for many years. I feel that I have a sense of what is pertinent in terms of how the government is functioning or malfunctioning."

This reporter's response to the apparent paradox of investigative journalism was typical of the distinguished reporters we interviewed. Marimow argued that he need not make moral judgments because he always compares the performance of officials to established criteria of conduct: the law, of course, but also ethical codes, professional standards, and expert opinion. "You report what the standards are or what people say the standards should be, and you let the reader make the judgment," he maintained. "Is the information important? Is it interesting? Those are the criteria I use. If the answers to those questions are yes, then I think you tell the story and present the readers with enough information so that they can evaluate."

Investigative reporters frequently cite this basic logic—journalists report empirically verifiable violations of established standards, while the public evaluates and perhaps responds to those violations—as the way that they maintain a separation between fact and value in their work. "If you simply bring something to light that has not been known, it's my feeling that you've done your job," said Jim Steele, one of Marimow's longtime colleagues at the *Inquirer.* "At that point it's in the public arena, and if somebody wants to act on that, and move on that, and do something about it, then that's another phase of the process." Steele insisted that although the process of investigative journalism may reveal the need for reform, "it's not part of the process to go out there and lobby for it."

With the idea that investigative journalism offers information for the public to "evaluate" and perhaps to "move on," Marimow and Steele acknowledged, even if only implicitly, that their stories help define the boundaries of the moral order by providing the community with opportunities to affirm or deny, and to correct or ignore, presumptive outrages against that order. But even as these reporters implicitly spoke to the idea of investigative journalism as a test of public conscience, they explicitly asserted that investigative journalists themselves need no conscience. By steadfastly maintaining that their judgments concern not "right and wrong but important or unimportant" and that their procedures "simply bring something to light," these reporters claim that their reporting involves no exercise of conscience but only application of empirical method—and that their finished reports are not moral discourse but simply information. In this way these reporters defend, or at least defer to, the enduring ideal of objectivity in journalism.

Occasionally, journalists suggest that the concept of objectivity is passé. The Code of Ethics adopted in 1996 by the Society of Professional Journalists makes no mention of objectivity—a provocative departure from the previous code, revised as recently as 1987, which cited objectivity alongside accuracy as a standard of professional performance. "Almost nobody talks about objective reporting anymore," wrote *Chicago Tribune* publisher Jack Fuller in his book, *News Values: Ideas for an Information Age.* "In its purest usage, the term suggested that journalism meant to be so utterly disinterested as to be transparent. The report was to be virtually the thing itself, unrefracted by the mind of the reporter. This, of course, involved a hopelessly naive notion from the beginning."[6]

Certainly, belief in the "purest usage" of objectivity has faltered (if it ever really existed in journalism), but as our conversations with reporters clearly revealed, the notion of "disinterested" knowledge continues to shape the news as a form of discourse and also to shape journalists' discourse about the news. These reporters probably would not suggest that their reports could be "virtually the thing itself," to use Fuller's phrase. But they would argue that, with effort, they could definitely know the thing itself and that their reports could accurately reflect its essential features. Similarly, they probably would not suggest that their reports are "unrefracted by the mind," but they might argue that this process of mental refraction separates, like colors of light, facts from values.

Even if, as Fuller argued, the journalistic craft is moving to some new understanding of itself, the ideal of objectivity has not really been left behind. Some of the most highly sophisticated and accomplished practitioners of the craft interviewed here tried to resolve the paradox of investigative reporting by affirming objectivity over morality. They simply insisted that they could make news judgments without also making moral judgments. But can that be so? This shall be one of our central questions: Is it possible to know and tell what is *important* about human affairs without also knowing and telling what is *right*? Put another way: Can such fact exist without value?

A Commitment

Investigative reporting, among all genres of journalism, poses such questions about fact and value most pointedly, for it is the fiercest of indignation fused with the hardest of fact. If these accounts of victims, villains, and institutions in disarray are a call for public moral indignation, they are also the product of the most rigorous journalistic methods. Contemporary investigative practice commits these reporters, in Marimow's words, to going "beyond the information that is released in a news conference, leaked to someone, oozed or seeped to someone." And in making this commitment investigative reporters are simultaneously freed from the most debilitating constraints of daily journalism: reliance upon official sources, formulaic balance among contending positions, and, of course, the daily deadline.

Kaufman, among many other reporters, spoke forcefully about the limitations of daily journalism as a venue for a public discussion of the issues that he thought important for his community to consider:

> Typical reporting gets the charge and gets the response and stops there. But what we tried to do with the racism series—what investigative reporting tries to do—is to go back and say, "Well, that response doesn't make sense." Or, "That response is a lie." Traditional objectivity here would not advance the argument at all. Traditional objectivity would basically have

white people saying what white people have always said and black people saying what black people have always said. What these pieces tried to do was to move the argument ahead.

Tofani was even more acerbic in her criticism of daily reporting routines. "You talk to a bunch of people. You see what they have to say. You write it down," she said. "There are often a lot of lies in those stories. People say a lot of things, often a lot of false things, but you try to arrive at as much truth as you can in the space of a day." In contrast to daily reporting, investigative reporting is less concerned with the "back and forth, yes and no" of policy debates, according to Tofani. "You don't forget what people are saying, but you test what people are saying against things like court documents, against what people saw and what people heard. It's a much more careful and painstaking process. You're trying to find out what is true."

Although investigative reporters retain a diffuse sort of deference to objectivity as a basic norm of their professional culture, they do not do so uncritically. Their desire to "move the argument ahead" and to "test what people are saying" leads them to challenge the limits of journalistic practice in an all-out effort to engage the social world as directly and completely as they can. Tofani expressed the commitment of the investigative reporter simply but eloquently: "You're trying to find out what is true."

Intellectual Foundations

Given this commitment, investigative journalism offers to other genres of journalism—and to all pragmatic yet serious-minded attempts to learn and tell of human affairs—some important lessons about the relationship between fact and value, truth and morality. We endorse the journalistic commitment to "trying to find out what is true," but we intend to critique the journalistic conception of what that means. We maintain that any attempt to gain truly important knowledge of human affairs—knowledge of individual innocence and guilt or institutional malfeasance and responsibility, for example—is built on a foundation of facts that have been called into existence, given structure, and made meaningful by values. The separation of fact and value is inevitably breached by all but the most elementary and isolated bits of information about the social world.

Subsequent chapters examine points in the journalistic process at which facts and values interconnect. It is important to understand that these are not moments of journalistic failure, moments in which emotions "taint" news judgments or opinions "distort" the facts. Rather, they are points at which the inherent interdependence of human interest and human knowledge is revealed. In overview, these points in the process are:

Objectification

Journalists maintain that they can produce their highly charged accounts of wrongdoing without making moral judgments. In chapter 3 we address this apparent paradox. Investigative reporters do indeed usually stop short of making explicit moral judgments—if such judgments are understood to be unequivocal pronouncements of right and wrong. However, in the application of (presumably) established standards to the conduct of officials and institutions, they certainly do make judgments. They locate and select, simplify and interpret the standards that the public is then invited to use in making its judgment. Although journalists neither create nor arbitrarily choose evaluative standards, they do participate in the establishment of such standards. This objectification of standards, as we shall call the process, is the particular contribution of investigative journalism to the ongoing cultural process that Celeste Michelle Condit characterized as "crafting virtue: the rhetorical construction of public morality."[7]

Representation

The claim to objectivity in journalism depends on the belief that "what is true" can, in its key features, be represented in story form. In chapters 4 and 5, however, we examine the rhetorical and narrative strategies that reporters use to represent the facts and, at the same time, to reveal and amplify the moral meaning of those facts. Chapter 4 notes that merely to document the violation of an established standard may not be sufficient to engage the public conscience. If so, journalists must reveal the violation to be not just technically wrong but terribly wrong—a moral outrage. For this they may turn to the rhetorical device of irony. That is, they will show the violation to be not only illegal or unethical but an ironic turn of events in which any expectations of honesty or justice were bound to be cruelly betrayed. Irony transfigures the conventions of journalistic objectivity into a morally charged vocabulary for condemnation of the villains to whom we have foolishly entrusted our public affairs. Irony always threatens further irony, however; as a means of moral discourse, irony threatens to undermine its own moral ends. For a warning about the perils of irony in public discourse, we will turn to philosopher Richard Rorty.[8]

In chapter 5 we show narrative to be an instrument not only for the representation of fact but also the assertion of moral authority. Historiographer Hayden White has argued that historical narrative (another form of storytelling committed to the truth) is inevitably constructed within a moral framework that identifies the facts and specifies their importance. History, according to White, is necessarily a "summons . . . to participation in a moral universe."[9] Investigative reports, with their skillfully crafted narratives of victimization and villainy, are another such summons, but they are only that—a summons. They may illustrate moral precepts and evaluative standards, but they do not provide a forum for the critique of those precepts and standards. Moreover, these reports may demand a response from officials and the public, but they typically say little about what that response ought to be. Thus these reports are neither an examination of the forces that uphold their moral universe nor a guide to action within it.

Verification

Investigative journalism reports the very hardest of hard facts. In so far as it addresses social problems, it does so by reporting specific instances of those problems: crime reports suppressed by the police department, for example, or sexual assaults in the county jail. Verifying the facts in each and every one of these instances is the moment when investigative journalists most fully capitalize on the opportunity to go beyond the limits of daily reporting to confront reality more directly and completely. It is also the moment when journalists most vigorously insist that facts can and must be separated from values. In chapter 6, however, we argue that the emergence of even the hardest of facts is not independent of a larger context that gives them structure, relevance, and meaning, and we argue that values are part of that context. We certainly do not argue that reporters fabricate facts or that no facts exist. We simply agree with philosopher Hilary Putnam's position that "every fact loads some value and every value loads some fact."[10]

Justification

To journalists the term *justification* may be unfamiliar, but to philosophers it concerns an essential element of any knowledge claim. It refers, in short, to a reason good enough to accept the claim. Investigative reporters simply point to the hard work of verification as a good reason to accept their published claims. Before publication, however, they often do struggle with questions of whether their hard work has indeed produced a reason that is good *enough*. Even if investigative reporters do not speak of justification, we show in chapter 7 that they can talk about concepts—"the weight of evidence," for example—that help them *consciously decide* about the sufficiency of their evidence and the credibility of their claims. In the struggle with such questions these reporters once again differentiate themselves from daily assignment reporters whose claims are casually accepted, at least as "news," if not exactly as "knowledge." And in that struggle, we conclude, investigative reporters provide a valuable model of journalistic responsibility.

Within the vast literature of postmodernity the argument that fact and value are deeply interconnected in the pursuit of social knowledge is far from radical.[11] Nonetheless, to journalists and to many in the audience the argument may still seem to dangerously undermine the foundations of journalism and knowledge itself. To them we say that our intent is not to undermine those foundations to the point of collapse but to contribute to their rebuilding. With Richard Rorty we relinquish the ancient hope for certainty of knowledge, and with Hilary Putnam we reject simplistic "realist" theories of truth. However, we do not reject the possibility of useful social knowledge, nor do we reject truth as a goal. Rather, we aim to understand how a particular process for the production of social knowledge functions and to understand what it means in the context of that process to tell the truth. Therefore what we offer is not merely an argument that fact and value are interconnected but a close examination of how, exactly, they are interconnected in a particularly rigorous form of journalism. From this close examination we shall try to draw some conclusions about the sort of news values that might transcend objectivity as a basic norm of journalism's professional culture.

The Research

In the spirit of media criticism intended to have a positive influence on both journalism and its audience, our analysis draws upon interviews with highly accomplished reporters working in respected "mainstream" news media, primarily metropolitan newspapers from across the United States. These reporters are among those whose work has defined investigative journalism in the era after Watergate. Some of them, like Zekman, Marimow, and Steele, long had been legends among their peers when we interviewed them. In talking with them we wanted to share in the wisdom that experience has brought. Others that we interviewed, like Tofani, achieved prominence relatively early in their careers. In talking with them we especially wanted to hear about the getting of wisdom—the still-fresh recollections of how they mastered their craft. At the same time we knew that some of these reporters, like Zekman, were masters of the shadowy investigative arts such as working secret sources, and others, like Steele, were masters of the most up-to-date investigative skills such as searching electronic databases.

From the beginning we conceived of the interviews with these journalists as an opportunity to sit in on a master class in the reporter's craft. Although editors, news directors, and others in the news organization certainly have wisdom to offer, we decided to emphasize the experiences of reporters as they ventured out of the newsroom—whether physically or electronically—to engage the social world. With this in mind we also decided to talk at great length with a few master practitioners rather than to superficially survey a cross-section of practitioners. Although we could not talk with all the reporters who should be counted among the masters of the craft, we did talk with enough to be confident that we could articulate the shared norms of their practice as well as appreciate the differences in approach among them. In the same vein we decided to carefully analyze a relatively small number of truly compelling stories rather than attempt to categorize or summarize the body of work in this genre of journalism. Although every year yields new investigations and more journalism prizes, we believe that the stories we have chosen offer enduring insight into the nature of news as moral discourse.[12]

In the course of our master class with these reporters we asked them to review in detail the procedures they used in one or more projects that brought them acclaim. We pressed them to explain and defend those procedures; when the opportunity arose, we interjected more general questions about the nature of news as social knowledge. Our goal was to coax these reporters, whose demeanor is typically one of no-nonsense modesty, to be open and introspective. In addition, our goal was to get them to tell some good yarns about their adventures. In the next chapter we retell some of those adventures for their own sake—simply because they are fascinating stories about masters at work. The yarns do have a point, however, for they dramatically demonstrate that "trying to find out what is true" requires hard work not easily described in terms of textbookish methods. There is, as Donald Schön has written, "an irreducible element of art in professional practice."[13] And the practice of investigative journalism, as we see in the next chapter, also reveals an element of perseverance, audacity, and sometimes even bravery.

2

In Search of Skills Not Taught in Textbooks

With a degree from Northwestern University's Medill School of Journalism completed only a year before, Jeff Marx was working from the *Lexington Herald-Leader*'s business desk, covering the Kentucky coal industry. And then one day, much like the young Woodward and Bernstein who were assigned to a routine story about a burglary, Marx was assigned to a small project about basketball tickets. "We didn't set out to do the series that we ended up doing," Marx recalled of his first step on a difficult journey to the Pulitzer Prize for investigative reporting. "All we were doing was trying to protect ourselves from getting beat on a major story in our own town by our competition."

The word around town was that the *Louisville Courier-Journal* had been investigating the University of Kentucky's basketball coach, who, according to a tip, had personally profited from the sale of season tickets. The *Herald-Leader*'s city editor and sports editor asked Marx to find out what the *Courier-Journal* had and to get something into the *Herald-Leader* within a few days. Marx recounted the origins of his big story this way:

> It was the week when the NCAA "Final Four" was being played in Lexington—when Villanova beat Georgetown in the finals in a huge upset. The semifinals were coming up on Saturday and the final on Monday, and the big rumor was that the *Courier-Journal* was coming out with this story on Sunday. The national media were in town, and here we were thinking that we're about to get blown out in our own backyard.

I got the assignment on Tuesday of that week, if I remember right. I worked on it alone for two days and got a list of the ticket holders to whom the coach had assigned the three hundred twenty-two seats that he controlled. I realized that I'd have to talk to as many of those people as I could as quickly as I could. For one person to attempt that was ridiculous, and so Mike York came in on it. We stuck together the whole way after that.

Mike York had been reporting for the *Herald-Leader*, a Knight-Ridder paper, from the chain's Washington bureau, when he was asked to join Marx. With time running short the two reporters had to play catch-up against the *Courier-Journal*. One of Marx's ideas for doing so was a stroke of mischievous genius:

> One of my favorite tactics was filing a public record request with the university for access to all the other record requests that had been filed with the university within a certain time period. My thinking was, "I've got to catch up to the *Courier-Journal.* If the *Courier-Journal,* in fact, has been on this thing, they've obviously filed some requests. I want to find out what they're looking for, and I certainly want to get access to what they've already seen." I don't know if anyone else at the paper had ever thought of that, but I know no one else ever did it. Mike York thought it was nuts but a great idea. My editor looked at me like I was crazy and said, "Get outta here and do it!"

As it turned out, the *Courier-Journal* didn't have much on the coach. Neither paper could find sufficient evidence that he had done anything improper with his tickets. For the *Herald-Leader* reporters, however, this was the beginning rather than the end of the investigation into the University of Kentucky basketball program. After seven more months of hard work Marx and York produced a two-part series entitled "Playing Above the Rules" that drew on interviews with thirty-three former players to reveal a pattern of payments from boosters to players in violation of NCAA rules. In the lead of the first article the reporters outlined that pattern:

> For years, ordinary fans have rewarded University of Kentucky basketball with a loyalty that is nationally known. What is less known is that a small group of boosters has been giving the players something extra: a steady stream of cash.
>
> The cash has come in various amounts—as little as $20 and as much as $4,000 or more—and it has come often.
>
> UK players have received what they call "hundred-dollar handshakes" in the Rupp Arena locker room after games.[1]

The report went on to detail one instance after another of these "special handshakes." For example:

> Forward Fred Cowan (1977–81) said Eastern Kentucky coal operator Maynard Hogg gave him "a couple of hundred dollars . . . anytime I wanted it."
>
> "I don't want to get into details, because you know and I know it was illegal," Cowan said, referring to violations of NCAA rules.
>
> Guard Dirk Minniefield (1979–83) said he shook the hand of booster Elmer Prewitt, a Corbin physician, in the locker room "a couple of times" and found himself holding a $50 bill. Three other players said they got up to $100 at a time in handshakes from Prewitt.
>
> Prewitt said he never gave money to players.[2]

The months of work that went into this story were "a brutal job," as Marx described it. "We were under tremendous pressures on several different levels. First, on the personal level, being a year out of school and this being my first major project, I felt like I had a lot on the line personally," he said. "The editors obviously trusted me enough to give me the chance, but I had every opportunity to mess it up."

This personal pressure was further intensified, according to Marx, by the atmosphere both in and out of the newsroom:

> Unfortunately, the last major project that the newspaper had attempted did not turn out to be what it was supposed to be. A reporter spent about three years working on a project concerning the local jail system. There were all sorts of complications—legal, ethical, and otherwise—that delayed things all the way along the line. It had become a newsroom joke, and we heard so much about that, some to our faces and some behind our backs: "When is the second jail series coming out?"
>
> The *Herald-Leader* is a fairly small newspaper. Two staff reporters pulled off full time to work on something is a big commitment. It really affects the rest of the staff. Others have to pick up your responsibilities, so there was that pressure inside the newsroom—all that shit we had to hear second- or thirdhand of what certain other reporters or editors felt about our project.
>
> And then external problems or pressures in doing what we were doing: being told by people about the amount of abuse we would take if a series like this ever came out; being told by people that we would definitely be sued if their names were in the story; being told by a booster that if we ever came back in his part of the state, we would be shot on the spot; being told by a guy—who would really know about something like this—that if this

story came out, I would come out of the newsroom sometime in the next year or two and find the state police taking cocaine out of my tires.

The external problems and the internal problems or pressures really built up to the point where there were times that I just couldn't deal with them. There were times that I just wouldn't show up for a day or two. There were times when John Carroll, the editor, was my only link to sanity. He was such a calm, easy-mannered person and also someone with a tremendous amount of journalism experience and know-how. He was, time after time, the guy who I relied upon to bring me back to reality and settle me down again.

When Marx and York's perseverance was eventually rewarded with the Pulitzer Prize, the reporters suddenly found that they had many more friends in the newsroom—even if not in the state of Kentucky—than they thought. "All of a sudden, everyone had been behind us the whole way. Everyone was pulling us aside and saying, 'Hey, I knew what you were going through; I just had a tough time talking about it,'" recalled Marx with some bemusement. "But I'll never forget the few people who were with us the whole way."

Despite the tribulations, Marx was quick to share the credit with the paper. "This was the culmination of a vast improvement at the paper. Here was something that people could look at as a sign from some outside group and say, 'Hey, we've really accomplished something.'" And much could be forgiven and forgotten in that sweet moment of vindication and success. "It was just jubilation, just complete excitement, because it was more than just this one series or these two reporters and an editor that did this thing," Marx remembered of the moment when the prize was announced. "It reflected the building up of a good newspaper."

How do reporters and their newspapers come to a moment such as this? Some argue that prizes are a matter of politics and luck. That may be so, but the stories that win them are not. The stories are a matter of mastery in the journalistic craft. They demand knowledge that must be learned but cannot readily be taught and methods that must be practiced but cannot easily be analyzed. What can be said of skills such as this?

Skills of the Master Practitioner

To the layperson the skills of any master practitioner—the design sense of the architect, say, or the diagnostic insight of the physician, or the courtroom maneuvering of the attorney—may appear wonderfully or perhaps threateningly mysterious. The client or patient, however, is invited to take some comfort in the notion that the mysteries of professional practice are resolved by systematic application of theory and principle to the situation at hand. After all, the principles of structural design, medical science, or legal argumentation are what these professionals use to guide their judgment and action.

That is so. And yet, as the practitioners know well, the application of theory and principle is only one aspect of their skill. In his classic analysis of professional expertise, *The Reflective Practitioner*, Donald Schön maintained that the "irreducible element of art in professional practice" is primarily the ability to simplify and organize a problem in such a way that theory and principle can be brought to bear on it. "Complexity, instability, and uncertainty are not removed or resolved by applying specialized knowledge to well-defined tasks," Schön argued. "If anything, the effective use of specialized knowledge depends on a prior restructuring of situations that are complex and uncertain."[3]

A key to mastery, then, is the *framing* of the problem in a way that renders its complexities and uncertainties understandable and manageable. Professionals may select the frame for the problem from among those used successfully in past practice, but that initial choice may be only the beginning of a process of framing and reframing in which practitioners search for meaning and coherence in the situation at hand. This the practitioner does "through a web of moves, discovered consequences, implications, appreciations, and further moves," according to Schön. "Within the larger web, individual moves yield phenomena to be understood, problems to be solved, or opportunities to be exploited" (p. 131).

Throughout this web of moves the veteran practitioner draws upon past problem-solving experiences. "The practitioner has built up a *repertoire* of examples, images, understandings, and actions," Schön wrote. "When a practitioner makes sense of a situation he perceives to be unique, he *sees* it *as* something already present in his repertoire." Moreover, Schön continued, "Seeing *this* situation as *that* one, one may also *do* in this situation *as* in that one" (p. 138, emphasis in original). Thus to make sense of a unique situation is not to apply a fixed formula or to impose a standard solution but to draw upon examples than can provoke creative thinking and on precedents that can guide productive action. This capacity to *see as* and *do as* provides the practitioner with a feel for new and difficult problems.

Although seeing as and doing as may provide a feel for the problem, they may not produce a complete solution. The practitioner must often conduct what Schön characterized as "on-the-spot-experiments" (p. 141).

Some of these are move-testing experiments in which the practitioner takes action to see what comes of it. Others are hypothesis-testing experiments in which the practitioner proposes an idea to help explain the situation at hand. But whatever their function, on-the-spot experiments are subject to "the logic of *affirmation*" (p. 155). That is to say, unlike scientific experiments (at least the idealized experiments portrayed in textbooks), which are supposed to be a search for evidence that can *disconfirm* a theory-based prediction, on-the-spot experiments are a search for evidence that can *affirm* the practical value of an approach to a problem. Even so, the experienced practitioner keeps an open mind and remembers that "the situation, having a life of its own distinct from his intentions, may foil his projects and reveal new meanings" (p. 163).

These thought processes—framing the problem, moving toward potential solutions, experimenting with alternative possibilities—may continue through many cycles that Schön described as an ongoing "conversation with the situation." In this conversation "the situation talks back, the practitioner listens, and as he appreciates what he hears, he reframes the situation once again" (p. 132). In the midst of this intimate exchange, however, practitioners may not be able to explain to others (to textbook authors, for example) what, exactly, they have heard and said. Although practitioners know what to appreciate and how to respond, their knowledge is not easily articulated for it is, in Schön's phrase, "knowing-in-action" more than knowing-in-words (p. 49). Creatively sustaining this conversation of actions-more-than-words is the essence of that irreducible element of art in professional practice.

The relationship between journalist and audience is not so very different from that of professional and client. The news media invite the audience to trust the expertise of the journalistic practitioner, but journalism, like the forms of professional practice analyzed by Schön, has an irreducible element of art. As journalists well know, reporting anything beyond the simplest event calls upon knowledge and methods that are not easily analyzed and taught. The objectivity of daily journalism, for example, may be reducible to a set of rules—lead with an important fact, quote official sources, and so on—but this textbookish objectivity is insufficient for the investigative reporter who is, as one said, "trying to find out what's true." The investigative reporter must, then, learn to creatively sustain a conversation with the situation.

The distinguished reporters whose personal accounts of big stories appear in this chapter have revealed themselves to be engaging commentators upon the irreducible element of art in journalism. Although they were not much better at abstracting their tacit knowledge or articulating intuitive methods than the professionals studied by Schön, they were adept at recounting their exploits. And when those experiences are compiled within the framework provided by Schön's key concepts—frames, repertoires, experiments, and so on—they do yield insight into mastery of the journalistic craft. That mastery, we argue, is not a matter of rulebound objectivity but of "mature subjectivity," in Michael Schudson's phrase, "subjectivity aged by encounters with, and regard for, the facts of the world." Indeed, Schudson's model of mature journalistic subjectivity is the seasoned investigative reporter who does not "submit uncritically to arbitrary conventions established in the name of objectivity" but instead exhibits a "tolerance of uncertainty, and acceptance of risk and commitment to caring for truth."[4]

In this chapter, then, we engage journalists in conversation about the nature of their skills, and we appreciate what we hear. In subsequent chapters we analyze more aggressively what these reporters have told us, but in this chapter we try to capture, in the reporters' own terms as much as possible, the nature of their "knowing-in-action"—that is to say, the sort of knowledge expressed in master practice rather than textbook principle.

Sensing a Story

No journalism textbook takes seriously the metaphorical "nose for news." But reporters sometimes do. "The first step is an intuitive sense that there's a story here," said one reporter. "My nostrils dilate or something." Sensing they will find a story in a tip or some other tidbit of information is, for investigative journalists, the first step in what Schön would recognize as the process of framing the problem. Sensing the presence of a story is also, as these reporters recognize, an excellent example of a skill that must be learned but cannot easily be taught. "I am much more confident of my own instincts now than I was in the beginning," said another reporter. "I didn't recognize the impulses that you get when something tells you: 'This is worth pursuing.'"

Well, just how seriously can we take the notion of an "intuitive sense" or an "instinct" for stories? "Let me give you an example where pure intuition led me to an interesting story," said Bill Marimow, offering an example from earlier in his career. "This is based solely on a reporter's experience and instincts and nothing else." His example began with a dozen reporters struggling to stay awake through a routine city council meeting. The clerk was reading a seemingly interminable list of new bills with typically unwieldy titles. "As I was sitting there, I heard this long rambling discourse: 'Amending Elected Officials' Pension Plan A as amended April 3, 1956. . . .'" recalled Marimow. "I just wrote down, 'Pension Plan A' in my notebook. The clerk kept going, and everyone else, including me, was kind of somnolent in there." After the meeting was over, however, Marimow looked through his notes and decided to read that particular bill. "It turned out that the city council was going to double its pension benefits at a time when the city administration had just raised property taxes and was claiming there was a fiscal crisis," he recalled. "Now, no other reporter in the room got that story. But whenever I heard 'pensions' and 'elected officials' when I was covering the council, I said, 'Interesting!'" The story was soon in the *Inquirer,* and the bill was soon back in committee from whence it never reemerged.

From this what can we say about an instinct for stories? Certainly, we can say that any such instinct would have much to do with the reporter's experience in the ways of the world, especially in the ways of elected officials. But we can also say that it would have much to do with the reporter's ability to use that experience to *see as.* Indeed, Marimow's own explanation of the instinct at work here suggested an ability to see facts as a story with an almost mathematical precision. He saw that "pensions" plus "elected officials" equaled "interesting!"—an equation that he had seen before and that he knew could add up to news. Although a "nose for news" may have become the cliché, an "eye for fact" is more essential to the journalist's metaphoric sensorium.

But what do reporters see? Lucy Morgan of the *St. Petersburg Times* first sensed a story about drug smuggling in Dixie County when she saw a connection among certain drug cases handled by the Florida grand jury system. Under the system in use at the time a statewide grand jury could bring an indictment, but for prosecution the case would go to the local venue in which the crime had occurred. Morgan noticed that the indictments of a particular smuggling ring always seemed "to fall away to nothing" once they were returned to the local court system, especially in Dixie County. Then, as she recalled, she saw another connection:

> A group of detectives from one of the local agencies had come to me complaining that they had been following defendants up into the Dixie County area and found themselves fending off the law enforcement officers more than the smugglers. Then a prosecutor had told me that the marijuana smugglers had built a church in the county with their money—which was intriguing. Then a state attorney had told me that his biggest frustration was that elected officials from Dixie County would go to testify on behalf

of the smugglers in other jurisdictions around the state every time the smugglers got caught.

I went to talk to the head of the Florida Department of Law Enforcement about the need for a statewide prosecutor, which we now have in Florida. . . . In the course of the conversation, I asked him about the problems in Dixie County, and he gave me some of the best quotes you would ever get about the endemic nature of the problem, about the code of silence among the citizens, and all of the other things that made it hard to investigate drug smuggling in that county. I walked out of there thinking about what he had said, the totality of it. I called one of our editors and said, "You know, I think I need to go down to Dixie County and play around awhile and see if there's not something to do." At that time my assignment was to roam around Florida.

I began by simply going to courthouses everywhere that there had been prosecutions related to Dixie County and just reading the records. I'm a great one for public records. . . . I usually make them the foundation of something that I'm starting. The second thing I did was to try to develop a local source who could direct me. I called everybody I knew in law enforcement, both state and federal, that might have a connection there, trying to search out the names of people who were reputable, who were not part of the smuggling. I had great difficulty with that and found only one name tended to emerge over and over again. At the end of the first week I went down and knocked on his door. I told him who I was and that I was there looking at the drug smuggling. He burst into tears and told me that I was an answer to a prayer.

This source did not appear in the story, according to Morgan, but he did help her sift through the cast of characters in Dixie County. In an extensive series entitled "Dixie County: Smugglers' Haven," Morgan introduced her readers to some of the most colorful of those characters:

> HORSESHOE BEACH—To his neighbors in this tiny coastal community, Floyd F. "Bubba" Capo is the kind of man who would build a country church, give you the shirt off his back and keep an entire neighborhood off welfare.
>
> But to state law enforcement officials, Capo is a notorious drug smuggler—a man given to boasting that he had his community and its sheriff in his hip pocket.
>
> "Capo thinks he's a godfather," says James W. York, director of the Florida Department of Law Enforcement (FDLE). "He's a classic case of how they (smugglers) survive. He buys out a community he helps. Those people admire him; they think he's a god."[5]

The story went on to reveal that in the late 1970s Capo's tax returns reflected an average income of less than $2,000 a year, but by 1980 other financial records showed a net worth of nearly $2 million. By the time Morgan talked to him, Capo was doing time for a second smuggling conviction although still proclaiming his innocence. He maintained that the money to build the church came from the real smugglers, "the boys from Petersburg," who felt guilty about his first unjustified conviction. He said that one day he found a paper bag with $30,000 on his back porch and a note that said, "Bubba, build your church." So he did.

And then there was Sheriff Glen Dyals. He was the elected official who had acted on behalf of several Dixie County residents accused of smuggling, including Capo's son, David. Witnesses said that Dyals was close enough to the Capo family to attend a "going away" party marking David Capo's departure for prison. And Bubba himself told undercover law enforcement officers, "I can handle this sheriff over here." Dyals, on the other hand, maintained that he did his best to patrol a large county on a small budget. He said he wrote the letter requesting lenience for David Capo because Capo's wife and children asked him to do so. "In politics," Dyals explained, "you try to keep everybody happy." Dyals also denied that he could be controlled by smugglers. "That's a lie," he told Morgan. "Nobody owns me—except my wife mostly."[6]

And so life went in what the *St. Petersburg Times* headlined as "most corrupt county in the U.S."[7] The reporter got the story because she could *see* patterns in the facts, especially the similarities among events and the connections among cases. As Morgan herself put it, "I look for a trend."

The origin of Morgan's investigation was a variation on a common theme in reporters' recollections of how great stories found *them*. That theme is the tip. "I would say that most of the stories that I work on start out with a lead that comes to me," said Marimow. "It's really very rare that something happens that I alight on, as I did in the city council listening to the new bills." But even when the tip came to him, Marimow credited his reportorial instincts with getting the story. "It'll be a kernel of fact or information or report or rumor, and, instinctively, I'll make a judgment about whether it'll be something that is documentable." Once again Marimow was able to dispel a little of the mystery surrounding his journalistic instincts. In this case they turned out to be a set of criteria for assessing the practicality of the project: "Is there a fair chance that it happened and that I can document it? Will it be newsworthy down the pike? And if it's newsworthy, how long will it take? Those are the basic judgments."

Another of Morgan's adventures, the story on the Pasco County Sheriff's Department that won her and colleague Jack Reed the Pulitzer Prize, began in just this way: first a tip and then some serious consideration of the practical aspects of actually doing the story:

> My name is well known in Florida, so I probably tend to get more than the average reporter in the way of tips. They've become a burden almost, because I feel guilty that I can't follow them all. Any time I get one from an area where we have a bureau, I give them to whatever editors I'm dealing with downtown, and sometimes I call directly to the bureau and say, "This is going on in your county if you want to pursue it."
>
> I did that in the case of the sheriff. I notified the supervising editor downtown, my immediate supervisor, and he called in the person who supervised the bureau [in Pasco County]. They discussed it and asked me if I'd be willing to take it on as a project. It was late February.
>
> I told them that there were several things they needed to know: that if we took on the sheriff's department project, we needed to do an extremely thorough job. . . . That I thought we would encounter incredible opposition from the sheriff himself, and because he disliked me, I probably would become the focus of a lot of his opposition . . . . That I did not want to be writing this story into the next year because it was something that should not be done in an election year.
>
> Sheriffs are so political in Florida. I think that any investigative project published at the moment of an election has less impact because it's easy for an elected official to say, "Oh, that's just politics." A lot of citizens subscribe to that. But the truth of the matter is that the best tips come in an election year. The minute a guy gets somebody running against him, he's got an enemy who's willing to come tell you everything.

Morgan came to terms with her editors and agreed to take on the sheriff. She worked on the project through the spring and into the summer, with only occasional help from other reporters. However, Reed joined her in August because, as she recalled, "Every rock I turned over revealed something else." Among the things that slithered out were deputies with highly questionable qualifications. Morgan had deliberately begun the investigation by checking deputies' backgrounds because she could pursue that angle in the state capital using public records. She could, then, make progress on the story before the sheriff got wind of it:

> I like to get as much information as I can before I inform the people I'm getting information about that I'm doing it, particularly when I expect them to start building walls. I expected the sheriff to build every wall he could . . . so the first month or so of inquiry was made solely in Tallahassee

in the police standards records. He never knew I was looking at it . . . which is miraculous in the world of law enforcement. There's a better grapevine there than in any prison.

When I began to pull the records, I thought some of the deputies were not certified or not qualified to be where they were. I would go through X number of records each day, and each night I would usually eat dinner with our Tallahassee bureau chief. We would sort of debrief each other on what the day had been, and I realized after a few nights of this that every day I was finding more deputies that had criminal arrest records. . . . It was the kind of thing that just began to shout at you—a pattern of conduct.

In many cases the paperwork indicated that the sheriff's department itself had made an effort to cover up the criminal record so that the state agency would certify them. The state requires an officer to fill out an affidavit that asks, "Have you ever been arrested, charged with a crime, or been taken into custody in any fashion?" It's a pretty all-encompassing question. A lot of deputies were answering no to that question, but their fingerprint, which was also a requirement of the law, was being kicked back out at the FBI—which reflected a criminal record. Clearly, you had a man being given a badge and a gun who was lying right up front about his background. I think, if anything, we have a right to expect law enforcement people to be credible characters.

Beyond that, there were things in those records that made these people great risks as law enforcement officers. In one of those files were letters from a doctor saying that a uniformed deputy had a hearing impairment that was so bad she was a danger to herself and others. The sheer liability to the department of having a person in uniform like that.

The cases that Morgan uncovered just kept getting better and better—or, rather, worse and worse:

One of the men that they'd made a deputy had been arrested for armed robbery, several counts of it. He had been a wheelman in a couple of armed robberies, shared the proceeds, ratted on his friends, testified against them, and they got forty-five years in prison. The particular state's attorney, who was notorious in Florida for dropping cases, had dropped the charges on him in return for his testimony. On the day they went to arrest him, so the arresting officers testified, he had tried to kill himself with a shotgun, but he had shot a hole in the trailer behind him instead of himself. So here you had a man who was a robber, a fink, suicidal—and not a good shot. We had given him a badge and a gun and sent him out on the street. With the first one or two you think, "Well, that's an isolated instance." I tend not to get excited until I see it become a pattern of conduct. In this case it was absolutely a pattern.

Morgan's project, like so many other investigations, began when the tip found her. But then she had to find the pattern of misconduct that would make the tip into a worthwhile story. Together Morgan and Reed traced a fascinatingly complex pattern of abuse of power by the Pasco County sheriff. A particularly curious wrinkle in that pattern was the relationship between the sheriff and a deputy, John Moorman, who was heir to a family fortune. While Reed traced the business dealings between the sheriff and the deputy, Morgan traced the influence of the deputy on the operation of the department. For example, the deputy had purchased his own patrol car and prowled the county at will. Morgan soon found that "a lot of the men in the department were alarmed at what they saw in the relationship between the sheriff and Moorman, a rank-and-file deputy who had special access to the commanding officer, who had all kinds of special privileges but no duty imposed upon him to go along with those privileges, who had a lot of money and was spending it around the department."

As Morgan listened to her sources inside the sheriff's department, she got a feeling familiar to many reporters—the feeling that she had the pieces of a jigsaw puzzle but could not make them fit together:

> I had a group of detectives sitting here at the dining room table one night. One of them said, "There was the strangest investigation that Moorman participated in, but I never really knew what happened to it."
>
> The detective went on to tell me: "At this meeting, Moorman and the sheriff started naming all these people as drug smugglers. I knew all these names, and one of them was an assistant state's attorney. They assigned me to go watch this attorney's house and get the tag numbers of everybody that came to his house. I told them I wasn't gonna do that. I thought the state's attorney would tar and feather me for doing something like that without any probable cause."

But one evening a few days later, as Morgan recalled, the pieces suddenly began to fit:

> I was talking to my husband, listing the names the deputies had given me. I couldn't figure out anything that these particular men had in common, though they were all names that were familiar to me. They were well-known businessmen in east Pasco. And Dick said, "Lucy, you have just named the directors of the Pasco Taxpayers Association."
>
> I was thunderstruck.

As the pieces of the puzzle came together, the pattern was revealed, and the sordid story of "Operation CUP" for "Clean Up Pasco" emerged as part of the series entitled "Inside the Pasco County Sheriff's Department: A Special Report":

> DADE CITY—Pasco County Sheriff John M. Short investigated a number of prominent East Pasco residents as suspected drug smugglers in a secret, privately financed undercover operation in 1981–82.
>
> The investigation, which produced no arrests, apparently focused on men who had earned the enmity of Short or John T. Moorman, a wealthy part-time deputy and Short associate who helped finance the operation.[8]

A few paragraphs into the story the reporter gave voice to one of the victims of this miscarriage of justice:

> "It's sort of upsetting that in this country this can happen; I wouldn't have thought it could happen here," added department store owner Otto Weitzenkorn, who said his family escaped from Nazi Germany four months before the outbreak of World War II.
>
> Operation CUP began in November 1981 after Sheriff Short won a bitter budget fight with the County Commission that went all the way to the State Cabinet. In that fight, Short was aligned against the taxpayers group, Pasco Taxpayers Association Inc.[9]

And so the reporters breathed moral life into the pattern of events in Pasco County. As in many other masterworks of moral discourse that this book examines, these reporters invoked the irony of a victim's plight—in this case a refugee from Nazi Germany persecuted by a county sheriff in the United States of America—to summon their community's moral indignation. "I'm naive enough to think that all people ought to have equal access to authority," Morgan said of her indignation at the situation. "I guess I'm a little offended when I see a man like that, who is able to give a sheriff a house or a tractor and get the sheriff to investigate his neighbor."

Framing the Story

Whether the investigation began when a trend was spotted or a tip received, reporters' recollections of getting down to work on a story typically revealed a struggle to find coherence and meaning in the emerging situation. Schön's reflective practitioner would readily recognize this process as framing the problem.[10] One reporter who spoke explicitly of framing a story was Jonathan Kaufman:

I feel it's almost an intuitive thing. I sense when I've got the frame. It fits. It's almost like you're trying to get a piece to fit into a puzzle. You're gonna turn it this way, this way, this way, and then suddenly it clicks right in, and it all seems to fall in place. If I'm still thinking a lot about a story, it's not framed right. But once I've got that frame down . . . I can sleep fine because I'm not thinking about it.

When pressed to define the concept of *frame,* he argued that, more than the angle, it was the core of the story. A story, it seems, must be framed much as a building is framed—that is, to provide a basic internal structure. But when Kaufman recounted the early work on the investigation of racial discrimination in Boston, his recollections suggested another sort of frame. A story must also be framed as a picture is framed—to clearly delineate it from the background in order to focus attention. Through the interplay of these two sorts of frames, as Kaufman recalled, the *Boston Globe* reporters developed their story:

> Everyone knew Boston had problems in race relations, but the only way you'd be able to convince people was by actually documenting the problems. Anecdotes weren't going to get you anywhere because everybody had competing anecdotes. For every black guy you had being discriminated against, some white guy had a black guy who'd taken a job from him. It just didn't advance the argument at all.
>
> I had learned when I was with the *Wall Street Journal* in Chicago that the federal government kept statistics about black managers, so I decided to get those numbers, and my initial memo [to the editors] was basically a description of those numbers, which showed Boston had the lowest number, percentagewise, of blacks in management positions across the board.

Based on that memo, the editors decided to pursue the project. Kaufman realized, however, that just as he would need more than anecdotes, he would need more than numbers for his story to arouse the public's indignation:

> My background as a *Globe* reporter had been a lot of street reporting, a lot of neighborhood reporting. I was always right out in the neighborhoods writing stories, and one of the things you'd always hear in the white neighborhoods of this city was: "The *Globe* is fulla shit. The *Globe* is too liberal. I don't trust the *Globe.*"
>
> I thought, for this to be useful, we have to get people to read it, but how would you get people to read about an issue they were sick of reading about? I remember talking to a reporter in the newsroom about it who said,

"Well, the best way to do it would be to go after Harvard or the Bank of Boston." All the coverage of busing had been focused on the working-class people fighting with each other, and no one had ever looked at the big institutions, the real players, and what they did.

That's basically how the series begins. We set our sights on the institutions—on the Bank of Boston, on Harvard, on the *Globe* itself—as if to say that these people are responsible for what's going on here. I think that appealed to people's sense of fairness. We weren't going to be picking on poor white working-class people anymore.

With the idea of focusing on "the real players," Kaufman and his colleagues had set a key structural feature of the story in place. Next they sought out individuals whose experiences could reveal the nature of racial discrimination in powerful institutions:

The next step for me was to get people to frame the issue in a way that would strike chords. I mean, so much had been written about this issue, and people had so many reflexive reactions to the whole question of job discrimination that I thought we had to find people who would really make it come alive, who would break through and give people pause.

It was a real revelation to me that none of those people were who I expected them to be. We spoke to all the usual suspects—all the usual characters—and they said all the usual things. And it was only when we started going to the second- and third-level people, to people who don't get quoted in the paper, that we came up with images that turned out to be the most gripping—a black firefighter talking about how people at fires still call him "nigger."

At the same time the other reporters were all doing their own reporting based on these statistics, and that was really the key to the piece. Once we had the numbers that showed what the situation was like, then it was a matter of finding what the reasons were and getting the examples.

Thus the work of the *Globe* reporters at this stage of the project was an elegant exercise in story framing. The (structural) frame for the story would be a series of case studies about highly visible and powerful local institutions. And within the (picture) frame created by those attention-grabbing cases, individuals would explain the practice and express the pain of racism. Here is an excerpt:

When the 10 deans of Harvard University meet in the Old President's House in Cambridge to discuss academic and admissions policy, all the participants are white.

When the Boston Building and Construction Trades Council, which represents construction workers, meets once a month to determine policy and lay out strategy, all the officials are white.[11]

And a few paragraphs later the firefighter was given voice to speak of life in his city:

Says a black fire fighter: "I hear that word 'nigger' everyday. I know people have to say it, so I let them say it. . . . Compared to a lot of things that could happen to me, it's nothing."

The fire fighter pauses and shakes his head: "They want to call themselves the hub of the universe."[12]

Another investigation of racial discrimination, Bill Dedman's Pulitzer Prize–winning series on bias in home mortgage lending, provides another example of story framing that is at once typical and extraordinary. Dedman was preparing a story for the *Atlanta Journal & Constitution* on low-income housing when he met a minister and community activist named Craig Taylor, who built and renovated houses in a very low-income neighborhood. Taylor explained to Dedman that his work was hindered by the refusal of banks to lend in the neighborhood. Dedman recalled his reaction to the neighborhood and Taylor's response:

I said, "Craig, I wouldn't want to lend money here, either. This is a pretty lousy neighborhood."

He said, "Okay, I agree with that, but I think we can make a case on the merits that these people qualify for loans. I don't think that the only motivation for not lending here is the income level. These lenders don't lend in the more affluent minority neighborhoods in Atlanta, either. Maybe there is some element of income, but I think there is also an element race."

So I put that on my list of stories to look into.

And so another reporter made another connection, and work on another story was soon underway.

To begin Dedman checked the newspaper's electronic library for stories mentioning both race and mortgage lending but found little. He went to the paper's clip files that extended much further back in time and found more. He learned that the practice of lending in some neighborhoods but not others was called *redlining* and that it been a major concern in Altanta in the 1960s and '70s but much less so after that. He then returned to the computer to search electronic databases for whatever had been written elsewhere. "I found that some other work had been done but mostly by academics," Dedman recalled. "And that's when I became aware that there was data. The academics were working with data collected under something called the Home Mortgage Disclosure Act."

Dedman contacted the university-based authors of the materials he had retrieved and learned of an upcoming conference. "All the people I was calling around the country seemed to be going to Chicago," he recalled. "So I went to the city desk and said, 'I want to go to this conference because everybody who seems to know about this topic is going there.'" At that conference he met several researchers from the University of Minnesota who agreed to assist him with the project. "They wanted to do what I wanted to do," Dedman said, and they became instrumental in helping him understand what would be necessary to show that Atlanta banks did in fact discriminate against minority neighborhoods. This was a pivotal moment in the reporting of the story, according to the reporter, for at that point he had found the frame:

> I was persuaded by what the academics had done that it was possible to get some data to measure the lending patterns of the banks—that it was possible to tell where they made loans and where they didn't. I didn't know if the data would be proof positive or not, but it would be newsworthy. It was clear that we could do the data work, and that would give us a point from which to ask questions about how the system works and what the motivations are.
>
> On the way home I sketched out the series on my notepad: "Part One. What The Data Showed. Who lends and who doesn't? Where do they lend?" (At this point I was just playing a hunch, but I was sure, because I grew up in the south, that there was going to be a very stark pattern. These academics had found it Boston and Chicago, and I was going to find it in Atlanta too.) "Part Two. Why is it that way and how does it work? What are the policies and practices of the banks?"

Now the reporter knew the story was "do-able" and that it could be structured with one of investigative journalism's most commonly used master frames: the demonstration of a pattern of harm or wrongdoing, followed by an explanation of how a system or institution has failed. Soon Dedman completed his conception of the project as a series with four basic parts: "What's going on? How's it going on? Why isn't someone regulating it better? What ought to change? To my mind those were the necessary elements of an investigative series."

At the same time Dedman had come to understand more fully that the central issue—the core of the story, as Kaufman might have called it—was a pattern of lending decisions based on race rather than income. "The Community Reinvestment Act says that banks have an affirmative obligation to make loans in low- and moderate-income neighborhoods," Dedman explained, "but we knew it wouldn't be very persuasive to our readers, and maybe to my editors, that banks weren't lending to poor people." Although the Community Reinvestment Act was one standard against which Dedman could evaluate the performance of the banks, another federal banking law was even more important to establishing the claim that the banks were in fact doing something wrong. "The Equal Credit Opportunity Act says that you are supposed to treat similarly situated people equally," Dedman said. "So the question was, how do we look at the data in such a way as to control as many factors as possible?"

Dedman and his academic advisers understood that, given the available data, the only strategy for comparing the treatment of similarly situated white and black mortgage applicants would be to compare the amount of mortgage lending in white and black Atlanta neighborhoods— neighborhoods similar in terms of all important factors except the race of the residents. Therefore the reporter and the researchers had to develop defensible criteria for the inclusion of particular neighborhoods in the comparison. The key factor to be considered was, of course, race. "What's a white area? And what's a black area?" asked Dedman. "There's no area that's all white or all black, but Atlanta is very segregated like most of the country." With the advice of the researchers Dedman defined as "white" or "black" any neighborhood in which at least 80 percent of the residents were of one race. "Also, we were careful to check about areas that were shifting from white to black," he said.

Another key factor was income. Because the reporter and the researchers wanted to focus on stable, middle-income communities, they needed to define *middle income*. Working with the researchers on this issue, the reporter got a lesson in how to find meaning in quantitative data (as opposed to the individual cases with which journalists more often deal):

> We settled on a variation of what social science experts in housing would normally use: some percentage of the metropolitan area's median income based on the census data. Generally, lower and moderate income is defined as fifty or sixty to eighty percent of the median. So we decided to throw out any neighborhoods below seventy percent of the median.
>
> We also arrived at that figure by computing how much income it would actually take to buy a cheap home in Atlanta—whatever that was, maybe

forty grand—and we did a mortgage calculation, just as a real estate agent would do if you were deciding how much home you could buy. That turned out to be about seventy-five or seventy-eight percent of the median income. We figured if you were below that, you couldn't afford to buy a cheap home anyway, so we were just going to ignore you.

Then we threw out the top because there were no very affluent black neighborhoods (that is, above about one hundred twenty percent of the median). But now, of course, my story seemed to be slipping away because, if you just make a comparison of whites to blacks, the ratio is, maybe, a thousand to one—a thousand loans to whites for every one to a black in the Atlanta area. . . . Now our ratio is getting down to, like, five or six to one, and every refinement brings the ratio down further. I thought that the story was going away, that we were losing our good story, but it turns out that five to one with controls is much more persuasive than a thousand to one with no controls. I didn't know that until them. Nothing in my journalistic training taught me that that would be better.

The controls were important, as Dedman realized, because the banks would try to pick the story apart. If the banks could show that the ratio had been overstated, even a little, they would have ground to question the credibility of the project and to dismiss the importance of the issue. Despite Dedman's commitment to making only the most conservative of statistical claims, his story did not go away. His series in the *Atlanta Journal & Constitution,* entitled "The Color of Money," delineated the white-to-black lending ratio of 5 to 1 as a moral outrage when compared to a baseline of true racial equality. The first article in the series began:

> Whites receive five times as many home loans from Atlanta's banks and savings and loans as blacks of the same income—and that gap has been widening each year, an Atlanta Journal-Constitution study of $6.2 billion in lending shows.
>
> Race—not home value or household income—consistently determines the lending patterns of metro Atlanta's largest financial institutions, according to the study, which examined six years of lender reports to the federal government.
>
> Among stable neighborhoods of the same income, white neighborhoods always received the most bank loans per 1,000 single-family homes. Integrated neighborhoods always received fewer. Black neighborhoods—including the mayor's neighborhood—always received the fewest. The study was controlled so any statistical bias would underestimate the differences between lending in black and white areas.[13]

Here the story's core—race, not income, determined lending—was succinctly yet dramatically revealed in the single compelling statistic that whites receive five times as many loans as blacks. Although the language of the lead was dryly factual—"flat" was Dedman's description—the carefully constructed statistic spoke with great eloquence, precisely because it was so carefully constructed.

Repertoire of Moves

Reporting, by which reporters mean information gathering, draws upon a repertoire of skills that can be divided into two essential sets. In Dedman's metaphor the tree of reportorial skills has two main branches: "One branch is getting people to tell you things they wouldn't tell somebody else, and the other branch is getting the facts from records." That ancient first branch ("people telling you things") remains as sturdy as ever, but the other branch ("facts from records") has grown vigorously in recent years. As Dedman's own reporting shows, the computerized retrieval of documents and analysis of quantitative data are now crucial skills of the investigative reporter.

The reportorial skills tree has still another branch—an offshoot, perhaps—that seems to grow less vigorously than in the past but still flowers occasionally: undercover investigation. The work of Bill Gaines at the *Chicago Tribune* exemplifies this shifting emphasis on the skills required of investigative reporters. In the late 1980s Gains won recognition for his document retrieval work in the *Tribune*'s Pulitzer Prize–winning investigation of unethical activities by members of the Chicago City Council. About fifteen years before, however, Gaines had begun his investigative career as a specialist in undercover work. "I've seen quite a bit of change in the *Tribune* over those years," he observed. "Undercover jobs were big back then."

One such job was an investigation of several small for-profit hospitals that specialized in a combination of poor care and Medicaid fraud. One hospital was owned by a doctor who, Gaines recalled, "ran it like a despot." Like so many other investigative stories, this one began with bits of information that suggested something bigger: "One of things we knew about the hospital was that the fire department stopped taking emergency patients there. On the basis of that, we looked up some lawsuits against the hospital. We found an attorney who had a client who said that he was a janitor there and that the hospital had used him to help in the surgery. That certainly did call for an undercover job."

For Gaines that undercover job literally became a job. He was hired as a janitor at the hospital:

> When I went there the first day, the other janitors told me what was going on in the hospital. It's amazing what janitors know about what's going on in a place like that. Just sitting around the table in the lunchroom that first day, they not only told me about [helping in the surgery] but they said that the hospital would bring in an entire family to have their tonsils out on the same day—all of them. The next day the hospital would bring in another family to have their tonsils out. . . .
>
> So the general idea was that the hospital had a clinic system in poor neighborhoods. Doctors there would refer these patients. They'd tell mothers that everyone needed tonsillectomies, whatever, and that they would remove a cyst or something while they were at it. They'd just move patients in and out of the operating room as fast as they could. That was the idea, but they were understaffed, and they had to use the janitors to do it.

But when the hospital had to use one particular janitor, the result was a story on the front page of the *Chicago Tribune*. It began:

> It is a critical period for the 6-year-old girl lying in anesthetized sleep on the operating table in von Solbrig Memorial Hospital. Only minutes ago she had undergone two operations, a tonsillectomy and surgical repair of a hernia.
>
> But the only other person in the operating room is a $2-an-hour janitor, in his unsanitary working clothes who has just put down his mop in the corridor outside and rushed in to watch over the young patient at the request of a nurse.
>
> The surgeon, the nurses, nurses' aides, and the anesthesiologist have all gone. And for several minutes, until the nurse returns to relieve him, the janitor is in charge of the patient.
>
> The janitor is Tribune Task Force reporter William Gaines.[14]

In a sidebar to the story, written in the first person, Gaines recalled: "The little girl and I were alone in the room, both of us helpless. I swore under my breath. It was a responsibility I didn't want. But I couldn't walk out."[15]

Based on Gaines's observations, the series went on to reveal a pattern of shamefully inadequate care at the hospital. And based on Medicaid documents and patient interviews, it also revealed a pattern of billing for unneeded or unadministered treatment. A few days later Gaines wrote a follow-up reporting that the city and state had begun an investigation of the hospital and its proprietor. The hospital eventually closed.

Like most investigations, this one depended most heavily on reporters' skill in locating documents and interviewing sources. (A good deal of that work, by the way, was accomplished by Pam Zekman who was then a *Tribune* reporter.) Gaines maintained, however, that the undercover work was also essential to the success of this story. "If we had just written the story based on a former janitor saying this, then the hospital would have denied it," Gaines argued. "Maybe we would have had a story and maybe we wouldn't. It could have just been some wild allegation, and it wouldn't have gotten any response."

Gaines said that in recent years this investigative technique has increasingly fallen into disrepute. "I think it was overdone, maybe abused, over the years," he acknowledged. "Some people went undercover specifically to steal documents." But Gaines also defended the ethics of the technique—at least as he and his colleagues at the *Tribune* practiced it. His team always went undercover in carefully planned roles in an attempt to witness the wrongdoing for themselves. "We tried to experience something," he said, "and we then tried to tell what we had experienced." For this reporter the era of the undercover job has nonetheless passed. "I've finally outgrown the role of the janitor in the surgery room," he concluded. "I'm thought of as a great guy with a mop, but I do a lot of records work now."

Most investigative reporters do a lot of records work now, but two of the masters are Don Barlett and Jim Steele of the *Philadelphia Inquirer.* "Don and I have become known in the profession as documents reporters," Steele said, "which is a little misleading because the implication is that we don't do any interviews, which isn't true." The interviews, however, take place after a determined search for relevant records—a search that has become the hallmark of a Barlett and Steele investigation. "Because we do all this document stuff, which has become the subject of great interest in reporting, we've been asked to do a seminar here and there," said Steele, acknowledging his influence on the craft.

Through these seminars Barlett and Steele have offered their colleagues not so much a method as a mind-set. They teach that successful documents reporting is not assured merely by a fat Rolodex. Steele maintained,

> The assumption of many young reporters is that, after you've done this for a few years, you know the territory, but that really isn't true. Yeah, I know that the Securities and Exchange Commission has certain kinds of documents, and I know that city hall has deeds and mortgages, but the truth of the matter is that every project is different. Every project is going to

encounter certain kinds of documents that we've never had any contact with before, so that's compelled us to adopt what we call 'a documents state of mind.'"

With that widely cited phrase these reporters remind their colleagues that master practitioners do have their methods, but those methods are not readily reducible to textbook procedures. "It is a certain discipline you try to apply to yourself," Steele concluded. "We assume documents are out there until we're proven wrong, and we try to think systematically about where we might find something that would deal with the issue."

Maintaining a documents state of mind has become somewhat easier in the last two decades, thanks to computerized public records and electronic databases such as Nexis that include, among much other information, the texts of newspaper, magazine, and journal articles. Barlett and Steele's mastery of these information resources is exemplified by their Pulitzer Prize–winning story on the revision of the federal tax code in 1986. The primary focus of their project was the approximately 650 tax exemptions written into the revised tax code that provided tax relief to specific individuals or companies. Reporting who, exactly, had received such special treatment from Congress was no simple task, however, because the tax code identified the recipients not by name but by specific yet cryptic descriptions. For example:

> In the case of any pre-1987 open year, neither the United States nor the Virgin Islands shall impose an income tax on non-Virgin Island source income derived from transactions described in clause (ii) by one or more corporations which were formed in Delaware on or about March 6, 1981, and which have owned one or more office buildings in St. Thomas, United States Virgin Islands, for at least five years before the date of the enactment of this Act.[16]

Confronted with hundreds of such exemptions, the reporters got into that documents state of mind, as Steele recalled, and then got to work:

> Early in the work on the tax series, we made a trip to Dover, Delaware, to try to find the identity of this one company that has been incorporated on a certain date. At the secretary of state's office, corporate records division, they can pull up a file by date and so forth, using the computer. When that document came up, there were three names: two people in the Virgin Islands and one fellow in California.
>
> None of the names meant anything to me—they weren't household names—so we came home and did a Nexis database search using all three

names. And with the name from California, up popped four or five items: something about the horse-racing commission, some major development in Long Beach, and the last item was the guest list for a state dinner at the White House for the prime minister of Canada. So you can see that the fellow moved in somewhat unusual circles, and that told us that this would be worth pursing a little further to see what we could find.

Another search concerned an exemption for a company that had issued a large amount of bonds:

> They were issued on such and such a date, so we had one of the librarians go into all the databases on the theory that not too many companies had issued that volume on that date. So we searched by the amount and the date and up popped something from the Dow Jones database about a company in Chicago that had issued bonds in that amount on that date.
>
> We had the name, so from there we went to the *Standard and Poor's Corporate Directory*. We looked up the name, and in the summary of the company was the date that it had been incorporated in Delaware. We went back to the tax code, which had a reference to the date that the company had been incorporated in Delaware. The dates matched. I wish they were all that easy. That took about fifteen minutes. If I told that story all the time, everybody would rush into this business. The story counteracts all those instances were we tried like hell and came up with zip.

With a number of exemptions decoded the reporters undertook additional document searches and interviews to learn more about the individuals and companies whose identities they had uncovered. They assembled the information into profiles that became the core of their series entitled "The Great Tax Giveaway." One profile featured the Californian who had dined at the White House. This wealthy investor, with connections to the Reagan administration, had set up shop in the Virgin Islands to exploit a questionable tax loophole, but just as the IRS was closing in on him, Congress came to his rescue with an exemption in the new tax code worth about $4.5 million. He had been, as his lawyer told the reporters, "in touch with the right people."[17]

Steele credited the numerous detailed profiles for creating the public impact of the series. "Everybody assumes that there are going to be some of these sorts of things in a tax bill or an appropriations bill or a budget bill, but by the second day of the series, people were calling to say they couldn't believe it," Steele recalled. "The power comes from the multiple examples." The reporters had skillfully amplified that power, however, by juxtaposing the examples with quotes from members of Congress promising greater fairness and simplicity in the revised tax code. "I think what bothered people," Steele concluded, "was that you had this bill called 'tax reform' that was supposed to level the playing field, to remove the favoritism, but it was laced with all these exemptions." The congressional rhetoric alongside all the outrageous exemptions seemed to unmask this attempt at tax reform as an ironic travesty—a powerful stylistic effect to which we shall return in chapter 4.

Like Barlett and Steele's work on "The Great Tax Giveaway," Dedman's work on "The Color of Money" offers a case study in the mastery of documents reporting. Like Barlett and Steele's work, moreover, Dedman's investigation uncovered multiple examples of injustice. In "The Color of Money," however, those examples—"the anecdotes," as Dedman called them—were not the only, or even the most important, evidence of injustice. The most incontrovertible evidence of racially biased mortgage lending in Atlanta was the computer-based analysis of the documents that lenders were required to file with regulators. "The key thing that the computer allowed us to do here was to get away from the anecdote," Dedman said. "The anecdotes were no longer what proved the story, though the anecdotes were what persuaded people to read it." While Barlett and Steele's "Great Tax Giveaway" stands as a landmark of investigative reporting for its computer-based *retrieval* of documents, Dedman's "The Color of Money" stands as a landmark for its computer-based *analysis* of documents—both skills, by the way, that Dedman began teaching other reporters after joining the staff of the Associated Press.

At AP Dedman became the documents reporter's reporter. Even so, he continued to emphasize the importance of both branches of the reporting skills tree: developing and interviewing sources as well as retrieving and analyzing documents. "The part of the mortgage lending series that I'm most proud of really isn't the numbers," he said. "It's the part that explained how the system actually worked." For that part Dedman interviewed a number of people in the banking and real estate businesses in a effort to show that, whatever the intentions of the individuals involved, the mortgage lending *system* inevitably resulted in fewer loans to qualified blacks than whites. Dedman found, for example, that most Atlanta-area banks did little to develop business in black neighborhoods, despite a federal law that established for all banks "a continuing and affirmative obligation to help meet the credit needs of their communities." Bank officials maintained that they received few applications from those neighborhoods, but as Dedman wrote in the article:

Real estate agents in black neighborhoods, however, said they usually don't refer home buyers to banks and savings and loans. One reason is that the banks don't come around looking for business.

Ruben James is black and he works in predominantly black south DeKalb County for Precision Reality. "I haven't seen anybody from a bank in a couple of years. There used to be a woman from C&S who came by this office, but I haven't seen her in a long time." . . .

Bank officers said that almost all of their loan originators—the salespeople who drum up loans—are paid on commission. A good originator will notice two things: First, more homes are sold in the mostly white areas than in black areas. Second, homes in white areas usually cost more.[18]

This part of the series revealed how institutional racism actually works. "To me," Dedman concluded, "this part proved the numbers."

If the greatest skill in dealing with sources is, as Dedman said, "getting people to tell you things that they wouldn't tell anybody else," Zekman's work on the "Killing Crime" series offers several instances of virtuosity. Early in that project Zekman found the number of crimes recorded in the city's official crime statistics to be much lower than the number of complaints recorded in the police department's daily summaries of criminal activity. At that point, however, she did not have the individual reports filed by the officers who had investigated and "unfounded" the complaints:

We couldn't do the story then. What did we have? We had massive discrepancies. So what? Maybe all those crimes were falsely reported and weren't really crimes. We couldn't do a story unless we could find the cases and talk to people to prove the point [that complaints were improperly unfounded]. . . . And so we had to get the reports.

It was a hold-your-breath proposition. . . . We were trying to get a hold of a massive number of police reports. First, we asked up front, "We want all of the burglaries reported in the tenth district for the month of March. We want the initial police report and the detective's follow-up report."

They said no. And they thought up all kinds of excuses. They said they didn't have the staff to pull them.

I said, "Okay, I'll provide the staff. I'll pay the expenses of the staff."

They said no. And then they came up with the confidentiality thing. . . . A police department rule had been put into effect that raised an interesting issue: if the narratives of police reports were made public, criminals would be able to get the police reports and find out who the witnesses were. So there was a rule in effect saying that those narratives in police reports—

which we needed badly in order to figure out which cases had been "killed"—should not be public records.

Finally, Zekman called upon one of the most important resources available to the veteran investigative reporter, the critically placed source, to get the daily reports. Using the initial police report and the detective's follow-up report, she found cases that seemed to have been unfounded on a flimsy pretext. Next she sought the testimony of victims. Getting the testimony of rape victims proved to be both particularly difficult and particularly important:

> We wanted rape cases where it was more than just the woman's word against the cops, where there was something extra. In the case of one girl, there were the hospital records. The police department just totally dismissed the hospital records and said, in effect, that she was lying. Well, the hospital records confirmed that she had been raped. In Maria's case there was a witness that saw the rape. Not many people witness rapes. So we had very high standards. We were looking for rape cases where there was some extra piece of evidence that the police had ignored so they couldn't come back and say it was one person's word against another's.

Zekman's next task was to talk with these women about what had happened to them:

> Maria wound up breaking down in my arms. It was one of those times in television when you're not really sure that you should be there recording it. It was a very difficult interview to do. She wound up breaking down in my arms and sobbing. I didn't know at the time that she had never gotten counseling after the rape. It had been a year, and she'd never really talked about it. All of the outpouring was the first time.
>
> In her own way she picked up on all the issues. She said, "They threw my complaint in the garbage." What does that mean? It means that the rapist is out there to do more harm. She knew exactly why it was an important story, and her outrage came through. I felt confident that we could make people care by having them watch that.

In Conversation with the Situation

Master practitioners choose from among their repertoire of moves, not by performing some calculation but by conducting what Schön characterized as "a conversation with the situation." Although these conversations may include interviews with sources, they are something more. In the reporters' accounts of information gathering one can hear the echoes of such conversations. Here, for example, Kaufman reconstructs his conversation with the racial situation in Chicago, where he'd gone to find a point of comparison for the situation in Boston:

The reason the story reads the way it does was, in part, because of my personal experience in Chicago. I was struck going back there after three years by how much the tenor of the city had changed. I had done a lot of reporting on the black south side of Chicago myself when I was a reporter for the *Wall Street Journal*, and going back soon after Harold Washington [the city's first African American mayor] had been elected, I was struck by how polarized things were.

I felt a lot less safe there. I remember that occurred to me when I was going to my first interview. I dropped off my bags at the hotel, and I hopped in a cab to head down to the Urban League offices on the south side. I was early, so I decided to just walk around, get a soda, and just get adjusted. I like to walk around, pick up the feel of things, and remember what city I'm in, and I was struck by how tense things seemed in a very black-and-white sense. I think I have been doing this long enough that I can pick up when that's just nervousness and when there's been a fundamental change in the city. While talking to the head of the Urban League, I sensed that too. There was almost this attitude: "We don't have to talk to white reporters anymore because Harold Washington has been elected." It was a much more confrontational atmosphere.

Then we went to several black neighborhoods, the photographer and I, just talking to people, trying to get a sense from people of what their expectations were and what they wanted. It was clear what Washington was offering them. I asked a woman if city services had gotten better—you know, if the snow was being plowed—and she said, "It would take ten mayors to fix what's wrong with my street, but I elected him because I wanted to see that a black man could hold that job."

I had an appointment to see Washington, but he was very hard to see. They canceled one interview. The second time they called and said, "We'll give you ten minutes. That's it." I walked into his office, and I told him that anecdote about the woman, and he said to me, "You know, no white reporter understands that in this town." We spent an hour and a half together. . . .

As I talk about it, I realize that a lot of the reporting I do is based on my own perceptions of things, a personal response I have to something, and I want to find out if that's what other people are feeling too. It takes a lot of balls to say, "I walked into a city, and people seemed to treat me badly.

Therefore, I concluded that there was a lot of polarization." But, in fact, I was right. . . . An important tool, when you're doing these kinds of stories, is to trust your own instincts. If you have good instincts, and your instincts are telling you that something is shaky here and that people aren't getting along, it's worth pursuing.

Such trust in one's understanding of the situation comes only with experience as exemplified by a conversation between a young reporter struggling with her story and a veteran reporter whose advice she was seeking. The young reporter was Loretta Tofani, who was facing a crisis in her attempt to document the occurrence of rapes in the county jail:

My editors gave me the go-ahead in January, and by March I had a reached a crisis. I had talked to the rape victims. I had talked to the medical workers. I didn't yet have the medical records, and I hadn't yet talked to the rapists. When I tried to write the story, it just didn't come across, and I wasn't clear on exactly what it was that I needed to do. My editors were very anxious to put the story in the paper, but I knew it wasn't ready.

I went to another reporter, and I asked him to please help me. I had read his stories in the *Post* and felt that they were the kind of thing that this story could be. He didn't just find out what people were saying. He went to the source of things and found out what was really going on. I felt like I needed advice from him.

He sat down with me one day in the newsroom. He spent an entire day asking me questions about what I had learned, who I had talked to, what the evidence was, and how things worked. At the end of the day he said, "Well, look: you've got to get the medical records. Otherwise, people are going to say that these guys [the victims] are just making these stories up. . . . And you've got to talk to the jail rapists."

At that point I protested. I said, "That's ridiculous. Those guys aren't going to talk to me."

He said, "They'll talk to you. They'll say something. You know the story of what happened, so you know enough to ask them the questions. They'll at least say, 'I beat him up, but I didn't rape him.' They'll say something. Go! You've got talk to them." So I did. And he was right.

Those were the two essential elements to corroborate the story. All along I had been thinking, "Okay, what do I need next?" My answers were, "Okay, I need more rape victims. I need to talk to the police about what they found. I need to talk to the medical technicians about what they see." I had established all the pieces of the puzzle, but I wasn't going deep enough. I wasn't creative enough.

In yet another testament to the role of mature subjectivity in journalism, the veteran reporter from whom Tofani sought counsel offered not technical assistance but worldly wisdom: if you know enough to ask questions, people will say *something*. This lesson in reportorial creativity resulted in a series of electrifying interviews with the rapists. Here is how Tofani used some of that material in her series:

> On the street, Dwight Welcher robbed and stole. In jail, he raped. His motive was always the same: to win prestige.
>
> "If I can completely destroy this person here [rape him], it tells everyone I'm okay," says Welcher, 29, a convicted armed robber who says he raped several men each week while he was in the Prince George's County Detention Center in 1980 and 1981.
>
> Welcher's values are known among jail officials as "the inmate code." This is how jail inmates define that code: The strong, violent inmates exploit the weaker, nonviolent ones. In many cases, exploitation takes the form of rape.[19]

Tofani's day with the veteran reporter was a private master class in the skills needed to keep the conversation with the situation moving along. For investigative reporters such skills include not only those necessary to elicit information but also those necessary to evaluate—or, in Schön's term, "appreciate"—that information. One such skill is evaluating—"sizing up" or "getting a sense of"—a problematic source. Jon Sawyer and Bill Freivogel of the *St. Louis Post-Dispatch*'s Washington bureau had to learn to deal with such sources in their ongoing efforts to track the use—or rather, the misuse—of Pentagon dollars. Sawyer offered this Watergate-esque example:

> We're working on a series on defense fraud—how federal agencies investigate and prosecute defense fraud and where the system breaks down. I've got a terrific source. . . . He'd seen our stories, and he wanted to talk to us. He's dumping all over the Justice Department. He works for the inspector general at the Pentagon. I've had, maybe, six hours of conversations with him. Wonderful detail . . . but he's never given me his name. He's never agreed to meet with me. He calls me up at night.
>
> He's been invaluable in giving me a sense of how the Pentagon looks at fraud. I've been able to use that in questioning other people. Mostly he's given me an attitude, a perspective . . . but now I think we're going to have a problem. I am pushing now for him to let me see him and to get to know who he is. If we do this series and I use a lot of quotation from him, I'd feel better if I sat down with him—if I just had more of a sense of who he is.

Steele urges caution, however, whenever reporters must depend on their "sense" of the source:

> A reporter says, for example, "I got this guy at the state capitol. I believe this guy. He wouldn't lie to me." Well, when I hear that I go crazy. I just go absolutely crazy. I don't believe that you can operate that way. That doesn't mean that I don't believe somebody might tell the truth, but I think you have to be skeptical every step of the way. It's fine to take the information but don't believe necessarily that the guy wouldn't lie to you—because these people are lying to people all the time. There is usually a very specific reason why sources give information, and it's not just because they think that you are the greatest guy as a reporter.

The knowledge that "people are lying to people" leads reporters to try, as Tofani did for each rape case, to piece together information from multiple sources. Sometimes these efforts reflect organizationally sanctioned rules of evidence, but more often they are strategies specific to the story at hand. Jeff Marx and Michael York, for example, established their own procedures for evaluating the testimony of basketball players concerning payments from boosters. "We would only print, or even consider printing, player A talking about what player A had taken part in," said Marx. "That doesn't mean we wouldn't listen to player A for what he had to tell us about what player B got. We'd certainly want to hear about that so we could then go talk to player B, but we didn't print any of that in our series—one guy talking about what another player got. That was one standard we maintained throughout."

Marx and York's standard was a variation on a general rule that historians and detectives would immediately recognize as useful: self-incriminating testimony is more credible than self-exculpating testimony. Another common standard is the requirement of multiple sources for crucial or off-the-record information. "If somebody is not going on the record, and it's a pivotal fact," Zekman said, "you've got to have some corroboration, if not double corroboration." Bob Woodward and Carl Bernstein made much of their claim that they had multiple sources for everything of importance in their Watergate reporting for the *Washington Post,* but another reporter with long experience in Washington, Jon Sawyer, was unimpressed:

> The *Post* and Watergate—all this big stuff about two sources and all these arbitrary rules that people had! Nobody at my paper has ever said that we have any rules like that. Those rules are meaningless anyway. It's

pretty easy to find two awful sources. A lot of times in an investigation you're dealing with a small circle of people and what people have heard second- or thirdhand.

It's easy to plant a story. One guy can tell you something, and if you like the sound of it, you can call up ten more people that are on the periphery of the story. You can tell each one of them, "Say, I heard this. Have you heard anything like this?" And by the time you get to the tenth person, he's probably heard it from the first or the second or the third. You've just created the story.

Sawyer was not questioning the importance of corroboration but remarking on the fate of formal rules in the real world. Similarly, John Ullmann, who literally wrote the book on investigative reporting with *Investigative Reporting: Advanced Methods and Techniques,* denounced as "total bullshit" any suggestion that two sources constituted some sort of journalistic rule.[20] "It could be that you should be satisfied with one," he said, "or it could be that you shouldn't be satisfied until you have fifteen." After all, two sources may corroborate each other, but they may instead contradict each other. And when confronted with differing accounts—when, in Ullmann's phrase, "what really happened is at issue"—reporters must make difficult decisions about their sources. "The decision often revolves around trying to figure out why somebody would say what they said, if there was a reason to lie and so forth," Ullmann said. "You try to find inconsistencies. You try to find motivations." Ullmann argued that reporters should be satisfied only when they have evaluated the information from each source and have fitted it together with the information from the other sources along with the information from the available documents. "That is why we put all of our evidence, or at least the bulk of our evidence, into our stories when we run them—so that everybody knows what the story is based on."

Nowhere more than in the process of assessing and assembling evidence does investigative reporting demand that "mature subjectivity" of which Michael Schudson wrote. In several subsequent chapters we return to this fundamental question: When what really happened is at issue, how can journalists know? But for now Marx's summary of the effort that went into the basketball story provides a brief but instructive answer:

How do you know? Well, the bottom line is, you don't know. There's no way that I could say, on my life, that every single incident that those guys told us about happened. There's no way. I wasn't there, but I can judge— and balance—the validity of what they said against the denials and against the corroboration of other people who were either there or did the same things or knew how the system worked. I can balance those things and try to write a story that reflects them.

On-the-Spot Experimentation

In Schön's conception on-the-spot experimentation is an impromptu test designed by the practitioner more often to affirm than to disconfirm expectations. When a reporter is the practitioner, such experimentation may be directed toward affirmation of the entire story or only a single fact. Here, for example, Tofani describes what Schön would characterize as "move-testing experiments" intended to affirm a fact about jail rape:

A judge said, "It happens all the time." Well, he may have been prone to overstatement, and what does he mean by "all the time"?

The first thing I did was go around the courthouse and ask other judges. They said essentially the same thing, "Oh, yeah. We see a lot of guys who say they have been raped."

Well, have they or haven't they? The judges didn't know, but it seemed like they [the inmates] had been raped. Sometimes there was medical evidence and sometimes there wasn't. Obviously, that's not conclusive. You have to go further.

I talked to the guards: "How often do you hear of rapes? What do you see? Can you give me examples?"

One guard, a lieutenant, said, "Oh shit, yeah! We get, like, two reports on the midnight shift every week, and those are the ones that are reported." Two a week on one shift—that means, maybe, six a week. Okay, but is he in the best position to know? No, he isn't.

The best person is the medical worker, right? A medical worker says, "Twelve a week."

But how does he know? Well, he knows because several times a week there are people who come in and say, "I've been raped." In addition to that, he gets a lot of people who come in and say that they have nosebleeds or find other reasons to talk to him. As he talks to them, he finds out that they've been forced to give oral sex or something else. He says, "I can't tell you the number of times that happens, but I'd say a minimum of twelve a week."

Okay, so then the question is, can I really trust this medical worker? I'd better find another one. The same story comes out, so then you feel like you're on solid—well, pretty solid—ground. . . .

That's an example of testing one fact. What the judge said, "it happens all the time," did end up becoming a message of the story, but that message was delivered with more precision than that through the reporting process.

Sometimes reporters regard the whole story as a hypothesis to be tested. "An investigative story will often grow out of a run-of-the-mill story where there are important questions left unanswered by the first story," said Bill Freivogel, who provided an example in which questions left unanswered became the hypothesis of an investigation:

> One story I did was about a disabled person who was shot to death in a police station in Maplewood, Missouri, which is a suburb of St. Louis. There was a police version of how that had happened, but the police version was a little suspicious. And then we began to get telephone calls about past things that had happened in the Maplewood police department. . . .
>
> The process to follow is to go out and try to get all of your unanswered questions answered, to test your hypotheses as to what may be wrong in this particular instance, and to not be afraid to draw conclusions that are warranted by the facts. But before you put that in the paper, you run that conclusion past those persons who might disagree. Get their view of it. If their view is persuasive, change your conclusion, and if their view is not persuasive, make sure that their view is included in the story. . . .
>
> Take that police story. A person is shot. And then you get two, three, four calls from people who say, "Hey, you really should look at the Maplewood police department, and you shouldn't accept their explanation at face value." What you tend to do here is to form a hypothesis—that there is something wrong in the Maplewood police department, that there are instances of brutality—and then you try to test if that's accurate by talking to victims and other firsthand sources.

Although moves and hypotheses may be put to the test more often with the goal of affirmation than disconfirmation, reporters know that they must always be open to disconfirmatory evidence. "You may start with hypotheses. You may start with some questions. You may have a rough road map," Steele said. "That's fine, but you've got to be flexible when those change." Moreover, at key points in the project moves or hypotheses may indeed be put to test with the goal of disconfirmation. "As we go along, we try not only to hypothesize alternative views, we try to seek them out," Ullmann said. "We try to prove or disprove them, which is a way of disproving the main hypothesis."

Stephen Kurkjian, a veteran of the *Boston Globe*'s investigative unit, succinctly captured the point at which the logic of affirmation gives way to the logic of refutation. "You push the story into a version of the events that you think is right," he said, "and then knock it down." Often the confrontational interview with the target of the investigation prompts the shift from the logic of affirmation (pushing the story) to the logic of refutation (knocking it down). Fairness demands that reporters confront those who will be accused of wrongdoing and ask for an explanation, but it is not fairness alone that demands these interviews. It is also the possibility that disconfirmatory evidence exists. Pam Zekman spoke of the importance of confrontational interviews in this regard:

> I'm going to let [the target of the investigation] give his side of it, and then I'm going to check out his side of it. One of things that some reporters do, which is a big mistake, is waiting until the last second to confront whomever you are investigating because you don't want him to know what you are doing.
>
> If your story is based on an important fact, and you've never asked him about it, and you do the tape, and that fact is the beginning of the story, and you call him Friday night when the story is going to air Saturday, and he pokes a hole in it, then where are you?

The information value of confrontational interviews has led Marimow to contact the target of the investigation as early as possible in the information-gathering process:

> Lately, I find myself doing something which I think most in-depth reporters might not approve of: I try as soon as possible to find out the two poles of the truth. For instance, I had someone write to me from prison, a convicted murderer who's become a jailhouse attorney. He said he was working on the case of another convicted murderer whom he believed was innocent. I read his letters. I asked some questions. I got some clips. I read a little bit of the trial proceedings, and then I knew what the convicted murderer's story was going to be. I went to see the guy who prosecuted him. . . .
>
> I wanted to make a judgment early on as to whether there was any chance whatsoever that this guy had been wrongfully convicted and, if he had been, whether I could get enough information to document it. . . . I feel comfortable with [this procedure] because I don't consider myself an advocate or a prosecutor. I consider myself a gatherer of facts.

Other reporters who regularly do other sorts of stories, however, had other sorts of wisdom to offer on the topic of confrontational interviews. Freivogel argued, for example, "I don't think you should ever call up the person who, you might say, is the target of the investigation until you've gotten enough for a story—everything that you can find out from other sources about the story." Still, Freivogel did not entirely dismiss the possibility that disconfirmatory information will emerge in such interviews. "Generally, you don't go into those confrontational interviews completely set in concrete." he said. "You go into them willing to listen and be persuaded that what you've got isn't the whole truth." Nonetheless, his years in Washington taught him not to expect much useful information from these interviews:

> Reporters have to get used to being in a situation where all their facts seem to point one way, and they get a response that says, "No, it isn't so." It makes you nervous, but you've got to be prepared to go ahead because often these responses are worded in a way that is completely misleading.
>
> I wrote a story about how the chairman of General Dynamics Corporation and other executives were charging the government for airplane trips taken for private purposes—trips to the farm and skiing vacations. The company's response was, "We categorically deny that the company or any of its executives have charged the government, and have been paid for, any trips for private purposes."
>
> Gee whiz! We had expected, "No comment," but this was categorically denying it. Well, it turned out that the key words were "been paid for" because the company had charged trips to the government, but the trips had been contested and hadn't yet been paid for. They were trying to get the money from the government, but they just hadn't yet received it. We would have been making a big mistake if we had allowed that categorical denial to scare us away from the story.

In that situation the denial became an important part of the story:

> WASHINGTON—General Dynamics Corp. has billed the government for thousands of dollars for airplane trips that its chairman, David S. Lewis, took from St. Louis to a small town in Georgia near where he has a private residence, the Post-Dispatch has learned.
>
> A House Energy and Commerce subcommittee has asked the company to explain why it has tried to collect from the government for Lewis' trips on the corporation's private jets from St. Louis to Albany, Ga.
>
> A spokesman for General Dynamics denied that the company had received payments from the Defense Department for any personal trips. But the spokesman refused to say whether the company had tried to collect the money.[21]

Similarly, Gaines thought that conducting the confrontational interviews toward the end of the investigation had worked well for the story on unethical conduct by members of the Chicago City Council. For that story Gaines and his colleagues had pieced together the history of outrageously self-serving, though not illegal, behavior by a number of aldermen. "It was all documented," as Gaines said, so that when it came time to confront the aldermen, the reporters were ready. "When I go into an interview of that type, I tell them at the start exactly what I know," Gaines said. "That clears the air. There's no bullshit." With this strategy Gaines expected to get something that would be more informative than merely a denial: "That's the technique I like to use because I know that they know that I know. They think we probably know even more than we do—so they're not going to lie to us because we'll catch them in the lie, and we'll put in the paper the fact that we caught them in a lie. . . . I think that when somebody does something wrong, in their minds they're rationalizing it anyway, so they've got a good story as to why they did it."

In the series of articles entitled "City Council: Spoils of Power," Gaines and his colleagues used these rationalizations to hoist a number of aldermen on their own petard. For example, one alderman who was also the Democratic Party committeeman had been pocketing half the funds allotted for maintaining an office in his ward. In the story his words showed him to be not merely unethical but smugly so:

> "It costs money to go downtown, park, buy lunch," explained Cullerton who as an alderman gets an additional $440 each month from the city for unaudited travel and auto expenses. "It costs money to be a committeeman too, and it's getting harder to raise funds." He added: "I have it all justified in my mind.'"[22]

Providing a useful reminder that interviewing techniques, like most other journalistic skills, are far more art than science, Steele offered advice seemingly at odds with that from Gaines. "A lot of young reporters want to impress the subject by how much they know, which is exactly the wrong way to interview," Steele argued. "Subjects need to know that you know a little bit about what you are talking about, so they have a certain amount of respect for you, but you really don't want to tell them anything very substantive. You want whoever you're interviewing to do the talking."

Whatever the timing and strategy of the confrontational interview, the information from that interview and any other crucial on-the-spot experiment is usually in hand before the reporters begin to write the story.

However, Don Shelby, a longtime investigative reporter at WCCO-TV in Minneapolis and a colorful storyteller, provided a counterexample that could evoke fear in the toughest reporter. The investigation concerned an alleged drug smuggler named Ramirez who had purchased the goodwill of a small town in, of all places, Minnesota. Here's Shelby's tale:

> Ramirez said that the source of his wealth was a patent on an aviation safety device, that he woke up a millionaire because somebody snapped it up. . . . Well, we talked to lots of people who said that was bullshit. We talked to a person who had investigated that before and said he found absolutely no record of any such thing.
>
> I commissioned a patent search through a Washington law firm, and within two weeks I had the search back. The piece of paper said that there was absolutely no record of aviation safety equipment under the name Joseph Diego Ramirez or any of his aliases. I squirreled that away somewhere. . . .
>
> We were going on the air Monday. The Thursday or Friday before, my boss came in and said, "We've got to shoot that document. Will you get it for me?"
>
> I said, "Yeah." I pulled it out and said, "Fuck! This is a trademark search. . . ."
>
> The fuck-up was with the Minneapolis law firm through which we had commissioned the thing. They had told the Washington firm to do a trademark search because they do trademark searches for all of the station's logos. They never do patent searches for television stations. I called them up and got the entire eighth floor, the corporate division, to run the patent search. Monday morning someone walked in and said that Ramirez has a patent—aviation.
>
> Joseph D. Ramirez with a Florida address—Ramirez was from Florida—has patented this piece of aviation safety equipment which was purchased by the United States Navy. I was just shaking. The only thing that bothered me was that it was a Panama City, Florida, address and all of my research into Ramirez said that he had never lived there. . . .
>
> So I called information in Panama City, "Is there a Joseph D. Ramirez in Panama City?"
>
> They said yes. They gave me a telephone number, and I called it. I let it ring seven hundred times. I just could not allow myself to hang up thinking that any minute he is going to answer.
>
> I called the library and said, "Give me your city directory. Give me an address for Joseph D. Ramirez." She did. I said, "I've got his telephone

number. Now, I want you to give me his neighbors on both sides." She said she couldn't do it. I'm going on the air in five hours. . . .

I'm a former military guy and I thought, "The navy holds the patent. The navy gets their patents generally out of their own R&D branch. Is it possible that a Joseph D. Ramirez is a civilian employee who patented it under his own name and then transferred it to the navy?"

I called the information operator back in Panama City and said, "Do you have a navy base in Panama City?" She said that they did.

I said, "Would you give me the number for civilian personnel?" She did.

I called civilian personnel and said, "Do you have a Joseph D. Ramirez on the payroll?"

She was gone for a hundred hours, but she came back and said yes.

I said, "Where does he work?"

"He works in research and development."

I said, "Could you give me that telephone number?" She gave it to me, and I called. A fellow answered the phone, and I said, "I am trying to reach a Joseph D. Ramirez."

"This is him."

I said, "Are you Joseph Diego Ramirez?"

He said, "No, Joseph Delgotto Ramirez."

"Do you own a patent on some kind of aviation safety equipment?"

"Yeah, an inflatable boat."

"Do you know Joseph Diego Ramirez?"

"Nope."

"Does anybody in the world know you had this patent?"

"Oh, yeah. It was all over the Florida papers."

This hair-raising adventure was, of course, an exceptional experience for a veteran. "Just in that forty-minute span of time, I know I got ten years older," Shelby remembered. "My hands shake just at the thought of those moments as they went by." More typically, the writing (and in television the production phase of the process) is, according to most reporters, the last of their worries.

The Secret of Good Writing Revealed at Last

"I have an early warning mechanism that doesn't allow me to write something until I feel that I have all the pieces settled in my mind," Kaufman said. He maintained that he could begin to write only when he could cast the frame or structure of the story into a few words—the "Ah-ha!" or "significance" paragraph, as he called it—that tells the reader why the story is important. But once the frame is in place, Kaufman said that he attempts to distance himself from the fact-gathering process. "I disengage myself from all this reporting and put myself in the shoes of someone in Newton or East Boston or someplace else," he said. "On a given Tuesday, how are they gonna want to read about the story?" And if effective writing demands that this reporter make contact with imagined readers, it also demands that he make contact with himself—that is, with his motive for taking on the project all those months before. With Kaufman's work on the racism series, that motive was to make Boston a better place. "When I'm trying to get in the mood to write a piece, that's the kind of image I have in mind for the information I want to put in—you know, make Boston the best possible city," he said. "The writing can affect people in a deeper way if you're aiming high like that."

Investigative reporters want to tell their stories, as Marimow maintained, in a way that "the average reader can relate to." But as Marimow also said, reporters will always "subordinate style to substance, accuracy, precision, fairness." Most reporters seemed uncomfortable talking very much about style, although as we will see in subsequent chapters, the powerful moral charge of investigative journalism does depend on the quality of the writing. Reporters were more comfortable talking about "tone," which they said should be even-handed rather than accusatory. Ullmann, for example, recommended avoiding a "gotcha" tone. He said, "The most useful tone you could take is this: 'We went out and looked at this, and this is what we found, and this is the reason why we think it is important that you know it.'"

Beyond these considerations, most reporters insisted that effective writing is largely a matter of figuring out what to include and where to put it. "Writing," Gaines said, "is organizing." And with a hint of parody Kaufman summarized an all-purpose formula for organizing a story: "Let's see. You have your anecdotal lead. You have your significance graph. You have the paragraph which says, 'This raises fundamental questions.' And then you go through it chronologically."

Most reporters, however, are not quite so glib about the task of organizing the information they have gathered. "You have so much material. You can't write everything you know," Gaines said. "First, you have to decide what you're going to do on what day of the series. Then you have to decide how you're going to present it—what you need here and what you need there." Although these decisions are not really subject to formulas, they are aided by a repertoire of organizational strategies. For example, Dedman's "Color of Money" series documented the pattern of wrongdoing (discrimination in lending) on the first day and explained the causes of that pattern on the second day. On the third day it examined the response of the responsible government authorities to the situation. And on the fourth day it presented the demands of community groups for change. The series also included a number of sidebars introducing the victims of discrimination—including the chairman of county commission.

Similarly, Barlett and Steele's series, "The Great Tax Giveaway," began with the pattern of wrongdoing (tax breaks for the politically well connected) on the first day and explained the connection between the congressional tax writers and their campaign contributors on a subsequent day. Several days were devoted to profiles of those who had received the breaks. On the other hand, the series to which Gaines contributed, "City Council: Spoils of Power," examined a different unethical practice each day, as exemplified by the activities of one or more aldermen. "I think the main thing in writing an investigative story," Gaines concluded, "is not to suddenly lead the reader down some side street, to have a purpose from the beginning of the story through to the end."

Despite these familiar organizational strategies, writing still resists reduction to formulas. One of the most accomplished reporters acknowledged that the process of writing has gotten no easier over the years. "When I was young journalist, I thought that the older I got, the more facile I'd become," Steele said. "That turned out to be one of the all-time great myths." But he also acknowledged that writing has gotten no easier largely because his standards for good writing have gotten higher. His advice was to produce a first draft quickly, "to spew things out," and then to review, reorganize, and rewrite. "You have to edit yourself and apply those higher standards."

In the final analysis, then, the secret of the masters is simply to get to work. "Find a way to make the first sentence interesting," said Jack Reed, a former English teacher, "and then keep it up."

Reflections

Reed's secret for good writing captures well, if wryly, Schön's concept of thinking in action. The skills of the masters are not applied by thinking and then doing, Schön argued, but rather by thinking in doing. Schön's goal in analyzing such skills was to encourage practitioners to reflect upon, and demystify as much as possible, their own practice. Although the reflections collected and analyzed here do not unlock all the mysteries, at least they invite further consideration of the skill and judgment that constitute the mature subjectivity of the best journalists. "I'm going to really do some thinking about what has made me whatever I am as a reporter," said Jeff Marx at the conclusion of our interview. "One common weakness among newsroom people today—whether it's TV, radio, newspapers, or magazines, whether it's an editor, a reporter or whatever—is that we don't take the time to really think through everything we're doing and why."

Marx's enthusiasm may draw a sardonic smile from his more world-weary colleagues. "Journalists don't have time to get philosophical," wrote Carlin Romano, a reporter and editor of long experience, "and no self-respecting managing editor would hire Bertrand Russell if he could steal a sportswriter instead."[23] Romano's remark was not idle sarcasm. It was the preface to an analysis of news judgment, a concept he found neither the public nor journalists understand very well. Romano knew not to expect too much from his invitation to reflect on journalistic practice but knew that it was important, not only for practitioners of journalism but for all of society, to extend that invitation.

Society's stake is this: through reflection, professional practice can be transformed from an exercise in unchallengeable expertise to a conversation with the client. "Just as reflective practice takes the form of a reflective conversation with the situation, so the reflective practitioner's relation with his client takes the form of a literally reflective conversation," wrote Schön. "He recognizes an obligation to make his own understandings accessible to his client, which means that he needs often to reflect anew on what he knows."[24] With the credibility of the news media everywhere in decline, journalism's clients seem to have already rejected any claims of unchallengeable expertise. The need for a conversation is urgent.

3

The Paradox of the Disengaged Conscience

If investigative reporting is American journalism at its most rigorous, it is also American journalism at its most paradoxical. The essential energy of investigative reporting is still best characterized as "righteous indignation," a term coined by Ida Tarbell a century ago as the anthem of the muckrakers. The contemporary version is IRE, the acronym for Investigative Reporters and Editors, a national organization founded in 1975. But this unmistakable tone of moral engagement stands in apparent opposition to the presumed objectivity of news. How can journalists function as the custodians of conscience and at the same time claim to be mere observers of fact? That is, how can they expose wrongdoing without making moral judgments?

In a classic study of the news media, sociologist Herbert Gans offered an insightful, if incomplete, answer to these questions. "Like social scientists and others, journalists can also feel objective when they assume, rightly or wrongly, that their values are universal or dominant," Gans wrote in *Deciding What's News*. "When values arouse no dissent or when dissent can be explained away as moral disorder, those who hold values can easily forget that they are values."[1] In other words, the presumed objectivity of news judgment is made possible by a consensus (or at least a widely shared or officially sanctioned agreement) on the values that constitute the premises of judgment. Investigative reporters can, then, set aside explicit consideration of the normative *ought* and concentrate on documentation of the empirical *is* by limiting their investigative stories to violations of such universal or dominant values.

In their dealings with presumably incontrovertible instances of wrongdoing, reporters typically describe two aspects of the empirical *is*. One aspect is the wrongdoing itself—the misdeeds of the villains and the suffering of their victims. The second aspect is some standard that those misdeeds have violated. As Gans pointed out, the quintessential investigative story, the exposé, "typically judges the exposed against their own expressed values, and these can be determined empirically by the reporter." If nothing else, then, the exposed are found to have violated the widely shared proscription against hypocrisy, but often they are also found to have violated such established standards as laws, codes of professional conduct, and the like. By invoking such standards investigative journalism can seem to treat questions of right and wrong entirely as questions of fact and thereby sidestep any analysis of—or any challenge to—the prevailing moral order. Thus, Gans concluded, journalism conserves the moral status quo insofar as it "reinforces and relegitimates dominant national and societal values by publicizing and helping to punish those who deviate from the values."[2]

Gans's central insight is that investigative journalists can see themselves to be objective to the extent that they can operate within what Daniel Hallin called "the sphere of consensus" and therefore can use what they take to be objective standards of conduct.[3] We argue, however, that Gans underestimated the amount of moral work that journalists must accomplish because the consensus upon which they rely is neither stable nor complete. Those "dominant national and societal values" upon which the claim to objectivity depends are not necessarily consistent, and their application to the situation at hand is not always clear. In turn, appropriate evaluative standards are not necessarily self-evident, and their empirical determination is not always straightforward.

Therefore investigative journalists do not—indeed, cannot—simply reiterate, and inevitably reinforce, a clearly articulated moral order by exposing incontrovertible transgressions against that order. Instead journalists help to articulate the moral order by showing that the actions of alleged transgressors are in fact transgressions. To maintain the (presumably necessary) fiction of moral disengagement, journalists usually stop short of explicit moral judgment—if such judgment is understood to be the overt denunciation of a transgressor. Journalists do, however, locate and select as well as simplify and interpret the standards that the public can use to make such judgments. This objectification of moral standards, we conclude, is the special contribution of journalism to the ongoing cultural process by which values are not only reinforced but realigned through application to new and ever changing conditions.

Investigative journalists are, then, participants in the "crafting of virtue," to use Celeste Michelle Condit's apt phrase, but the terms of their participation in that process are problematic.[4] Although reporters are called upon not simply to maintain but to participate in the establishment of standards for moral judgment, they are denied the opportunity to explicitly defend or critique such judgments by the conventions of journalistic objectivity. Despite investigative journalism's focus on apparently incontrovertible instances of wrongdoing, escape from the paradox of the disengaged conscience is not so easy as it might first have seemed.

The paradoxical connection between moral custodianship and moral disengagement provides a point of departure for a study of the connection between the mass media and the maintenance of the moral order. Specifically, our goal in this chapter is fourfold: to briefly review the long-standing relationship between objectivity and indignation in journalism; to examine the diverse styles that contemporary investigative reporters have adopted to live within that enduring but difficult relationship; to review the strategies for objectification of evaluative standards that is the special moral craftwork of these reporters; and to draw a conclusion about journalism's role in the continuity and change of social values.

Objectivity and Indignation

Fueled by the *Washington Post*'s now legendary efforts in the early 1970s to uncover corruption in the Nixon White House, the rise of contemporary investigative reporting represents nothing less (and nothing more, for that matter) than a renewal of the watchdog or adversarial tradition in journalism. The adventures of Carl Bernstein and Bob Woodward—and, no doubt, of their celluloid counterparts, Dustin Hoffman and Robert Redford—marked the beginning of an extended celebration of those hard-hitting reporters whose bravado spirit affirmed the importance of a free and unintimidated press. Books with titles like *The Typewriter Guerrillas* and *Raising Hell* presented an unabashedly heroic profile of investigative reporters whose stories were said to "attack, charge, inflame, accuse, harass, intimidate, incriminate, and sometimes damage or destroy, organizations, agencies, and government on your behalf and mine."[5] These newsroom irregulars were cast in the role of our last hope for a challenger to the power of government—a role that was important, we were told by veteran investigative reporter Clark Mollenhoff, because "realistically, the public cannot count upon any administration to do a strict job of policing itself."[6]

Whether the ideal of an adversarial press manifested itself as healthy skepticism or exaggerated cynicism, whether it reflected journalists' commitment to their constitutionally sanctioned duty or merely their psychic baggage, this ideal has long endured as the ethos of American journalism.[7] It may be true that investigative reporting, despite flashes of high visibility, has appeared relatively infrequently on America's front pages. It may also be true that only a minority of journalists expressly adopt an adversarial role.[8] But it is probably just as true that an adversarial attitude "has always lurked in the psyche of American journalists."[9] The notion that the press should be a relentless adversary of the powerful—a "lifeline of democracy in reporting upon the use, misuse and abuse of power"—has deep roots in American journalism.[10] But the notion that the press is an unbiased recorder of fact is sustained by roots no less deep. Indeed, any account of the intimate relationship between adversarialism and detached observation would begin where the history of modern journalism begins: the penny press.

As James Gordon Bennett himself explained, the penny press sought both to reach "the great masses of the community" and to gain independence from the mercantile and political elites whose interests dominated the press of the 1830s.[11] Thanks to this self-proclaimed independence, the penny press could offer, it claimed, a more dependable and authentic journalism—news unstained by the political, social, and economic values that had for so long defined the content of the daily papers. That the penny press in fact championed the values of its predominantly working-class public served not to diminish but to strengthen faith in the authenticity of its news among its readers. Drawing upon these values, the penny press could, without apparent contradiction, claim to be at once the recorder of what Bennett said would be "facts of every public and proper subject, stripped of verbiage and coloring" and also the "private defender of the public good."[12] This new journalism spoke for, and thereby helped to realize, a vision of the public interest by telling stories that exemplified and defended that interest.

Any account of the relationship between adversarialism and objectivity must also highlight the alliance between journalism and reform movements of the Progressive Era. Journalism's sense of independence, its disdain for special interests, and its commitment to news of public interest— all a legacy of the penny press—coincided well with the progressive call for reform. In the hands of the muckrakers, monthly magazines began to bring vivid stories of public corruption and private abuse to American readers who otherwise would have had only fragmented newspaper accounts. "These writers, using the most sordid details to make their points, shocked and bewildered the conservative reader," wrote Louis Filler in his classic account of the muckrakers. "To the common people, however, the new writing was as gripping as it was educational: they had never known that business and politics could be so interesting."[13] Once again a new journalism helped to consolidate the values upon which depended its claim to speak on behalf of the public interest.

The muckraker's exposé, and even the sensational journalism of William Randolph Hearst and Joseph Pulitzer, benefited enormously from what was becoming the hallmark of the new century: reverence for the logic of science and faith in the power of detached observation. The Progressive Era marked the beginning of what Hallin described as the "scientization of journalism" when the "changing conventions of journalism paralleled the rise of science as a cultural paradigm against which all forms of discourse came to be measured." The ideal of objectively reported fact allowed journalists, like scientists, to position themselves and their work as value free. That ideal was soon rationalized into journalism's dominant paradigm—"a canon of professional competence and an ideology of professional responsibility," in James Carey's terms, that conveyed a "reassuring sense of disinterest and rigor."[14]

By this account the paradoxical linkage of objectivity and indignation is less a logical contradiction than a necessary tension in the historical development of American journalism. Tarbell's journalism of righteous indignation had been made credible—indeed, it had been made intellectually possible in the age of science—by that reassuring sense of disinterest and rigor. After all, no one can "unearth a scandal as effectively as a man with no vested interest in any part of the scandal-making mechanism."[15] But if the triumph of objectivity as the professional ethic of journalism has worked to make modern muckraking credible, it has also worked to further obscure the values upon which it depends. Social values are submerged below the surface of journalistic discourse as a component of what Stuart Hall, drawing upon Claude Lévi-Strauss, characterized as the ideological "deep structure" of news.[16]

This deep structure is never completely submerged, however. In our time journalism has come under fire for its values even though, as Gans found, contemporary journalism has retained the value system of the progressive reformers. The resemblance, wrote Gans, "is often uncanny, as in the common advocacy of honest, meritocratic, and anti- bureaucratic government, and in the shared antipathy to political machines and dema- gogues, particularly of populist bent."[17] Nevertheless, contemporary journalism is often seen to be dangerously adversarial in its stance toward traditional values. For example, Daniel Moynihan's celebrated *Commentary* essay, "The Presidency and the Press," published three years before Richard Nixon's resignation, lamented "an almost feckless hostility to power" among members of the press. Journalism had become yet another manifestation of what Moynihan took to be a "culture of disparage- ment."[18]

Even journalists have sometimes argued that the values they detect within journalism are not proper values. In his 1982 presidential address to the American Society of Newspaper Editors less than a decade after the apparent journalistic triumph of Watergate, Michael J. O'Neill com- plained bitterly about the press's "harshly adversarial posture toward government and its infatuation with investigative reporting." A more appropriate editorial philosophy, O'Neill proposed, would involve a "clear but uncrabbed view of the world."[19] Similarly, journalists' com- mentary on the Janet Cooke scandal (in which a *Washington Post* reporter relinquished a Pulitzer Prize after admitting to fabricating a story) often suggested that in the 1960s and '70s journalism had gone too far in its attempt to overcome the limitations of traditional objectivity.[20] Indeed, some observers argued that the excesses of investigative journal- ism, along with the experiments in New Journalism, had undermined not only the authority of government but the authority of truth.

And so, it seems, the boundaries of the moral order that journalists are to defend are not clearly demarcated. The call for a renewed commitment to a "clear but uncrabbed view of the world"—which is to say, "objectiv- ity"—is one response to uncertainty about what, exactly, falls within the sphere of consensus. However, a simplistic call for resolution of uncer- tainty in favor of more objectivity and less indignation is, as we will see, not the only response among contemporary journalists.

News Judgment and Moral Judgment

Our interviews with distinguished investigative journalists show these reporters to have a sophisticated, if inconsistent, understanding of the tension between objective detachment and active adversarialism. These interviews reveal diverse approaches to that paradoxical relationship, but they also reveal commonalities that unite these reporters in a shared intellectual enterprise. Here we attempt to reconstruct that unity within diversity.

The interviews with some of these journalists began as a celebration of active adversarialism. An example was Jonathan Kaufman, the reporter who proclaimed that his goal was to make his city the best it could be and that to accomplish this goal he wanted to write stories that would make his readers say, "This is an outrage." Here, then, was a reporter who took pride in his ability to influence his community but who also recognized that any claim to moral leadership within the community is deeply problematic for journalism. Expressing discomfort with the idea that his work on the *Boston Globe*'s Pulitzer Prize–winning series on racism was driven by either his newspaper's or his own sense of morality, he argued that it was driven simply by a sense of what was important to the city.

In contrast to the interview with Kaufman, other interviews began as a ringing reaffirmation of objectivity. An example was Bill Marimow, who insisted that moral judgments are *not* a concern of investigative reporters. "Right and wrong may be a threshold question but not a fundamental question," he argued, adding that the importance and the truth of the story were the fundamental questions. Right and wrong is "a threshold question" because established standards of conduct easily determine the answer. Importance and truth, however, are the fundamental questions that demand the expertise of the reporter.

Marimow elaborated his arguments with reference to his Pulitzer Prize–winning investigation of the Philadelphia police department's K-9 unit, whose dogs and officers were, according to his reports, out of control:

> Let's go to the K-9 cases. Are these attacks warranted? Yes or no? No, they look questionable. Is there a standard by which I can gauge whether they're justifiable, questionable, or really unwarranted? Not a clear one, but you can get a sense of it. . . .
>
> Is it newsworthy? Well, in my opinion, if people sworn to uphold the law are alleged to be violating people's civil rights over and over again, that's important. Why is it important? It's important because these people are entrusted with great power and authority, and these dogs are capable of inflicting great physical and psychological harm. The city must know about it because there are dozens of civil suits being filed, and nothing's happening. The officers go back to the street time and time again. So I think, for me, the ultimate question becomes a question of importance and not right or wrong.

Just as Kaufman implicitly recognized a limit to active adversarialism even as he defended it, so Marimow recognized a limit to objective detachment. Although Marimow argued that morality is an unproblematic "threshold" question, whereas newsworthiness is a "fundamental" question, he acknowledged that moral issues are indeed both present and problematic. And in his comments we catch a brief glimpse of the dominant values—individual civil rights, for example, and cost-effective government—that are submerged in the journalistic judgments of importance. We also glimpse the moral work to be done: Marimow suggested that standards do exist to judge this situation, but he acknowledged that those standards are not unequivocal. Although this reporter's goal was to report on obvious violations of the moral order, he knew that the exact boundaries of the order were not well defined. He knew that wrongdoing was not entirely self-evident and that he would be required to demonstrate that the transgression was in fact a transgression.

If the interviews with Kaufman and Marimow defined the range of responses to the connection between objectivity and indignation, the interviews with other reporters offered interesting variations on the theme. Loretta Tofani, for example, acknowledged that her Pulitzer Prize–winning investigation of sexual assaults against jail inmates evoked a strong "gut reaction" within her and that her work was a "conscious choice to show the wrong" in a situation that is often seen as an inevitable, and therefore acceptable, consequence of incarceration. Elsewhere in the interview, however, she rejected the role of moral leadership for her paper or for herself. She said that she was sure her readers, when confronted with the facts, would agree with her response to the situation. "I think my judgment reflects people outside of journalism," she said. "I really felt that people outside would see it as wrong as well." Thus any morally inflected judgments she may have made were not, as she viewed it, her judgments but those of her community.

At the same time she backed away from the notion that she had helped define for her readers an ambiguous situation as wrong. "I don't know if I'm helping them see what's right and wrong so much as I am showing them a problem that they otherwise would not be able to learn about in any sort of detail," she argued. "You stop at the point of describing the problem. You don't end up saying in the story, 'This is wrong.'" With many of her colleagues this reporter sought refuge in the notion that she had not made explicit moral judgments but had merely described a situation that was important to her community. It is the community, Tofani argued, that must ultimately say, "This is wrong."

Bill Gaines characterized the moral status of the investigative reporter within the community in similar terms. "An investigative reporter has a threshold of outrage—a point at which you say to yourself, 'This is wrong,'" Gaines said, quickly adding that this threshold is also the point at which the public is likely to say the same thing. It is the point, according to Gaines, at which "we would *all* think, 'This is wrong.'" As a result, investigative reporters need not, and usually do not, explicitly announce in print or on the air, "This is wrong." In this way journalists retain grounds for contending, as Gaines did, that the making of moral judgments is a "pretty strong term" for describing their work.

The *Chicago Tribune*'s Pulitzer Prize–winning investigation into conflicts of interest within the city council provided Gaines with an example. "We decided that we had better tell the story because it was pretty obvious to us that the situation was wrong, and we thought that everyone would agree with us," he recalled of the investigative unit's response to the emerging facts of their story. For the reporter and his colleagues, then, the evidence of wrongdoing had surpassed that "threshold of outrage" at which point the public, not the journalists, would be seen to occupy the seat of moral judgment. "We didn't flat out say, 'The city council is rife with corruption,' or anything like that," Gaines said of the finished series. "We just laid the thing out and said, 'Here it is. Judge for yourself. What's wrong is wrong.'"

For Gaines a sense of where, exactly, the public's threshold of outrage lies depends on journalistic experience and public affairs knowledge. "You have to work on, maybe, a government beat for a long time," he said. "You have to know how government is supposed to work before you can criticize it." More urgently, however, reporters must learn to respect the idea that, beyond the newsroom, there exists a community and its values. Gaines attributed his awareness of community standards to his youthful days as a radio reporter in a small town. "We would gather a story and put it on the air and, my God, the phone would ring," he recalled. "We were not in some far-moved place, like on Mount Olympus, judging everyone." Gaines worried that young reporters often lack the opportunity to develop a keen sense of the community and its values. "We've got a farm system that brings in good reporters, terrific writers, but their social circle is one another," he said of his paper. "I think, maybe, they get a little out of touch."

Boston Globe reporter Stephen Kurkjian also emphasized the importance of a value-based relationship between journalists and their community. "With more experiences in various systems, when you pay your bills and when your kids go to school, you become more of a judge as to what shouldn't be and what should be," he argued. "The more part of a community you get, the more cautious you become but the more accurate becomes your sense of personal outrage." Kurkjian conceptualized the values of his community as a "common man set of standards" personified in the standards of his aunt whom he described as an average citizen with a high school education. "I think, 'Gee, I gotta see it the way she would see it.'" Her sense of outrage, he argued, had become his.

Some variation on this basic argument—any judgment made by the journalist directly reflects the values of the community—was fundamental to the thinking of all the reporters who were willing to acknowledge, even if only implicitly, the role of moral judgments in their work but who were reluctant to take responsibility for those judgments. One more example is Jon Sawyer, who acknowledged that investigative reporters constantly make judgments concerning "immorality, the potential for immorality, the appearance of immorality." But he argued that journalists cannot dictate values to their audience. If the investigation does not uncover something that is "really wrong," he maintained, "the story will sink without a trace." To have an impact the story must reflect "the community consensus on those values and how they apply in particular instances."

When journalists have a sense of what they take to be "the community consensus," their value judgments become, in another of Sawyer's apt phrases, "ingrained." Value judgments, in other words, become news judgments. "I make a judgment about whether something's worth going after, whether it meets my own standard of what's significant," Sawyer said, but when asked to articulate these standards, he revealed just how ingrained they really are. "I don't know that I can [articulate them]," he said. "It would depend entirely on the situation—the circumstances that you're talking about." But whatever those unarticulated standards may be, they seemed to Sawyer to concern "what's newsy, what's jazzy, what's interesting, what's out of the ordinary—more than what's immoral."

In the simultaneous embrace of active adversarialism and objective detachment these masters of the investigative craft all found a way to live with, though not resolve, the paradox of the disengaged conscience. These examples of journalistic self-revelation do not exhaust the possibilities, but they do capture the key features of the modus vivendi that continues to make contemporary investigative journalism intellectually viable. Although these reporters failed (or, let us say, declined) to articulate a value system, they did acknowledge that their connection to a community and its moral order allowed them to identify outrages against that order. Although their conceptions of "the community" and its values may not have encompassed everyone in their city or everyone in their audience, these conceptions did reference an "interpretive community" within which values seemed to be consensual and therefore unproblematic.[21] In this community, to whatever extent it may be real or imagined, judgments of right and wrong are, as one reporter said, "pretty black and white"; the facts, as another said, "speak for themselves." Therefore these journalists could claim that they made judgments of importance but not of moral value. And yet they did not make this claim naively. Like Gans, they realized that their claim to moral detachment depended, paradoxically, upon a long-standing moral relationship to their community. And once in that relationship, community values came to be "ingrained" or, in Gans's terms, "built into importance judgments."[22]

Investigative journalists are not, then, moral arbiters who can dictate values to the community with each story, but neither do they simply and uncritically reinforce values. Rather, they contribute something to that ongoing moral relationship with their communities. These reporters seemed to understand at some level that even if values seem "pretty black and white," they must do moral work. It is to this work, a role in the crafting of public morality not fully appreciated by either Gans or the reporters themselves, that we now turn.

From Moral Claims to Empirical Claims

Documenting the existence of a transgression is largely a matter of gathering evidence and assessing its quality. But establishing that the transgression is in fact a transgression requires the process that we have termed the *objectification* of moral standards. In this process reporters attempt to make good on their claim that they make news judgments rather than moral judgments; that is, they attempt to transform moral claims into empirical claims so that ultimately the evaluative standards used to appraise the transgression appear as empirically unambiguous as the evidence used to document its existence. By the logic of this process the moral order is made fact, and fact can be reported with detachment.

In simplest terms the objectification of a moral claim is accomplished through the reporting of established standards of conduct that can locate a "threshold" of right and wrong. Among the investigative reports that we have reviewed, such standards were drawn from the law; formalized regulations, codes, and guidelines; recognized expertise; statistical comparisons; and commonsense interpretations of fairness and decency. In a reading of a completed investigative report such standards appear self-evidently credible and obviously appropriate to the situation at hand. In an examination of the reporting process, however, the standards are seen to emerge from the investigator's hard work at locating, selecting, simplifying, interpreting, and in those ways helping to establish the threshold of right and wrong.

Of course, investigative journalists do not speak of the objectification of moral claims, but they recognize the reporting of an evaluative standard as an essential element of the investigation. "There may be different or competing standards that can be used," said John Ullmann. "But there has to be a standard if you're going to say in an investigative story that something is wrong, and somebody is the cause of it." Beginning with the law, Ullmann offered a basic list of resources for the establishment of standards. Regulations were next on his list because, like the law, they are published, often with the methods for investigating violations and the procedures for reporting them. Expertise, particularly that of professionals who can cite a codified body of knowledge to support their judgments, was next on Ullmann's list. And fourth he listed "a standard that you might call common sense and fairness," a variation on Kurkjian's common man set of standards.

Although Ullmann argued that an appeal to common sense alone was never sufficient to support a claim of wrongdoing in an investigative report, we argue that an appeal to any other standard alone may not be sufficient to summon public indignation. Thus an appeal to moral common sense often accompanies the appeals to other standards. Moreover, as we will see shortly, an appeal to moral common sense can indeed stand alone. Ullmann did acknowledge, however, that common sense was implicitly at work in the other standards and that reporters do try to reveal the common sense within the letter of the law or the pronouncement of an expert.

In any case, as Ullmann suggested, the law is usually the most concrete, even if not always the most compelling, standard for the objectification of moral judgments. "I can hang my hat on the law," said another reporter. "I'm always trying to find the legal edge to the story," said still another. An excellent example of putting a "legal edge" on the story is the *Boston Globe*'s series on racial discrimination. For Jonathan Kaufman and his colleagues federal law was "the rock to cling to" throughout any storms of criticism directed at their analysis of racism: "One of the key things that we decided was that whatever definitions we used would have to be federal law, things like affirmative action and discrimination. . . . That was our fallback: saying, 'Look. These are definitions that the courts have decided. It's not something we decided would make a good city. This is what the law is.'"

Kaufman's term *fallback* was well chosen, for it captures well the logic of objectification. Kaufman and the *Globe* wanted their city to be, as Kaufman said, "the best city it could be," but because of discrimination they judged Boston to be less than that. Although their attack on institutional racism was not motivated by the mere illegality of racial discrimination, the attack depended on the law as a source of moral authority above and beyond the personal or organizational judgments of journalists. The law served not merely as their shield against criticism but as their instrument of moral craft.

In the *Chicago Tribune*'s investigation into conflicts of interest on the city council the law again provided a necessary instrument of moral craft—even though most of the conflicts reported were *not* illegal in Chicago. "The bad thing," said Gaines about the subjects of the investigation, "was that they had the power, and they used the power for their personal gain." One such "bad thing" was that some council members used their expense accounts to rent office space in buildings that they owned, thereby using public funds to help finance the purchase of private property. Moreover, some members rented space in their buildings to their campaign organizations or to political cronies who operated insurance agencies, law offices, and other businesses that exploited the flow of citizens into the aldermen's offices. "You had to run a gauntlet," Gaines said of anyone seeking an audience with these aldermen. "You couldn't get out of there without having your arm twisted by someone who had something to sell."

Although this practice violated no applicable statutes, it did flout an "unwritten conflict-of-interest law," as Gaines saw it. "It was supposed to be a city function and not a commercial enterprise," he said. "That's where I saw something wrong." And although the practice broke no written law, the reporters nonetheless found a legal edge to help objectify the unwritten one. Under the headline "Ward Offices Mix Private, City Business," the reporters began the third article in their series by describing the office arrangements of several city council members. They then turned to the task of outlining relevant standards for the assessment of the members' conduct: "Federal officials, Illinois state legislators and council members from other large cities are prohibited by law from most of these practices. But in Chicago, $900,000 of taxpayer money—$1,500 per month per alderman—will be awarded this year to council members for expenses with no questions asked, no strings attached."

A few paragraphs later the reporters began a more detailed review of the standards:

> Members of Congress are governed by a strict code that prohibits the mixing of government and political or business offices and requires a detailed accounting of expenses. . . .
> Members of the Illinois legislature cannot keep any of their expense funds, pay themselves rent or use their allowances for political purposes. . . .
> Los Angeles city officials negotiate council members' district office leases and prohibit aldermen from owning the building, pocketing leftover expense money or running a business out of their government office.[23]

Interspersed with the review of legal standards drawn from other jurisdictions was the description of many more violations in Chicago. As if to affirm the relevance of those standards to their community, the reporters quoted a council member who, for ethical reasons, had decided that he would no longer combine his council office with his campaign headquarters. "You wouldn't let the mayor do it, you wouldn't let the governor do it, you wouldn't let your congressman do it," the penitent alderman said of the practice. "But in Chicago, an alderman can do it." And to conclude, the reporters quoted an alderman who had introduced an ordinance requiring his colleagues merely to account for their expenses. "I would be fooling you or anyone else," the alderman said, "if I told you this ordinance had much chance."[24] Although the unwritten conflict of interest law would remain unwritten, the reporters had found a way to objectify it.

The legal edge may be the sharpest edge among the journalist's tools, but because so much that is wrong is nonetheless legal, the law cannot be the only tool of moral craftwork. Kurkjian, for example, succinctly summarized the range of wrongdoing encountered by the investigative reporter as "illegal, improper, irregular." Marimow offered a strikingly parallel hierarchy of wrongdoing, ranging from the illegal to the apparently improper: "I'll go through the categories that I have in my mind. First, there's the issue of legality, and then there's the issue of ethicality; then there's the issue of propriety, and then there's the issue of appearance of impropriety—four levels."

According to Marimow, a frequent task of the investigative reporter is "to find some objective standard" that can transform impropriety into unethical behavioral or at least transform the appearance of impropriety into actual impropriety.[25] Chief among the standards for objectifying wrongdoing that is not necessarily illegal are formalized codes of ethics and guidelines for behavior. At best these codes or guidelines are those of the individual or organization under investigation, but if those do not exist, Marimow said that he would not hesitate to borrow relevant codes or guidelines, much as Gaines and his colleagues borrowed legal definitions for conflict of interest. Marimow also said that he would not hesitate to call upon the testimony of experts to establish the relevance and applicability of standards. To illustrate he turned again to his investigation of unwarranted attacks on citizens by Philadelphia police officers and their dogs:

> If you look at the "K-9" story, you'll see I like to have something to measure conduct by . . . .
>
> After the questions were raised about the necessity for these attacks, I said, "Well, what specifically do the guidelines say?" I found a deposition given by Morton B. Solomon, former police commissioner of Philadelphia, in which he equated the use of dogs to the use of deadly force. You can use them when the police officer's life is in mortal danger, when another citizen's life is in mortal danger . . . or to apprehend a fleeing felon. That was what the police commissioner said was the appropriate use of dogs.
>
> I wasn't satisfied with that. I went out and found the head of the New York Transit Authority's canine unit, and he said, "No, Solomon's wrong. Dogs are like nightsticks—another law enforcement tool." So through those two people I was able to establish parameters.

In the series that appeared in the *Inquirer* Marimow first pointed out that the police department did not have guidelines:

> A three-month Inquirer investigation has found that a hard core of errant K-9 police officers and their dogs is out of control. Furthermore, the police department has made no attempt to hold these men or their colleagues to any sort of written guidelines or standard procedures spelling out when to attack and when to hold back.

A few paragraphs later Marimow applied the stricter standard set by the former police commissioner:

> Former police commissioner Morton B. Solomon, in a deposition taken in February 1982, stated that there were only three circumstances in which he believed a dog should be commanded to attack—protect an officer's life, to protect another person's life or to apprehend a fleeing felon. But these are only Solomon's beliefs, not the rules that actually govern the officer and dog on the street.[26]

Marimow defended this borrowing of standards—and implicitly acknowledged his role as moral craftsman—with the notion that it was not the violation of particular codes or guidelines per se that made the story important. "Ethicality isn't determined by whether or not there's a strict set of definitions," he concluded. "Rather, it really deals with one's values and what's right and wrong." Just as Kaufman fell back upon the law, so Marimow fell back upon other modes of objectification for a story in which values were not so unproblematic after all.

Lucy Morgan and Jack Reed's investigation of the county sheriff also illustrates the reliance on expertise as an objectification of an essentially intuitive sense of wrong. Reed was responsible for examining the suspicious financial relationship between the sheriff and an independently wealthy deputy:

> I felt almost immediately, because of the things I looked into, that there was something wrong. . . . One of the first things I did was look into [the sheriff's] dealings with Mister Moorman, the deputy, and I realized something was wrong.
>
> I went to a professional property appraiser in that county and ran it by him and said, "What's going on here in this transaction where [the deputy] apparently sells a piece of property for a fraction of its value and buys a business from the sheriff for a lot more than it was worth—apparently it is worth nothing. What do you say about this?" He agreed that this was an unusual transaction, so immediately I know that there was something unusual going on.

Just as the threshold of wrongdoing extends beyond the illegal to the unethical, so it may extend beyond the unethical to the abnormal—that is, to the "unusual" in Reed's terms or the "irregular" in Kurkjian's. Faced with the merely irregular, however, the investigative reporter will try to move the wrong up the hierarchy by pursuing the possibility that the irregular is in fact unethical. And in Florida, as Reed knew, the unethical behavior of an official may even be illegal, although that is a judgment made by the state Commission on Ethics once a complaint has been lodged. In the investigation of the sheriff's department, however, Reed had begun with the idea that he was on to something that was merely unusual:

> When it came to land dealings and bank dealings, I would try to talk to professionals in the field. . . . They backed up my feelings that we were on to something that was unusual. You know, at the time I didn't even think, "Is it illegal?"

The next thing I got into was whether it *was* illegal for a public official to be doing this. I would call the director of the commission on ethics for the state in Tallahassee. He wouldn't answer specific questions, but he would answer hypotheticals—you know, what if a public official does this? He'd say, "Yes, potentially there's conflict with this certain code of ethics."

Reed was adamant in his conviction that it would not have been appropriate for the newspaper or an individual reporter to lodge a complaint with the state agency, and so a conclusive judgment could not be reported in the story. Nevertheless, with the director's help Reed found precedent for strongly implying in the story that the sheriff's behavior was unethical. At the same time the reporter allowed the sheriff to make his own appeal to a standard of normal conduct:

The sheriff says it's all proper—sheriff's business comes first. . . .
Short also says that "many sheriffs" and other elected officials do business with subordinates because they are "people they know and trust."
Yet Florida law prohibits a public official from having a work relationship that "will create a continuing or frequently recurring conflict between his private interests and the performance of his public duties."
In interpreting that law in 1982, the State Ethics Commission said that "an ongoing business relationship with a subordinate" can cause conflicts for a public official, since it could impede that official's "duty of impartially evaluating the subordinate's job performance."[27]

The abnormal is low on the reportorial hierarchy of wrongdoing, but documentation of abnormalities may play a useful role in the moral craft of the investigative journalist. Pam Zekman's investigation of the suppression, or "killing," of crime reports by the Chicago Police Department, provides an example. "In the case of 'Killing Crime' there were no laws being broken," Zekman said, "but there are FBI guidelines for crime reporting, and we hung a lot on that." It was not, however, merely the violation of bureaucratic guidelines that objectively demonstrated something to be wrong in the police department; it was that Chicago, as compared to other major cities, had an abnormally high percentage of crime reports classified as "unfounded" (that is, lacking evidence of a prosecutable crime). In her report Zekman combined these two elements in her explanation of Chicago's "secret weapon" against crime:

Here's how it works: the police say the victim's complaint is unfounded—in effect, that the crime never happened. The police rubber-stamped that conclusion on more than nine thousand robbery cases last year—one out of every three. By comparison, New York, Los Angeles, and Saint Louis unfounded fewer than one out of a hundred. We wondered why Chicago is so out of line when it's supposed to follow the same FBI guidelines as all other cities.[28]

According to Zekman's report, Chicago's unfounding rate for rape was six times higher, and for burglary was fifty times higher, than *normal*—as defined by the rates of other major cities. Such statistics were central to the conclusion that the Chicago police department "lies about the number of crimes."

According to Kaufman, statistical comparisons provided another of the "rocks" to which he and his colleagues could cling in their assessment of racism in Boston:

> With the rock of statistics you were able to go to the Bank of Boston and say, "Only one percent of your managers are black."
>
> They'd say, "Well, you know, there are very few black bankers."
>
> And then you could say, "Well, the national average is five percent, and Chicago has six percent, and Washington has two percent."
>
> That was probably the thing that gave the story the most credibility, because otherwise you would have been hooked into competing anecdotes. You never would have had any evidence.

Altogether, these sorts of data helped the reporters to objectify the claim that among a number of large cities, Boston was "the least livable" for blacks.

If statistics are not available, a comparative case study may suffice. In Kurkjian's many stories on the machinations of government bureaucracies, his basic principle was always "the system should work." And in those stories Kurkjian established the norms for system performance through comparisons to other systems. "In each of our series we try to show a system which has worked out there," said Kurkjian, "and why it works there and doesn't work here." Comparisons, like statistics, objectify the normal; through the implicit equation of morality with normality they turn moral claims into empirical claims.

Common Sense and Moral Craft

Although established standards—federal antidiscrimination laws, state ethics codes, judgments of experienced police officers, federal employment statistics, and the like—may speak with substantial authority, they

still may not speak forcefully enough to summon the righteous indignation of the public. After all, these standards are really only echoes of the
values that are at stake in the story. But when the echo seems too faint for
the public to hear clearly, journalists can enlist common sense to amplify
the moral call of even the most elaborately objectified story.

A journalistic appeal to commonsense morality differs markedly from
an appeal to the other sorts of established standards because it uses
implicit rather than explicit evaluative criteria. Any appeal to common
sense is the invocation of vaguely articulated (though widely shared) precepts rather than carefully codified rules. Moreover, the authority of this
appeal resides not merely in a reassuringly familiar "good old commonsense approach" to judgments of right and wrong but in the use of that
approach to organize and present the facts of the cases to be judged. The
appeal is made within and through a story in which the facts of wrongdoing seem simply to speak for themselves. Thus commonsense morality
does not appear to be imposed on the facts but to be dictated by reality.

A good example is Don Barlett and Jim Steele's Pulitzer Prize–winning
investigation into the hundreds of individual and corporate exemptions
written into the "reform" of the federal tax code. The commonsense
value violated in this situation was, of course, just plain fairness. "Congress was putting paragraphs in the tax code for one person," Steele said.
"I think that most people would say that is not proper; that is not what
the tax code should be." But the violation of this value was compounded
by the violation of another: the proscription against public hypocrisy.
"The rhetoric about the tax code, all those congressional committee
reports, talked about the belief among the American people that there
was favoritism in the system for some groups," Steele continued, "and it
talked about the tax reform act of 1986 setting out to eliminate the
favoritism, to level the playing field, to make a more fair and just system."

In their series of reports Barlett and Steele skillfully juxtaposed
excerpts from the tax reformers' rhetoric with paragraph after paragraph
of exemptions from the tax code. As the reporters well knew, such juxtapositions served both to emphasize fairness as the fundamental value at
stake and to dramatize the outrageously hypocritical violation of that
value. And yet these juxtapositions did not seem argumentative. "This is
the rhetoric," said Steele, referring to committee reports. "And then you
come to a paragraph like that," he said referring to a particularly outrageous tax exemption. "I think it speaks for itself."

Any story in which the outrageousness of the situation seems to "speak
for itself" is the work of a skillful storyteller—although some stories

require more skill than others. Precisely because the outrageousness of the situation did *not* seem to speak for itself, Tofani's series on sexual assaults in the county jail provides a particularly instructive example of the appeal to commonsense morality. Although the rape of one jail inmate by another was illegal, Tofani knew that "there would be some really highly insensitive people in the world who would not view that as wrong and who would say, 'Look. The guy was in jail. What do you expect in jail?'" Tofani's personal response to such a point of view was a classic statement of moral common sense:

> The first thing I would say is, "How would you feel if that happened to you?" Then I would say, "Human beings are entitled to a certain amount of dignity. That [experience] really robbed this man of that. The jail is entrusted with keeping these people secure, and that was violated. People ought to have a certain peace of mind and not have to spend their lives thinking of this really traumatic thing that happened to them."

Tofani's appeal—"How would you feel if it happened to you?"—is, of course, a variation on that cornerstone of commonsense morality: the Golden Rule.

Tofani attempted to objectify her "gut sense" of this terrible wrong by searching for experts who could explain the psychological consequences of jail rape or provide statistical comparisons to the situation in other jails. All she could find, however, were "self-styled experts" for whom "theories were more important than people." Few had any clinical knowledge of jail rape. "Some of the worst experiences I had were talking to those so-called experts," she recalled. "I just wanted to puke every time I got them on the phone." The importance of this failure to objectify the evil of jail rape with expert opinion or statistical comparison was clearly demonstrated by the reporter's need to explain the absence of such information from her series. She wrote:

> It is not known whether the rape problems in the Prince George's County jail are more or less serious than in other jails throughout the country. Few people have studied the problem of jail rapes; those who have studied it tend to produce more theories than facts. Perhaps as a result, the problem of jail rape is not a public issue; only rarely is it even a topic of discussion at conventions for jail officials, according to penologists.
>
> Yet it is a problem with serious consequences. Men who were raped in the county jail say the experiences left them shocked, disoriented and unable to concentrate on their upcoming trials. Of 15 victims who were interviewed, three were later treated in mental institutions.[29]

Although this passage from one story acknowledged the absence of objectified standards, it also laid the foundation for an appeal to common decency. Narratives of victimization and villainy, as we show in chapter 5, are central to the moral force brought to bear within and through investigative journalism. In Tofani's series the narrative's appeal to common decency began with terrifying case studies of young men who typically were charged with a minor offense but who were punished with a brutal rape. The appeal continued by juxtaposing these cases with the head jailer's grotesquely callous statement that the same thing happens in schools. Through narrative the reporter showed her readers what it would be like if it did in fact happen to them: terror, pain, humiliation, and abandonment. She showed them that the wrongdoing here was not the failure of officials to obey a law or follow a guideline but the failure to meet the most basic expectations of human decency. In one story the appeal concluded with an explicit condemnation of the situation voiced by a source:

> "We're not rehabilitating people," says District Court Judge Joseph Casula, referring to the rapes. "We're not even punishing them. We're subjecting them to torture and degradation."[30]

While explicit, this summary judgment was brief and hardly necessary. Through storytelling the reporter made her appeal to common decency in an attempt to evoke public indignation at a situation that was, until she began work, morally ambiguous for many of her readers. Through storytelling the reporter not only documented events in a county jail, she established the standards that revealed those events to be a moral outrage.

Journalism and the Moral Order

In this chapter we have tried to understand how the tension between active adversarialism and objective detachment is mediated within the institution of journalism. We have taken seriously the arguments of accomplished reporters who maintained that they make news judgments rather than moral judgments. We have responded, however, that news judgments depend upon a historically given moral order and that news judgments have implications for the future of that order. Such judgments concern the selection for public attention of breaches in the moral order, and they concern the objectification of standards appropriate to the assessment of those breaches. In deciding where, as one reporter phrased it, "the curative powers" of journalistic scrutiny are to be brought to bear, and in working to establish the evaluative standards that are to be used, investigative journalism contributes to the process by which the moral order may be reinforced but may also be altered, even if only a little.

To be sure, journalism is not the only agent active in this process, for as the journalists vigorously argued, the community must also participate. "I raise the question. I can tell you what he did, and I can tell you what the law is, and you can take it from there," argued Reed of his investigation into the county sheriff's department. "It really wasn't my job to make that final decision: Is this illegal or not? Is this immoral or not?" Investigative reporters understand their power, as well as their responsibility, to be limited to telling a story. In response to the story the community may turn a sheriff or alderman from office at the next election, or it may commission the construction of new jail facilities. On the other hand, it may do absolutely nothing. To this Marimow said, "So be it. My job, I think, is to present important information to the public." Like all the other reporters, Marimow had examples of stories that evoked no public indignation or even interest, but he argued that such stories were no less valuable to the community. "The value to me is getting important information to readers," he maintained, "so that they, based on their judgment, can either bring public pressure to bear or ignore it."

But whether a story summons public indignation or "sinks without a trace," as Sawyer put it, each story is nonetheless a test of "the community consensus on values and how they apply in particular instances." An investigative story, in other words, is always a call for the community to affirm that certain conduct is in fact a transgression of the moral order or to affirm through indifference or hostility that the conduct under scrutiny once might have been a transgression but that it no longer is. A story that summons the public's righteous indignation rewards both the journalist's selection of a transgression for scrutiny and the application of standards to that transgression. If that story is merely one more exposé of an official with a hand in the till, it may simply reinforce established standards. If, however, that story is the work of a reporter who made, as Tofani did, "a conscious choice to show the wrong" in an unfamiliar setting, the story may function not so much to reinforce as to revise and renew moral standards.

On the other hand, a story met with indifference or hostility may not be told again. That such stories sometimes *are* told again is evidence of a moral persistence, even a moral courage, in journalism that should command public respect. The *Boston Globe* undertook its series on racial discrimination, for example, even though its earlier reporting on school busing had been, as Kaufman described it, "a whole trauma ... where people had shot at the building and all." The series was important precisely because, as Kaufman realized, "the overwhelming sense in Boston was, 'Don't bring this up; things are okay.'" This evidence of moral courage, however, is no guarantee that investigative reporting will inevitably enhance, or even maintain, social values. Investigative reporting may be a party not only to the development of values but also to their dissolution— a darkly ironic prospect to which we turn in the next chapter.

In sum, investigative journalism embraces the eternal tension between cultural continuity and change. On the one hand, it hardly constitutes the culture of disparagement envisioned by Moynihan. It can conserve the moral order insofar as it invokes "dominant values"—among them, basic human decency—and evokes public indignation at their violation. On the other hand, investigative journalism is not a witless apologist for domi-nant values. It can expand, even if only a little, the community's under-standing of its values along with its willingness to apply them more justly—or it may reveal that the community no longer cares.

By emphasizing the open-ended, ongoing character of this process, we sharply diverge from the classic theorists of social legitimation such as Horkheimer and Adorno and Marcuse, who maintained that the mass media uncritically reflect and thus unrelentingly legitimize the existing order.[31] In accord with Hallin and others whose understanding of legiti-mation derives from Habermas, we argue that journalism can achieve no complete or lasting ideological closure.[32] It can serve as an agent of legit-imation for dominant values, but there is also reason to believe that it can serve as an agent of change for those values—change that may be, but is not inevitably, for the better.

Moreover, and even more important to the long-term legitimacy of the moral order, any effect of investigative journalism on values, whether in the direction of continuity or change, is made less coherent and more ten-tative by the tactic that presumably makes this sort of journalism more credible: the transformation of moral claims into claims that are ostensi-bly only empirical. This tactic alienates reporters from the moral dimen-sion of their moral discourse and thereby denies them what philosopher Richard Rorty, following Iris Murdoch, called "a morally sensitive vocabulary."[33] Daniel Callahan and his colleagues made much the same point in their assessment of the relationship between the press and con-gressional ethics:

> Journalists are reluctant to raise ethical issues or to analyze them on their own. For the most part they approach ethical issues only indirectly, through

quotes elicited from others. As a result, legislative ethics is molded by journalistic practice into the form of charges and countercharges, accusations and denials. This distorts the process of moral dialogue and reflection in the legislative setting and leads to a preoccupation with . . . "scandal ethics."[34]

Whether journalism promotes continuity or change in the moral order, it undermines the rationality of that order by subverting the critical discussion of values. In this way it tends to devalue the values on which it depends.[35] Although journalism has intellectual resources sufficient to tell tales of moral outrage, it lacks the resources necessary to rigorously discuss—whether to passionately critique or dispassionately analyze—the values at stake in those tales. This impoverishment of moral resources equips journalism to preside most comfortably, perhaps, over the dissolution of values—more comfortably, certainly, than over their development. And so we are enfolded again in paradox: investigative journalism does serve as the custodian of conscience, but it does so despite itself.

4

The Irony of
Irony-in-Journalism

Why should anyone still believe in a role for journalism in the furtherance of democratic ideals? After all, several generations of irascible media theorists, from Horkheimer and Adorno to Herman and Chomsky, have insisted that the news is more likely the means to hegemonic power than democratic empowerment.[1] And now a new generation of besotted media consumers seems to insist that the news ought to be, well, just less trouble. So why should we listen to a philosopher, even one so distinguished as Richard Rorty, who still believes in a democratic role for journalism—at least, why should we listen in any frame of mind other than one of ironic knowingness about the fate of philosophy in the real world?

"I think that contemporary liberal society already contains the institutions for its own improvement," Rorty wrote in *Contingency, Irony, and Solidarity*. "Indeed, my hunch is that Western social and political thought may have had the last *conceptual* revolution it needs." For Rorty the proper task of government now is "optimizing the balance between leaving people's private lives alone and preventing suffering" while "discoveries about who is being made to suffer can be left to the workings of a free press, free universities, and enlightened public opinion."[2]

Why, moreover, shouldn't we dismiss in an especially derisive tone of ironic knowingness any such vision of intellectual history at its end? Rorty, it turns out, has anticipated and subverted our irony with irony of his own. Indeed, he has claimed for himself the role of ultimate ironist. An ultimate ironist, according to Rorty, knows that even if liberal democracy has had the last conceptual revolution it needs, it has not had the last revolution possible. That is because a world in which democracy is fully realized is a world constituted and maintained by a particular language—a language that enables its citizens to articulate their loathing of injustice as well as their love of liberty. The ultimate ironist also knows that such a world can never be entirely secure because its language is a contingent rather than necessary development in human history. Anything, including both suffering and freedom, can be "made to look good or bad, important or unimportant, useful or useless, by being redescribed."[3] Thus the ultimate ironist lives with the terrible realization that, whenever language hostile to justice or liberty is spoken by the adversaries of democratic values, no ultimate philosophical weapon—no knowledge of what is fundamentally real and no vision of what is truly human—is available to the defenders of democratic values. The defenders can only exercise, and strive to enhance, the descriptive and persuasive powers of their moral language.

Rorty's position on the constitutive yet contingent character of language coincides with the position taken by sophisticated observers of that peculiar language game known as journalism. News, as James Carey wrote, "sizes up situations, names their elements and names them in a way that contains an attitude toward them" and thereby "brings a world into existence."[4] To insist on this position, however, is not to argue that the concept of truth has no meaning in journalism and beyond. Rorty saw truth as the outcome of ongoing public discussions in which journalism can play an important part:

> From our angle, all that matters for liberal politics is the widely shared conviction that . . . we shall call "true" or "good" whatever is the outcome of free discussion—that if we take care of political freedom, truth and goodness will take care of themselves. "Free discussion" here does not mean "free from ideology," but simply the sort which goes on when the press, the judiciary, the elections, and the universities are free, social mobility is frequent and rapid, literacy is universal, higher education is common, and peace and wealth have made possible the leisure necessary to listen to lots of different people and think about what they say.[5]

Listening to lots of different people is essential for Rorty because that is what we must do—and all we can do—to try to build good lives together. No philosophical foundations, no insights into what is eternally true, can secure the democratic community. We can only enlarge and strengthen our sense of solidarity, one with another, as we listen to lots of different people tell their stories. These stories do not reveal some essential bond between us all but simply make us more reluctant to inflict suffering on one another. For this reason telling the stories of those who suffer pain or injustice is especially important. "The liberal novelist, poet, or journalist is good at that," Rorty concluded. "The liberal theorist is not."[6]

This vision of a role for journalism in ongoing discussions about what is true and good provides a point of departure for a study of the language by which journalism brings a world into existence. Specifically, our concern is the vocabulary used by journalism when, in the form of investigative reporting, it earnestly tries to enact the role that Rorty assigned: telling stories about people who suffer injustice and the villains who work that injustice. The language of this storytelling, as reviewed in chapter 3, includes terms drawn from the law as well as ethical codes, professional standards, and expert judgments. Such terms for the description of misconduct transform moral claims into claims that seem to be entirely empirical and allow journalists to maintain their pretense of dealing in facts but not values. Often, however, such technical terms as *illegal, unethical,* or *unprofessional* seem insufficient to engage the public's interest in the misconduct that has been uncovered. Then journalists may turn to a rhetoric of irony that reveals the misconduct to be not only technically wrong but terribly wrong—a true moral outrage. The great value of irony to journalism is that it can moralize without appearing to sermonize. It allows investigative reporters to elevate the illegal, the unethical, and even the merely improper to the outrageous and yet retain the formal features of objective reporting. "The rhetoric of irony," as Thomas Rosteck argued of Edward R. Murrow's *See It Now* report on Senator Joseph McCarthy, "saturates the objective discourse of journalism with meanings, while, at the same time, it disguises this connection."[7] But more than that, irony does not merely operate within the constraints imposed by the conventions of journalistic objectivity; it *transfigures* those conventions into a moralistic vocabulary for condemnation of the villains to whom we have foolishly entrusted our public affairs.

For journalists who must honor objectivity yet evoke outrage, ironist rhetoric holds great stylistic appeal, but as the ultimate ironist understood, such rhetoric also holds moral peril. Although Rorty was able to come to personal terms with what he took to be the ultimate irony—the need to construct a life with meaning and values but without philosophically certain foundations—he worried about the ability of society as a whole do so. "I cannot go on to claim that there could or ought to be culture whose public rhetoric is *ironist*," he wrote. "I cannot imagine a culture which socializes its youth in such a way as to make them continually dubious about their own process of socialization."[8] Private life is the proper domain of ironist rhetoric, Rorty concluded, for there it can remind all of us that we could be other than what we are and so motivate each of us to enrich the "final vocabulary" that constitutes the individual self. Public life, on the other hand, must be protected from the potential of ironist rhetoric to degenerate into a vocabulary of morally corrosive cynicism.

Any public discussion about what is true or good is subject to irony's simultaneous appeal and peril. Irony's great appeal to historians, for example, is that "characterizations of the world cast in the Ironic mode are often regarded as *intrinsically* sophisticated and realistic," according to historiographer Hayden White.[9] Such characterizations are so regarded because they acknowledge the constitutive and contingent character of language. "Irony thus represents a stage of consciousness in which the problematical nature of language itself has become recognized," White argued. "It points to the potential foolishness of all linguistic characterizations of reality as much as to the absurdity of the beliefs it parodies" (p. 37). But therein lies irony's peril for historians.

Even as irony promises to be a mode of thought that is genuinely enlightened, it casts doubt on any effort to capture the truth of things in language. "As the basis of a world view," White concluded, "irony tends to dissolve all belief in the possibility of positive political actions . . . and to inspire a Mandarin-like disdain for those seeking to grasp the nature of social reality in either science or art" (p. 38). A compelling example is Edward Gibbon who, in his account of Rome's decline and fall, produced "the greatest achievement of sustained Irony in the history of historical literature," by White's estimation, but who eventually succumbed to "debilitating skepticism about reason itself" (p. 55). Although historians seem to be the sort of ultimate ironist-intellectuals envisioned by Rorty, they do not necessarily escape irony's threat to their public discourse— nor perhaps even to their own final vocabularies.

Far from ultimate ironists, investigative reporters are probably best described as earnestly moralistic ironists. They may use irony to parody the villain's self-serving characterizations of reality but never to call into question their journalistic characterizations of reality—which they take to be the really real. They use irony to lend an aura of sophistication and realism to their language even as it disguises the moral basis of their entire language game.[10] For these journalists irony seems to threaten neither their final vocabularies with debilitating skepticism nor their public discourse with corrosive cynicism. To disregard peril, however, is not to escape it, and—as we will argue—irony's simultaneous appeal and peril persist in journalists' attempts to contribute to public discussions about what is true and good.

In this chapter we take readerly pleasure from the artful use of irony in one of the more writerly genres of journalism. And as critics of journalism's pretense to value-free knowledge, we take special pleasure from the idea that irony *in* journalism creates an interesting irony *of* journalism: the very language intended to differentiate fact and value becomes the means to unify fact and value. And so we begin with an appreciation of investigative reporters' mastery of ironic language. But to conclude this chapter we also consider the possibility that irony in journalism creates another irony of journalism: the language intended to advance the discussions about what is true and good may become the means to undo those discussions. The melancholy irony of irony in journalism is that this mode of discourse seems so right for the task of summoning righteous indignation, so sophisticated and so realistic, and yet it is potentially so destructive of its ultimate purpose.

Requirements of Irony

To structure our reading of irony in journalism, we turn to D. C. Muecke's *The Compass of Irony* for a primer on the concept. Although that work offers no brief definition of irony, it does specify several formal features or requirements. The first is that irony is double layered. "At the lower level is the situation either as it appears to the victim of irony (where there is a victim) or as it is deceptively presented by the ironist," Muecke wrote. "At the upper level is the situation as it appears to the observer or the ironist. The upper level need not be *presented* by the ironist; it need only be evoked by him or be present in the mind of the observer."[11]

The second requirement follows from the first: the two levels stand in opposition or contradiction to each other. "What is said may be contradicted by what is meant," according to Muecke, "or what the victim thinks may be contradicted by what the observer knows."[12] The two sorts of contradiction specified here reflect the traditional distinction between verbal and situational irony. The former is often defined as simply saying one thing while meaning quite another and is exemplified by Jonathan Swift's *Modest Proposal* to take care of the poor by eating their children. The latter can be defined as expecting one thing while quite another awaits and is exemplified by any war. "Every war is ironic because every war is worse than expected," wrote Paul Fussell in *The Great War and Modern Memory*. "Every war constitutes an irony of situation because its means are so melodramatically disproportionate to its presumed ends."[13] Here, for example, was the situation, as Fussell recounted it, at the Third Battle of Ypres, a battle that began with a ten-day British artillery bombardment:

> The result was highly ironic, even in this war where irony was a staple. The bombardment churned up the ground, rain fell and turned the dirt to mud. In the mud the British assaulted until the attack finally attenuated three and a half months later. Price: 370,000 British dead and wounded and sick and frozen to death. Thousands literally drowned in the mud.[14]

That the massive bombardment expected to destroy German defenses only added to the British casualties is an example of what Fussell called, in a compelling paraphrase of Gibbon, "the dynamics of hope abridged."[15]

Muecke reminds us, however, that the irony of a situation is realized only within an artful account of that situation. Such accounts can "take something which on the face of it is not ironic but which, being inherently self-contradictory or false or absurd, might be seen as ironic and . . . present it in such a way as to bring out the latent irony." A narrative strategy for doing so, Muecke suggested, "is to restate the situation cutting out all the obscuring irrelevancies so as to reveal a clear and close confrontation of incompatibles."[16] This, according to Fussell, is what memoirists did in their elegiac accounts of the Great War and exactly what Fussell did in his brief account of Ypres.

The third formal feature or requirement of irony is a certain sort of innocence: the victim of the irony must be *confidently unaware* of the possibility of contradiction (or else the ironist pretends to be unaware of it). This sort of innocence is equivocal, however, "for one of the odd things about irony is that it regards assumptions as presumption and therefore innocence as guilt," Muecke argued. "Simple ignorance is safe from irony, but ignorance compounded with the least degree of confidence counts as intellectual hubris and is a punishable offence."[17] Fussell used a line from the poetry of Philip Larkin to ironize the confident ignorance with which young men first volunteered to serve in the Great War and old men first planned it: "never such innocence again."[18]

When a higher level of knowledge contradicts a lower level to the misfortune of a confidently unaware victim—but is not itself contradicted by another, still higher level—irony may function as a potent corrective to misconception. In the light of the new or greater awareness created by the confrontation of incompatibles, as Muecke pointed out, "an assumed or asserted fact is shown not to be true, an idea or belief to be untenable, an expectation to be unwarranted, or a confidence to be misplaced."[19] Irony that performs this sort of corrective function is "stable," according to Wayne Booth, in the sense that "once a reconstruction of meaning has been made, the reader is not then invited to undermine it with further demolitions and reconstructions."[20] Such irony is also "specific" for when "the victim is dealt with the incident is closed, the irony is over," according to Muecke. "In these instances of irony the victim is isolated; he is 'in the wrong' and over against him are the rest of society or mankind who are 'in the right' and safe."[21] Specific irony stands in contrast to what Muecke called "general" or "cosmic"—the enduring ironies of humanity's fate in an indifferent universe.

In the application of irony to investigative journalism the two incompatible levels brought into confrontation are a naive expectation of justice and the harsh reality of injustice. The victims of the irony include not only (and not even primarily) those particular individuals who may have witnessed or experienced the injustice; the victims include all those readers or viewers who have been confidently unaware of the injustice—especially those who have been oblivious to even the possibility of it. The victims of the irony, in other words, are all who (as the saying goes) need to wise up about what's going on. The innocence of these victims therefore is particularly equivocal, and the need for a corrective to their misconception is particularly urgent. However, the ironist's stance toward them is one that Reinhold Niebuhr characterized in his analysis of irony in history as neither so hostile as to deny the victims' virtue nor so sympathetic as to deny their vanity.[22] The working hypothesis of the morally earnest ironist, after all, is that, once these victims—that is to say, the public—are made aware of the situation and their complicity in it, they will adjust their views and acknowledge their responsibilities. The expectation for journalistic irony, then, is reform—but therein lies the potential for further irony.

The Transfiguration of Objectivity

Working with a variety of textual materials gathered from sources and documents, investigative reporters weave a text in which irony is likely to be an important design motif. Within this design reporters try to realize the potential for righteous indignation inherent in the original materials by calling upon what G. G. Sedgewick described as "one of the keenest and oldest and least transient pleasures of the reflective human mind—the pleasure in contrasting Appearance with Reality."[23] In a well-written investigative story that pleasure is especially keen because the contrast of appearance with reality serves to amplify but then avenge the suffering of victims by unmasking the machinations of villains.

The genius of the ironic imagination in this application is that it transfigures the conventions of journalistic impartiality into a means of moral condemnation. Irony and objectivity do not merely coexist; irony exploits objectivity to work its effect. Irony, especially situational irony, instructs investigative journalists where to find damning facts and how to assemble them into compelling narratives, and yet it *requires*—not merely allows— journalists to present the facts in an objective style that lends them credibility. Irony, as Northrop Frye observed, requires "suppression of all explicit moral judgments," which amounts to the appearance of "complete objectivity."[24] Thus a carefully documented "web of facticity," an incisive selection of direct quotations, and a conscientious attempt to balance the story (that is, get the villain's side) are all essential tools of journalistic ironists.[25] At the same time these conventions of journalistic textual production continue to serve their function as presumed warranties of fairness and truth.

Objectivity, no less than irony, is a literary device. Together they enable journalists to produce texts that encourage the moral engagement of the reader and yet deny the moral engagement of the author. "As with other forms of journalistic narrative, the ironic account seems to enable the world to speak for itself," observed Robert Manoff. "The writer appears to be merely the medium for the story and takes no responsibility for shaping it."[26] Because irony works through objectivity, journalists may assert that irony is merely, as one investigative reporter said, "in the facts that you find." But because irony guides the discovery and portrayal of these facts, the reporter might better have said that irony is "the finding that you factualize."

Our examination of the ironic transfiguration of objectivity focuses on three texts: "The Great Tax Giveaway" by Donald L. Barlett and James B. Steele, "The Color of Money" by Bill Dedman, and "City Council: The Spoils of Power" by Dean Baquet, Ann Marie Lipinski, and William Gaines—all winners of Pulitzer Prizes. These investigative reports stand, modestly but rightly, beside Swift's *Modest Proposal* and memoirs of the Great War as important examples of irony in moral discourse. In these reports talented journalistic ironists have described certain arcane machinations in Washington, D.C., Atlanta, and Chicago as outrageous abridgments of our hope for justice, equity, and honesty. In these reports, however, the ironists have intended to speak in the terms of a specific irony that seeks to correct naive expectations by revealing a true state of affairs, as well as a stable irony that undercuts one position (that of hypocritical officials) in order to affirm another (that of citizens who demand justice, equity, and honesty). Thus these reporters have sought to enlist irony in an inherently hopeful campaign for progressive civic reform—a campaign that depends upon, and presumably also sustains, the ongoing discussions that Rorty celebrated.

The Motif of Hope Abridged

Consider first a paradigmatic case of situational irony, Barlett and Steele's "Great Tax Giveaway," in which the facts of tax reform speak in a voice that throbs with indignation:

> When Congress passed the Tax Reform Act of 1986, radically overhauling the Internal Revenue Code, Rep. Dan Rostenkowski (D., Ill.), chairman of the tax-writing House Ways and Means Committee, hailed the effort as "a bill that reaches deep into our national sense of justice and gives us back a trust in government that has slipped away in the maze of tax preferences for the rich and powerful."
>
> In fact, Rostenkowski and other self-styled reformers created a new maze of unprecedented favoritism. Working in secret, they wove at least 650 exemptions—preferences, really, for the rich and powerful—through the legislation, most written in cryptic legal and tax jargon that conceals the identity of the beneficiaries.
>
> When they were finished, thousands of wealthy individuals and hundreds of businesses were absolved from paying billions upon billions of dollars in federal income taxes. It was, an Inquirer investigation has established, the largest tax giveaway in the 75-year history of the federal income tax.[27]

This passage, drawn from the first article in the series, served as the introduction to a review of many especially outrageous exemptions. Although the passage offered the usual formal features of contemporary journalism—official quotes and specific facts cited in the familiar terse paragraphs—the passage certainly did not offer the usual sense that the situation is just as the officials claim it to be. In part, this is a result of the sarcasm (a primitive sort of verbal irony) in the characterization of those officials (members of Congress, no less) as "self-styled reformers." Most strikingly, however, the officials are dramatically undermined simply by juxtaposing their promises—"justice," "trust"—with facts of the situation—"650 exemptions."

A common strategy of investigative journalism is to hoist public officials on the petard of their own words, but hypocrisy alone is not ironic. Barlett and Steele's story, however, is about much more than mere hypocrisy. Their story is not simply that officials have misled the public, nor even that the revised tax code is unfair. Their story is that the "self-styled reformers" who promised to fix the tax code in fact have made it worse. "It is ironic when we meet what we set out to avoid," as Muecke noted in his catalogue of ironies, "especially when the means we take to avoid something turns out to be the very means of bringing about what we sought to avoid."[28] The situation uncovered by Barlett and Steele is outrageous for exactly this reason: a promise of justice has yielded further injustice.

This juxtaposition of word and deed—the abridgment of hope for reform by the actions of the reformers—is a motif that the reporters used throughout the series to introduce the specific results of their investigation. Here is a variation of the motif from the third part of the series. First, the word:

> Lawmakers often cite the need for simplification as the reason for tax-code revisions. That was especially true when President Reagan began marshalling support for the tax-overhaul movement that led to the 1986 Tax Reform Act. Declaring the system was "too complicated," the President said that Americans "often resent complexity" because "they sense it is unfair—that complexity is the means by which some benefit while others do not."

And then the deed:

> Instead of simplifying the code, the reformers in 1986 actually rendered it the most complex ever, fueling what has become, in the 1980s, America's most explosive growth industry—the tax industry. As a result, more lawyers, accountants and tax specialists than ever are needed to interpret the law.
>
> Who better to do that for business than the people responsible for writing the code in the first place?[29]

This story went on to introduce a number of congressional staff attorneys who left government service for "the tax industry."

With such juxtapositions of word and deed the reporters rendered tax reform as a ironic joke played on the American people. The reporters could always claim that situation was simply there, in the world, and that they have merely described it. After all, even if they have tested the limits of objective news writing with references to "self-styled reformers," they have honored the elemental conventions of objectivity with the use of direct quotations and documented facts. And yet the joke turned on these conventions. The quotations established one level of the ironic confrontation while the facts created the other, and the terse news style pruned away, in Muecke's terms, "all the obscuring irrelevances so as to reveal a clear and close confrontation of incompatibles."

Perhaps because the situational ironies were so infuriating, the reporters could indulge in occasional verbal irony that challenged the limits of objectivity. For example, they introduced the fourth part of their series, an article that identified the beneficiaries of many tax loopholes, with an exercise in verbal irony that even a master like Jonathan Swift might have enjoyed:

> Herewith a civics quiz.
>
> As a result of efforts by Congress' tax reformers, the Internal Revenue Code contains a provision that will:
>
> (A) Allow members of a socially prominent Chicago-area family, who have made the Forbes magazine list of the 400 richest Americans, to take tax writeoffs denied to most taxpayers.
>
> (B) Permit a millionaire Beverly Hills stockbroker, who boasts the world's largest private collection of Rodin sculpture, to escape payment of taxes that others must pay.[30]

The reporters provided several more options and then concluded this one-question quiz with the option feared by all quiz takers:

> (E) All of the above.
>
> If you answered (E), score yourself 100.
>
> Each of those provisions was wrapped into the Tax Reform Act of 1986 that was so widely praised as a model of fairness by the lawmakers and others who engineered it.

Here the civics lesson—that familiar recitation of eternal democratic truths—is parodied to suggest that special privileges for the rich are among those truths.

Investigative reporters can never persist long in this Swiftian mode. To meet the formal requirements of journalistic objectivity investigative stories must always return quickly to the facts of the situation, and this means that they can never be as subtle and elegant as the masterworks of ironic literature. But if this particular application of the motif of hope abridged does not offer the rewards of great literature, neither does it demand specialized reading skill. This is mass-mediated irony for the average reader and the ordinary citizen whose likely response to the situation is at least a rudimentary sort of ironic knowingness: "Tax reform? Fairness and equity? Yeah, right!"

The motif of hope abridged is also woven throughout Dedman's "The Color of Money," where its application is of interest precisely because this series is *not* a paradigmatic case of situational irony. The motif, however, is one strategy by which the reporter coaxed what irony he could from the materials at hand. Early in the first article, for example, he previewed the results of his investigation by establishing a "clear and close confrontation between incompatibles":

> A federal law, the Community Reinvestment Act of 1977, says deposit-gathering institutions have an "affirmative obligation" to solicit borrowers and depositors in all segments of their communities. . . .
>
> As part of a five-month examination of compliance with the Community Reinvestment Act, the Journal-Constitution used lenders' reports to track home-purchase and home-improvement loans made by every bank and savings and loan association in metro Atlanta from 1981 through 1986—a total of 109,000 loans. The study focused on 64 middle-income neighborhoods: In the white areas lenders made five times as many loans per 1,000 household as in black areas.[31]

Like Barlett and Steele, Dedman breathed moral life into a stuffy topic by juxtaposing a legally mandated promise of justice with the fact of its betrayal. Unlike Barlett and Steele, however, Dedman did not claim that the very promise of justice worked the injustice. Although lenders failed to live up to their obligations under the Community Reinvestment Act, the act itself was not seen to be the source of their failure to do so. But if the situation offered less potential for irony, Dedman's diligence in exploiting whatever potential existed is a testament to its rhetorical value. Here, for example, Dedman used a variation on the motif to amplify indignation at the behavior of the worst offender:

> Equitable lending practices are required under the Community Reinvestment Act, which says banks and savings and loans have "continuing and affirmative obligations to help meet the credit needs of their local communities, including low- and moderate-income neighborhoods, consistent with safe and sound operation. . . ."
>
> Bankers said they bend over backwards to obey the laws, and some said they are eager to make more money in black areas.

"If I could make $10 million or $20 million in these loans, I'd make them," said First Atlanta's [vice chairman Thomas] Boland. "I don't think a black borrower brings me any more risk per se."[32]

The story went on to report that First Atlanta placed dead last in a ranking of seventeen banks and savings and loans based on the percentage of home loans made to minority and lower-income neighborhoods.

Here the invitation to irony came less from the explicit juxtaposition of the bank's statements with its actual record than from an implicit confrontation that readers could provide for themselves. The upper level of the confrontation between appearance and reality, as Muecke observed, "need not be *presented* by the ironist, it need only be evoked by him or be present in the mind of the observer."[33] And in the passage cited here, the upper level was the evocation, rather than assertion, of an explanation for the fact that certain communities just don't seem to get loans: enduring racial bias, or at least, indifference to racial equality. Using the ironic motif, the reporter has elevated, as best he can with the materials at hand, the merely hypocritical into the morally reprehensible. Here again irony invites the response of ironic knowingness: "The big banks bend over backwards? Yeah, right!"

Perhaps because the potential for situational irony was less compelling in Dedman's story than in Barlett and Steele's, his use of verbal irony was less aggressive than theirs. For example:

> Each year the U.S. government grades America's 17,000 banks and savings and loans on how fairly they serve their communities, including working-class and minority neighborhoods.
>
> Across the country last year, 98 percent of the lenders passed. In the South, 99 percent passed, according to federal agencies.
>
> Supporters of working-class and minority neighborhoods suspect grade inflation.[34]

Here the important claim that the government has not enforced the law emerges from humorous understatement—a gentle, though still easily accessible, form of irony. "Grade inflation? Yeah, right!"

The irony in "City Council: The Spoils of Power" by Baquet, Lipinski, and Gaines, on the other hand, is far from gentle. Many Chicagoans have long viewed their city council as an ironic joke, and in the first article of this series the reporters acknowledged that "Chicagoans' ingrained, bemused cynicism toward their public officials is well deserved." In an attempt to summon whatever righteous indignation may have been left in their cynical readers, however, the reporters fell back on that familiar "confrontation between incompatibles":

> On Sept. 17, 1985, as the Chicago City Council prepared for its annual budget hearings, Ald. Edward Burke (14th), chairman of the council's Committee on Finance, warned that the city was facing a $50 million revenue gap.
>
> Thirteen days later, Ald. Patrick Huels (11th) sent his secretary to a Wabash Avenue store to pick up office supplies for his Committee on Licenses. The secretary returned with five picture frames and two pen-and-pencil sets, including a 10-karat gold-filled, green onyx Cross desk set. Taxpayers picked up the bill for $326.29.[35]

The juxtaposition of a $50 million revenue gap and a $326.29 gold-filled desk set, although amusing in a sardonic sort of way, did not complete this particular joke. In the next paragraph the reporters delivered the punch line:

> Between that date and the end of the year, Huels' committee, with a budget of $107,044 in public funds, met only twice and approved no legislations, although 11 ordinances were pending before it. . . .
>
> Huels' purchases were typical of how the $5.3 million in taxpayers' funds budgeted for city council committees are spent by the aldermen who run them.[36]

The joke was not merely that the committees waste money but that the committees don't do anything except waste money. The joke was not quite complete, however, and a few paragraphs later the reporters tried to top themselves:

> Burke seemed to ignore his own predictions of dire financial difficulty—which as it turned out, proved exaggerated.
>
> For example, he used a committee contingency fund to pay $6,000 in legal fees to defend himself in a libel case. He also authorized his committee to pay $471.34 for his bodyguard's stay at the deluxe Mayfair Regent Hotel in New York City.[37]

In the attempt to keep the joke running just a little longer the reporters revealed just how far they had reached to pull together a serviceable juxtaposition. The $50 million revenue gap was juxtaposed with a few hundred dollars of fancy office supplies, and—what's more—the anticipated financial demise of the city, as the reporters acknowledged, "proved exaggerated." But if these reporters did not have the material to construct the infuriatingly ironic joke of "The Great Tax Giveaway," they did have the material for many farcical jokes about the villains who lurk in the council chambers. They told of one alderman, for example, who promoted a soft drink marketing scheme that he had concocted, by introducing a council resolution touting his commitment to entrepreneurship. "Entrepreneurship? Yeah, right!"

Villains and Victims

A key task of investigative journalists is the rhetorical constitution of villainy and victimization. One important way that the ironic transfiguration of objectivity contributes to this task is the deconstruction of the comments made by the targets of the investigation on their own behalf. The conventions of objectivity, along with most reporters' sense of fairness, demand that the targets be allowed to speak for themselves at some point in the story. By the time that point comes, however, it is difficult to read anything they might have to say without that sense of ironic knowingness. Baquet, Lipinski, and Gaines, for example, often gave the last word to the aldermen, with comic but deadly consequences for any foolish enough to speak. An article that profiled the rapid rise of Alderman Joseph Kotlarz concluded this way:

> None of the transactions that propelled Kotlarz from the city's motorpool to a prosperous law practice are prohibited by city regulation. There is no rule barring aldermen from using the city payroll to employ associates and campaign workers; no rule against the use of city funds to subsidize privately owned ward offices; and few rules that restrict an alderman's use of his office.
>
> Kotlarz acknowledges that he has been fortunate. His business has prospered and, though he complains of brutally long hours, he says, "I love the city council."
>
> And if along the way people have been generous contributors and kind enough to include him in their business ventures, he says it should not be seen as a reflection on his office.
>
> "I'm going to say it's because I'm a likable guy," he said. "It would sound crazy, but you know what? It's true. It's as simple as that.
>
> "I mean, even if I wasn't an alderman, wouldn't you be googy about me?"[38]

Here the reporters have reviewed their facts with verbal irony: the alderman has been "fortunate," and his associates have been "generous" and "kind." However, the alderman himself added the best ironic flourishes: the hours are long, but he loves the city council, and people have been so generous and kind because he's such a likable guy. Even if the alderman's behavior is not illegal, the ironic deconstruction of his words shows his behavior to be unacceptable. He is not merely a hypocrite but an insufferably smug one. "Googy? Yeah, right!"

Another strategy for ironizing Kotlarz was the introduction of an ordinary citizen through whose eyes jaded Chicagoans might see anew the behavior of their city council. The citizen was Philip Greco, a Northwest Side police officer who had worked hard to help Kotlarz win a seat on the city council. "In Kotlarz—the 26-year-old son of a machinist, a student working his way through the John Marshall School of Law by pumping gas for the police department motor pool—Greco saw the future of the 35th Ward," according to the story.[39] And in Greco the reporters found a victim who would soon learn to be an ironist. This is the sort of character that Muecke called an "ingenue" ironist, someone whose values are those of the author but whose "mere common sense or even simple innocence or ignorance may suffice to see through the woven complexities of hypocrisy and rationalization."[40] More precisely, Muecke would have recognized Greco as an "active" ingenue because the officer did not unwittingly expose pretense, as did the child in "The Emperor's New Clothes," but rather came to understand the situation for himself.

The education of Officer Greco began when the alderman invited him to a local restaurant and then on to a White Sox game. To Greco's surprise, he found a gathering of men at the restaurant, including a millionaire developer, most of whom he had not seen during the campaign. After schmoozing with the alderman's rich new friends Greco found himself in a limousine heading for the game.

> As the small caravan sped south toward Comiskey Park, the police officer recalled his campaign visits to the ward's Polish shopkeepers along Milwaukee Avenue and thought: "The people should see us now."
>
> The story of the quick rise of Joseph Kotlarz from a city gas station attendant to a wealthy and well-connected alderman provides a case study of the opportunities available to members of the city council simply by virtue of their election, of the legal possibilities for making money and building influence that are part of the aldermanic endowment.[41]

The people *could* see them now. In Officer Greco the reporters created a surrogate for all the other victims of the irony—The People of Chicago—who might now be able to view the situation in their city with renewed indignation. Greco was constituted as the victim both of "the aldermanic endowment" and of the irony inherent in his confident unawareness of that endowment. Greco could not escape victimization by his alderman, but because he eventually wised up, he did escape victimization by his unawareness. Greco, serving as a model for reader response, escaped irony to become the ironist. "The future of the 35th ward? Yeah, right!"

In Dedman's "The Color of Money," unlike "City Council: Spoils of Power," the villains remained, for the most part, faceless representatives of their institutions. The reporter typically did not give them the last word, which instead went to someone who summarized the moral of the story. For example:

> "Let's face it: Redlining hasn't disappeared," said Sen. William Proxmire (D-Wis.), chairman of the Senate Banking, Housing and Urban Affairs Committee. "Neighborhoods are still starving for credit."[42]

Dedman was working with a story line in which some, rather than all, citizens had been directly victimized (that is, denied a loan) by the villains. Therefore he focused extensively on narratives of those who had been directly victimized in an effort to personify the abstraction of redlining for those readers who had not. In his second article, for example, Dedman constituted a victim who had not escaped the villains but who, like Officer Greco, had escaped confident unawareness:

> When he went to the banks last year looking for campaign contributions for his 1989 race for mayor, Michael Lomax picked up a donation from every one. He wishes he'd done as well when he wanted a loan.
>
> The Fulton County Commission chairman says he had to go to three banks last year to get a loan to add a guesthouse in Adams Park, an upper-middle-class black neighborhood in southwest Atlanta.
>
> "The first reaction from the bank was, 'Why do you want to invest that much money in that neighborhood?' But that's the neighborhood my house is in."[43]

Lomax observed and wryly expressed the irony of his situation. Dedman gave Lomax the last word of his own story and used it to introduce yet another victim:

> "If I, a powerful black elected official, can't get a loan, what black person can?" James Fletcher said he couldn't—at least not from a bank. (p. 1)

Fletcher, a retired railroad laborer, was a more usual but less articulate victim of redlining, and the reporter needed to apply his rhetorical arts more assertively. When Fletcher needed $5,000 to fix his roof, he contacted Citizens and Southern Bank (C&S), where he had done business for ten years, but

> "They said they didn't make no house loans. They didn't let us fill out the papers."
>
> So he and his wife, Lizzie Mae, went to Atlantic Mortgage Co. which loaned them $5,773.69 at 18 percent interest—plus $3,180 in "discount points" and other add-ons, raising the effective interest rate to 27.1 percent, according to loan papers.
>
> Total payback: $30,722.30. (p. 1)

If the bank had made the loan at typical interest rates, the payback would have been less than $12,000. The Fletchers made payments on the usurious loan until, after several years, they were able to pay it off in a lump sum.

Next Dedman delivered the punch line:

> A spokesman for C&S, Dallas Lee, confirmed that Fletcher had been a depositor, but said he could find no record that Fletcher had ever applied for a loan. "It seems highly unlikely [that he would be discouraged from applying]. We make a lot of home-improvement loans," Lee said. (p. 14A)

There was no record of an application, of course, because the bank had refused to let the Fletchers fill out the papers. Dedman concluded the story by reporting that, according to federal records, the bank made no home-improvement or home-purchase loans from 1984 to 1986 in the Fletchers' neighborhood. The Fletchers remained doubly victimized. "No record? Yeah right!"

Barlett and Steele, much like Baquet, Lipinski, and Gaines, worked with a story line in which the readers were cast in the role of victimized citizen-taxpayers. Therefore Barlett and Steele diligently worked to rhetorically constitute the villains. For example, the reporters reviewed with classic verbal irony "an old Capitol Hill tradition that those who write the tax laws one year go to work the next year for those seeking to tailor the tax laws to their own desires." When members of the congressional tax-writing committees were later quoted as praising their aides' commitment to "public service," readers had been wised up and knew exactly what they could expect from their public servants:

> William J. Wilkins was the minority chief of staff for the Senate Finance Committee when the 1986 act was written—[Senator Daniel P.] Moynihan hailed him as "an exemplar of public service at every stage, providing insightful, direct and accurate analysis always."

Wilkins subsequently became the committee's staff director. In March, he announced his resignation to join Wilmer, Cutler & Pickering, a Washington law firm.[44]

Because readers could now read between the lines, the self-styled reformers and their beneficiaries could be given the last word with self-destructive effect. Here an executive was given the last word on his company's "transition rule" (i.e., special tax break):

> "We were very fortunate that Sen. Packwood was willing to consider the particular problems of our company."
> "I'll bet there are some transition rules that are not good ones. But, boy, I'll tell you this one—we're sure pleased that we got it."[45]

The executive went on to defend the fairness of his company's transition rule, but his words still sounded like those of a corporate fat cat caught with taxpayers' feathers in his teeth.

Similarly, Packwood was given the last word on cost:

> "In the overall scheme of events," said Bob Packwood just prior to enactment of the 1986 act, a few billion dollars in transition rules represents "a relatively minor part of the whole bill."[46]

Although the senator had merely observed a truism about the federal budget, in which a few billion dollars *is* relatively minor, his last words became the self-condemnation of another smug politico. "A few billion? Yeah, right!"

Barlett and Steele's most artful portrayals of villainy were the revelations about those who benefited from the transition rules. The reporters created a powerful sense of unmasking pretense with the facts by juxtaposing an inscrutable provision of the tax code with carefully chosen details concerning the individuals or businesses for whom the loophole had been created. One typically cryptic provision began:

> (i) IN GENERAL.—In the case of any pre-1987 open year, the amendment made by section 1275(b) shall not apply to any income derived from transactions described in clause (ii) by 1 or more corporations which were formed in Delaware on or about March 6, 1981 and which have owned 1 or more office buildings in St. Thomas, United States Virgin Islands for at least 5 years before the date of the enactment of this Act.[47]

This provision of the U.S. Internal Revenue Code, it turned out, resulted in tax savings of $4.5 million for a single company, La Isla Virgen controlled by California businessman William M. Lansdale. The company had been using its ownership of a small office building in the U.S. Virgin Islands to shelter income earned elsewhere, but by 1986 the firm had come under the scrutiny of both the Virgin Islands Bureau of Internal Revenue and the IRS:

> As it turned out, though, there was no cause for concern on the part of Lansdale.
>
> While tax investigators were bearing down on La Isla Virgen, Lansdale, or someone on his behalf, was bearing down on Capitol Hill.
>
> The same month that the IRS issued its summonses, Sen. Bob Packwood (R., Ore.) and Rep. Dan Rostenkowski (D., Ill.), the chairmen of Congress' powerful tax-writing committees, approved a special tax dispensation that absolved La Isla Virgen from paying back taxes.
>
> The tax concession—arranged by a friendly colleague whom they refused to identify—was then incorporated in the Tax Reform Act of 1986, which was passed by Congress in September of that year and signed into law by the President the next month. (p. 6)

Although the reporters never discovered who, exactly, was "bearing down on Capitol Hill" or which "friendly colleague" had come to the rescue in the nick of time, they did find interesting connections between Lansdale and his wife and the president. "About the same time that Capitol Hill tax writers were wrapping up work on drafting Lansdale's second tax preference," the story went on to report, "President Reagan appointed Lansdale's wife to the National Advisory Council on Women's Educational Programs" (p. 6). The reporters also found the sources of the Lansdales' wealth to be of interest. "His real estate interests have ranged from housing and condominium projects to the Marina Pacifica Mall in Long Beach, an open, two-story mall with courtyards," the story continued. "There are $150,000 yachts moored in an adjoining waterway, enabling weekend sailors to step from their boats into a boutique or restaurant." And the reporters found the legal squabbles within the Lansdale family—over money, of course—to be of interest. "Says a lawyer familiar with the proceedings, who requested anonymity: 'This is one of those real stories that makes Dallas or the Colbys (Dynasty) pale in comparison'" (p. 7).

The reporters brought this tangled tale to a close by returning to an important theme of their series: the secrecy that surrounds the presumably public business of lawmaking. Although most characters who appeared in this story declined to be interviewed, a lawyer named Gustav Danielson, who claimed to have invented the tax loophole exploited by Lansdale, did say a little:

Asked if he had any notion of how La Isla Virgen arranged its provision, Danielson replied:

"I would trust that they got in touch with the right people."

The staffs of the tax-writing committees—who know the identity of all "the right people"—are not talking either. All refused comment to Inquirer reporters.

James M. Jaffe, a staff member of the House Ways and Means Committee, summed up the prevailing attitude on Capitol Hill:

"We don't talk. We have people who clearly know, but who have yet to talk to a reporter—ever." (p. 9)

The ironic imagination has not summoned forth such facts as an appointment to a national advisory council and a family feud over money merely to make the point that the wealthy have access to public officials. Nor has it given voice to the likes of Danielson and Jaffe merely to make the point that public officials sometimes won't comment. The ironic imagination, when shared by reporters and readers, brings into existence a world that incorporates but transcends the particular facts and comments as reported here. It evokes a reality of greedy presidential acquaintances who are so damnably well served by the public treasury, a reality of smug officials who consider the public's business to be nobody's business but theirs. In such a world we cannot be surprised when promises of justice yield outrageous injustice. In such a world we must attend to reform immediately—or do we? Why should we believe any longer in its possibility? Haven't we been told insistently that it is an ironic joke? Shouldn't we dismiss any mention of it with—"Yeah, right!"—ironic knowingness?

The Irony of Irony

In these masterworks of investigative journalism, as in the literature of warfare, experience is emplotted and thereby given meaning by irony's fundamental story line: the dynamics of hope abridged. Unlike many wartime memoirs, however, this journalism does not intend to speak in the terms of a cosmic irony that would describe all hope as forever abridged. Rather, it intends to speak in the terms of particular irony that corrects naive expectations by revealing the true state of affairs. Moreover, it intends to speak in terms of stable irony that effectively undermines one position—the villain's—while unequivocally supporting another—the wised-up victim's. Irony can work as a corrective, however, only when writer and reader share a clearly articulated moral vocabulary. Journalistic irony, as a force for civic reform, depends on such key terms in the vocabulary of democratic ideals as *fairness in public policy* and *honesty in public service.*

But even as Richard Rorty celebrated the historical success of the vocabulary of democratic ideals, other observers began to sense that this vocabulary had begun to lose its coherence and expressive power. With a certain Gallic flamboyance the French sociologist Jean Baudrillard captured a sense of decay in both public discourse and public purpose with the argument that, in an era of unrelenting "hyperinformation," the public has fallen silent—in fact, disappeared—as a meaningful entity. The will for collective political action has been supplanted by "radical uncertainty as to our own desire, our own choice, our own opinion, our own will," he wrote. Thus the public has collapsed into merely an aggregation of irritated and confused media consumers who, in response to their sense of uncertainty, "take their revenge by allowing themselves the theatrical representation of the political scene."[48]

Even as media audiences consume politics as theater, Baudrillard argued, they sabotage the efforts of politicians as well as journalists, pollsters, and social scientists to tell meaningful stories either to them or about them. "Where the whole population of analysts and expert observers believe that they capture [these audiences], there passes a wave of derision, of reversal, and of parody," Baudrillard asserted.[49] Through the theatrics of derision, reversal, and parody the audiences disappear into "those simulative devices which are designed to capture them," and in doing so audiences come to realize "that they do not have to make a decision about themselves and the world; that they do not have to wish; that they do not have to know; that they do not have to desire."[50]

Even if the public-as-audience has not yet fallen completely silent or entirely disappeared, many individuals in the audience are reduced to the inchoate mutterings recorded by Nina Eliasoph in her study of the styles adopted by ordinary citizens for presentation of their political self-image. Eliasoph identified a number of presentational modes and found them all to incorporate a note of derisive irony. The mode that she labeled "cynical chic," for example, is a strategy for presentation of the self by which "speakers capitalize on ignorance and powerlessness, making them seem intentional." The mode of cynical chic suggests that speakers "have not been fooled into wasting their time on something that they cannot influence, and cannot be held responsible for whatever happens."[51] Here is one of Eliasoph's examples of cynical chic-speak concerning public officials: "We hear them contradicting so much, we contradict ourselves, and that's just what they want: keep us confused and not really knowing what's happening," said one such speaker concerning the Iran-Contra hearings. "Otherwise, they couldn't be doing the things they're doing."[52]

Perhaps Baudrillard's superheated prose is not necessary to explain why Eliasoph's respondents present themselves as they do; perhaps the more traditional terms of *apathy* or *alienation* or *just plain fed up* will suffice.[53] Nonetheless, in the encounter with these withered political personae we can hear the vocabulary of democratic ideals, with its terms of public virtue, giving way to the language of cynicism with terms that Baudrillard would readily recognize as those of "derision, reversal and parody."

Are those the terms in which investigative reporting will be understood by more and more of its audience? If so, it's easy to imagine how the ironies of victimization and villainy could be reinterpreted—or, in Rorty's term, "redescribed"—to transform them from moral outrages to cynical jokes. The tenuous ironies of the city council story, for example, concocted as they are from a gold-filled desk set and a limousine ride to the ball park, can be easily redescribed as Baudrillardian parody. Indeed, these purported outrages are already only parodies of outrages—mere shenanigans. And these villains can easily be reversed, if not into heroes at least into mere rascals—guys about whom a cynical chic audience might even be, well, "googy."

The paradigmatic ironies of the tax reform story, on the other hand, constructed as they are from a more potent mix of official hypocrisy with taxpayer self-interest, seem more stable and thus less easily redescribed as parody. These outrages nonetheless could be reversed into the most deeply cynical of political jokes. The victims of these ironies are, of course, the taxpayers who are victimized, not only by the alleged unfairness of the tax code but also by the infuriatingly ironic joke that produced the code—or, rather, the victims are those confidently unaware taxpayers so naive as to believe that the process of "reform" really would produce a simple and fair tax code. Cynical chic taxpayers would not be so naive. They would already know that the promise of a simple and fair tax code is an ironic joke that is going to be *on them*. The object (that is to say, ultimate target) of these ironies is not merely a particular attempt at tax reform but the whole idea of reform. And to a cynical chic audience, moreover, the object is not merely the idea of reform but the very possibility of fair treatment at the hand of government—a possibility already widely in doubt.

The understated ironies of the mortgage lending story, coaxed as they are not only from the stories of victims and villains but from the weighty materials of federal regulations and bank lending records, also seem stable. We can imagine that these outrages might be redescribed as parody precisely because they have been so painstakingly constructed around suspects who are so very usual: big banksters cast in the role of sneering villains and downtrodden minorities in the role of sympathetic victims. A media savvy, cynical chic audience might, then, see through the transparently moralistic "simulative devices" designed to capture them. Possibly. However, the outrages against racial equality presented in "The Color of Money" depend the least heavily on the devices of irony. They are outrages made real to the audience not only in the stories of victims and villains but also in the quantitative documentation and systematic explanation of bias in lending. In this story, as compared to the others, irony seems least threatening to belief in the possibility of justice; yet in this story irony still amplifies indignation at the reality of injustice.

Precisely because it eludes the irony of irony-in-journalism more successfully than the others, "The Color of Money" directs our attention back to Rorty's warning about the line between irony and cynicism in public discourse. Dedman has walked a narrow line more sure-footedly than others, but his balance still seems precarious. Irony has been important in the moral vocabulary of investigative reporting because it adapts so handily to the constraints of objectivity, and it seems so sophisticated and realistic in its descriptions of the cruel world. Now, however, the morally earnest ironies of investigative journalism must compete with a variety of mass-mediated ironies that cultivate the mode of cynical chic: delusional rantings on drive-time radio, paranoid fantasies on prime-time television, smirking monologues on late-night television, snide political commentary in the next morning's paper, and glib assurances about the future in the company newsletter. How much longer will the audience try or care to distinguish investigative journalism's moral earnestness from— "Yeah, right!"—a cynical chic knowingness?

The ultimate ironist knows that the language of politics can change— and not necessarily for the better. The historian also knows. In a somber conclusion to a study of the origins of political reporting Thomas Leonard argued that, through stories about the decay of party politics, the muckrakers of the Progressive Era effectively eroded what had been taken to be the proper basis for political action.[54] By turning the virtue of party loyalty into a vice, they undermined the rituals of political participation, leaving their readers disengaged and disaffected. "Overall political participation declined in America as this reporting gained strength," Leonard concluded. "For all the new constituencies we may credit to the progressives, for all their skill in mobilizing protest, it remains true that this age of reform was an age of voter apathy."[55] So progressive journalism presents the irony of a more enlightened yet less active electorate. In Leonard's conclusion about the consequences of journalism in the Progressive Era—yet another argument about the irony of journalism—we find precedent for a melancholy irony of journalism in an era now emerging.

In the absence of a larger and more diverse vocabulary for describing right and wrong, journalism's moral descriptions now seem vulnerable to derisive redescription. The stable and particular irony that has been an essential feature of journalistic language threatens to destabilize and universalize—to go *cosmic* in a blaze of hyperinformation—and thence to condense and harden into a cynicism that holds all hope forever abridged. When, at last, the ironies of victims and villains can generate no indignation but only derision, investigative journalism will have no vocabulary with which to discuss the true and the good or to express human solidarity. Then any possibility for a role in the defense of democratic values will be at an end.

5

The Morality of Narrative Form

News stories are just that—stories. They are true stories presumably, but stories nonetheless; as such, they give truth a particular form. Michael Schudson put the point elegantly in an essay entitled "The Politics of Narrative Form":

> The power of the media lies not only (and not even primarily) in its power to declare things to be true, but in its power to provide the forms in which the declarations appear. News in a newspaper or on television has a relationship to the "real world," not only in content but in form; that is, in the way the world is incorporated into unquestioned and unnoticed conventions of narration, and then transfigured, no longer a subject for discussion but a premise of any conversation at all.[1]

Across two centuries of news stories about the presidential State of the Union message, for example, the conventions of journalistic narration have conveyed changing premises about the proper location of power and the proper conduct of politics within the American polity. These conventions have had little to do with the accuracy with which the president's words are transcribed but much do with the context in which those words are read. Only in the twentieth century, according to Schudson, have journalists formed their stories about the State of the Union address "as an indicator of the President's personal program and political career," a form that both reflects and conveys the expectation of "power exercised in the conscious intentions of actors."[2] The function of narrative form, as

Schudson concluded, "is less to increase or decrease the truth value of the messages they convey than to shape and narrow the range of what kinds of truths that can be told."[3]

Schudson's comments about narratives in the news echo those of Hayden White about narratives in the writing of history—another source of stories that, presumably, are true. "The content of the discourse consists as much of its form as it does of whatever information might be extracted from a reading of it," White wrote in one of many provocative essays on the historian's craft. "When the reader recognizes the story being told in an historical narrative as a specific kind of story—for example, as an epic, romance, tragedy, or farce—he can be said to have comprehended the meaning produced by the discourse. This comprehension is nothing other than the recognition of the form of the narrative."[4]

Historical events, according to White, provide story elements but not the story itself. "The events are *made* into a story by the suppression or subordination of certain of them and the highlighting of others, by characterization, motific repetition, variation of tone and point of view, alternative descriptive strategies, and the like—in short, all of the techniques that we would normally expect to find in the emplotment of a novel or play," he argued. And so, for example, an event becomes a great historical tragedy not merely because it is intrinsically tragic but because it has been skillfully placed "within the context of a structured set of events of which it is an element enjoying a privileged place."[5] The great tragedies of the Great War, as reviewed in chapter 4, provide many cases in point.

Narrative is an instrument for comprehension of historical fact, but for White it is the instrument of another intellectual impulse as well. The historian is called upon to produce an authoritative account of "what really happened" only because alternative accounts are possible. In attempting to provide such an account, the historian will invoke the authority of reality, but reality does not provide a storylike account. "There can in fact be no untold stories at all just as there can be no unknown knowledge," wrote another historiographer, Louis O. Mink. "There can only be past facts not yet described in a context of narrative form."[6] And any truly authoritative story, according to White, must invoke not merely the facts but a moral vision of those facts. Indeed, that vision gives the facts their reality: "The events that are actually recorded in the narrative appear real precisely insofar as they belong to an order of moral existence, just as they derive their meaning from their placement in this order. It is because the events described conduce to the establishment of social order or fail to do so that they find a place in the narrative attesting to their reality."[7]

Historical narratives, White maintained, "are images of that authority that summons us to participation in a moral universe."[8] Unlike the medieval narratives that served as a point of departure for White's analysis, however, contemporary narratives do not commence with an invocation of the authority of God or king nor conclude with a jeremiad that calls for a new moral order in which the just are delivered and the wicked are punished. Any such overt display of moral force would be dismissed as an egregious breach of objectivity. Nevertheless, asked White, how else could any story of real events be brought to conclusion except through a "passage from one moral order to another?"[9] The "moralizing impulse" endows facts with relevance and stories with closure and coherence—the very features we use to judge the value and the truth of the stories we hear and tell.[10]

Narrative form is fundamentally metaphorical, White argued, and as such *"tells us* what images to look for in our culturally encoded experience in order to determine how we *should feel* about the thing represented."[11] His point was not to dissolve the distinction between the discourse of reality and the discourse of desire but rather to highlight the extent to which narrative transforms the real into an object of desire through a formal coherence and a moral order that the real lacks. Historical narratives are not, then, false and certainly not without value. Indeed, the value of narrative is precisely this transformative potential. Because the same set of facts lends itself to alternate story forms, whether tragedy, comedy, romance, or farce, the wise selection of story form provides the opportunity "to teach what it means to be moral beings" and "to judge the moral significance of human projects." And yet, as White hastened to remind us, story forms "permit us to judge [such projects] even while we pretend to be merely describing them."[12] The moral vision of the contemporary historian—and, as we shall argue, the investigative journalist—is more covert and ambiguous than that of the ancient narrator who was unencumbered by modern conceptions of objectivity. The message of these contemporary tales is essentially moral nonetheless.

Tales of Virtue and Vice

Investigative journalism defends virtue by telling stories of outrageous vice. In this respect it bears a resemblance to some other genres of storytelling such as the social melodrama genre of popular fiction. "Melodrama moves from a sense of injustice and disorder to an affirmation of a benevolent moral order in the universe," wrote John Cawelti. "It is a highly popular form because it affirms some conventional moral or philosophical principle as the inherent basis of cosmic order by illustrating this principle at work in the lives of good and wicked characters."[13] Although the focus of investigative journalism is more civic than cosmic, it does tend to affirm conventional interpretations of right and wrong by applying them, with little analysis or critique, to the situation at hand. Even if this genre of journalism is not a witless apologist for dominant values, its essential moral vision is a culturally *conservative* vision in the most fundamental sense of the term—that is to say, committed to the conservation of such values as fair play, common decency, and individual liberty.

To argue that investigative journalism is fundamentally conservative, however, is certainly not to argue that contemporary investigative reporters have lost the reformist spirit of their muckraking predecessors. "I guess what really interests me is showing a systemwide problem, finding out everything you can possibly know about it, and making a picture clear that has just been really fuzzy before," said one reporter. "The best stories are when you see situations where people are being abused or their rights are really being trod upon." Although such stories rarely analyze or critique public morality, they do, as another reporter said, "amalgamate it and vocalize it." Thus the reporters' moral task in these stories is to evoke indignation at the violation of social values by the social system and to implicitly invite, if not explicitly demand, a return to those values. In this work contemporary reporters can trace their intellectual lineage not only to the Progressive muckrakers but to the prophet Jeremiah.

The ideas that reality must be given narrative form and that this can be accomplished only within the compass of a moral vision serve as our point of departure for an examination how the fuzzy facts of systemwide problems are cast into the form of morally compelling stories. As in chapter 4, our interest is the representational strategies of moral discourse. We will have just a little more to say about irony here but will try to put that particular device into a larger narrative context. Also, as in the last chapter, we will focus on three important journalistic texts that are familiar from earlier chapters. They are "Rape in the County Jail: Prince George's Hidden Horror" by Loretta Tofani, "A City Roughed Up: The K-9 Cases" by William Marimow, both of which won the Pulitzer Prize, and "Killing Crime: A Police Cop-Out" by Pam Zekman, which won the du Pont-Columbia and George Foster Peabody Awards for broadcast journalism.

The basic narrative form in each of these texts, as we will see, is the dramatic encounter between victim and villain. Within that basic form these texts draw together the "story elements," to use White's phrase, in order to *realize*—that is, make real through narrative—two crucial features of investigative journalism as moral discourse. These are the innocence of those good citizens who have been victimized by some systemic problem and the guilt of those reprehensible lords of civic vice (often, though not always, bureaucrats) who have caused the problem or else failed to address it.

Realization of Innocence

In reporting the encounters between citizens and a system in disarray these investigative news stories all carefully define the citizens involved as innocent victims—innocent *enough*, at least, to make the encounter an obvious injustice. This in turn frames each encounter not merely as an example of a systemic problem but as a moral outrage. The portrayal of victims in this way provides a good example of the complex interdependence of fact, value, and narrative, because the simple fact that innocent people have been victimized turns out to be not so simple after all. In these stories innocence has to be painstakingly made real through narrative.

The investigation of rapes in the Prince George's County Detention Center began as Loretta Tofani sat in court covering her regular beat. "The lawyer was telling the judge that her client, who couldn't have been over eighteen years old, had been gang-raped in the county jail," she recalled. "Although I knew theoretically that men get raped in jail, it was the first time I was ever really confronted with it, and it really did bother me. So then I talked to the judge and found out that it happened all the time."

Although the reporter thought that this story was important, her editors were indifferent. They indicated that the situation did not strike them, in the reporter's words, "as such a big wrong." At that point Tofani was unable to defend the story idea to her superiors because she had not yet properly defined the victims in the story. "At the time I did not know that these men were often acquitted of crimes and were innocent," she said. "I had the impression at the time that these guys were being convicted of crimes." These guys, in other words, simply did not seem innocent *enough*. "You know," Tofani said, "it's not as great a story to say that a bunch of guys who have committed [the] highest crimes are being raped in jail."

Tofani just couldn't let go of the story, however. She found time to interview rape victims and jail medical personnel. And as she gained enough information to begin "writing the story in the air"—talking through the findings with others—she was always drawn to those cases in which the victim had been arrested for a relatively minor offense, had not yet been tried, or was later acquitted. "I would find myself repeating these things: 'This guy was in for shoplifting and this guy was acquitted,'" she recalled. "These were the most important elements. These were the ones that I wanted to put up front. These were the ones that I wanted to dramatize." It became clear to the reporter and then to her editors that the central action of the story, the rape of jail inmates, had limited moral meaning unless the victims were properly defined.

In the series of articles produced at the conclusion of a nine-month investigation the reporter did indeed "put up front" and "dramatize" the facts of the victims' innocence. She achieved the drama by presenting twelve carefully selected case studies that used two narrative strategies to evoke outrage at the victims' plight: highlighting cruelly ironic details of the victims' experiences and privileging the victims' accounts of those experiences. These strategies were immediately clear in the first paragraphs of the first article in the series:

> Kevin Parrish, a 20-year-old student from Upper Marlboro, was arrested on a drunk driving charge at 3 a.m., Feb. 20 and taken to the Prince George's County Detention Center. He was to wait there for a few hours, until his mother could arrive with $50 to bail him out.
>
> But his mother came too late.[14]

This case was followed by others in which the victim was always employed and always charged with a relatively minor crime: an eighteen-year-old waiter who was later acquitted of malicious destruction of property, a twenty-six-year-old cook who later pleaded guilty to malicious destruction of property, a twenty-six-year-old repairman who had not yet gone to trial for theft when the story was written, a thirty-one-year-old air force lieutenant who developed mental problems after leading "rescue workers in the gruesome six-day-long job of sifting through [aircraft] wreckage and identifying the 21 dead."[15]

But then there was also a thirty-two-year-old salesman who had been jailed without bond after stabbing someone who sat on his motorcycle. The case of the salesman is of particular interest because it required the most work to maintain the definition of the victim as innocent. The reporter began the task immediately in the first and second paragraphs of the case study by pointing out that this man, someone who had never been arrested before, suddenly found himself in a cell block with about thirty inmates charged with, or convicted of, murder. At this point in the story the reporter turned to the salesman for a recounting of the nightmare into which he was plunged:

> "I lit up a cigarette and someone said I had to go into a cell if I wanted to smoke. So I went into a side cell and sat down on a bunk to smoke. Then four or five of them came up to me and hit me in the face with fists. They told me to roll over. I yelled for the guard and they started kicking me. They banged my head against the wall, tore my clothes off and all of them raped me. It went on for about half an hour."[16]

Later paragraphs revealed that the salesman underwent surgery for a punctured lung and spent nine days in the hospital. The charge against him was later reduced from assault with intent to commit murder to malicious stabbing, and after pleading guilty he was sentenced to five years' probation. "Today," the story concluded, "he thinks of his real sentence as the rape rather than the probation." Even if not entirely innocent, this victim, like the others, had suffered far more than he deserved.

And so it was for the victims of police dog attacks on the streets of Philadelphia. Bill Marimow's investigation into their plight began with a tip that certain K-9 unit officers and their dogs were conducting "target practice" on the streets. It soon became clear to the reporter that attack cases came, as he said, "in all shades of gray." A few attacks were clearly accidental, although many others were quite ambiguous. Some attacks, for example, occurred on subway platforms or outside bars late at night after the police had been called to the scene to deal with a disturbance. It also became clear to the reporter that innocence was an essential theme of the story. "I think the more factually innocent a person is who has suffered one of these attacks, the more compelling and the more important it is that these things don't happen again," Marimow said. "It makes a situation where this could happen to you—a good citizen."

As in the jail rape story the reporter here had definitional work to do, and as in the jail rape story the narrative strategy was to emphasize the ironic twist of fate that brought the victim face to face with the attacker and to recount the attack from a point of view sympathetic to the victim. For example, the first story in this series began:

> It was nearly 1 o'clock in the morning last June 1 when an exuberant Matthew Horace bounded up the subway staircase on the east side of City Hall.
>
> Like thousands of others, Horace had come to Center City to celebrate

the Sixers' sweep in the NBA Championship Series. He was looking for a good time. He never found it.[17]

And so another victim—guilty only of youthful exuberance—was drawn to his fate.

Once again the most interesting examples of the reporter's narrative craft are the cases in which innocence is most problematic. The narration of one such case began not from the point of view of the victim but from that of witnesses: a young couple, both lawyers, walking home after a long day at the office. They saw a swirl of activity from across the street, and then:

> Still on the south side of the street, across from the police, Sarah Solmssen said she saw several officers "throwing a person against a brick wall. I saw the nightsticks, and then I started running."
>
> By the time she had broken free of her husband's grip and crossed Spruce Street, she said she could see a K-9 dog biting the leg of a young man who was lying inert, in a semi-fetal position, on the sidewalk in front of the Engineers' Club.
>
> "I saw the dog's jaws moving up and down three or four times," she recalled. "No officer was attempting to get that dog off the boy. He was just lying there motionless.
>
> Peter Solmssen, who is 29, was slightly behind his wife, but with his height, 6-foot-2, he could see the boy on the ground, his hands cuffed behind his back, unmoving.[18]

With this image of the attack in place the boy is revealed to be a 220-pound, seventeen-year-old who is so drunk that later he could not clearly recall the attack. It was clear, however, that he had been fighting inside the bar and when hauled out by relatives, as his aunt reported, "he was cussing very bad." He may or may not have tried to throw a punch at his aunt or at the police officer who had responded to the report of the brawl. He was handcuffed by the officer, but then suddenly the dog was on top of him.

Of the nine cases reviewed in the story, Marimow singled out this one as the best example of his commitment to reporting "all possible points of view" and revealing "all of the foibles of the victims" so that readers could make up their minds about what happened:

> I spoke to [the victim's] aunt who'd been at the scene. I spoke to one of her friends . . . who'd been at the scene. I got the reports of the officers, even though they wouldn't talk to me. And in publishing my account I stressed

that [the victim] had been profane. He'd been drunk. He'd been obnoxious, and even his aunt and [her friend] said that the police would have been totally justified in arresting him for disorderly conduct and that they exercised remarkable restraint. I put that in there because I'd come to the conclusion that [the victim] should have been arrested, but what happened afterwards, once he'd been knocked to the ground and handcuffed, was not justifiable.

Nevertheless, in privileging the account of witnesses who had come on the scene just as the victim was being bitten, the reporter had defined the target of the attack not as a drunken and violent teenager but as "the boy" handcuffed and in a "semi-fetal position" when the dog attacked.

It is important to note that the reporter did not characterize the privileging of the Solmssens' account as a persuasive tactic. Indeed, he denied ever attempting to persuade his readers of anything. Rather, he characterized his reliance upon the Solmssens' account as the use of the best available evidence, evidence provided by witnesses "who had nothing to protect." It is also important to note, however, that the evidence provided by the Solmssens earned its place in the story—and thus its reality—from its meaningfulness in "an order of moral existence," to use White's phrase, in which innocence is a principal concern and righteous indignation the proper response to its violation. It can be no surprise, then, that the Solmssens served not only to define the target of the attack as "the boy" but also to vocalize indignation at his fate: "Horrified by what they had seen, the Solmssens walked directly home to their townhouse on Juniper Street, less than a block from the Engineers Club. Peter Solmssen said he wanted 'something done about' what he and his wife had just witnessed."[19]

In Pam Zekman's investigation of the suppression of crime reports, the victims—people who reported a crime but who had their report "unfounded" in violation of FBI guidelines—were unequivocally innocent in their encounter with the police. Nevertheless, the reporter used the familiar narrative strategies to evoke the full measure of moral outrage that was due these victims' plight. In the cases selected for the series the victims—whether of rape, robbery, or burglary—were asked to recreate their emotional responses to the crime as well as their responses to the unfounding of the crime report. The second segment of the four-part series, for example, began by evoking the terror and humiliation of rape:

VICTIM 1 (*taped interview*): I thought he was going to kill me. He raped me and I thought he was going to just leave me in the alley.

REPORTER (*voice over*): This woman was raped at knifepoint and this teenager was raped repeatedly by two men who grabbed her as she walked home.

VICTIM 2 (*taped interview*): They were laughing at me 'cuz I was bleeding. I was hurt. I started crying. They were laughing at me.[20]

And near the end of the segment a sobbing victim responded to the unfounding of her report:

VICTIM 1 (*taped interview*): I was raped. I should know. Ask them. What they say there is not true. How could they say that? How? I was raped. And that is a filthy word—"rape." Because if it happened to me, it could happen to anyone. To me, when I think about the police, you know, they don't give a damn. They throw my case in the garbage.

These emotionally charged accounts served to underscore the master irony of this story—the double victimization of these innocents, once by a criminal and once again by the police. The reporter understood very well that in a few seconds of videotape she had not only established the credibility of the victim's story but had amalgamated and vocalized the moral indignation appropriate to these events:

I've had more comment about that than almost any interview I've done. It really got people angry, I mean, they believed her. . . . There's a conflict constantly in that kind of an interview. You feel like you're intruding on something very private you shouldn't be intruding on. On the other hand, she's willing to do it, and you know it will help make people care about the subject—care enough, perhaps, to start doing something about it. And in fact that story is one of the few stories that we've done where the newspapers picked up the story and started doing editorials and reaction stories. I think that the combination of television plus the newspapers together was what forced the police department to do something that they might have ordinarily ignored.

In this report, as in the others, the facts of victimization have been plotted as a story most akin to tragedy—a story in which an ironic turn of events leads inexorably to terrible suffering for the innocent.

Realization of Guilt

In the moral universe mapped by these stories the matter of innocence cannot exist without the antimatter of guilt. And just as the full reality of innocence must be constructed within and through narrative, so must the reality of guilt. All three reports found responsibility for the plight of the victims in a failure of "the system" (that is, the policies and performance of senior officials) to properly dispense criminal justice. Toward that end all three reports portrayed the low-level denizens of the system such as the jail guards and police officers—and even the jail rapist—as, themselves, victims of the system. Any culpability of those individuals was not allowed to mitigate the guilt of the officials in charge.

In the course of the jail rape investigation, for example, Tofani became very clear on the proper allocation of guilt. "Here you have these [rapists], presumably of free will, violating another man's dignity and security—and yet the focus of the story was not the evil rapists but rather the flaws in the system," she acknowledged. "I feel as though those rapes would have been prevented, or many of them could have been prevented, if the jail had done its job." While the "free will" of the rapists may have been part of the problem, according to the reporter, the malfeasance of the jail administrators was the cause. "They are officials who we have entrusted to take care of these people," she said, "and they have failed, and the effects are devastating to people."

The reporter's extensive interviews with the rapists allowed her to present a theory about the cause of jail rapes that in turn allowed her to direct responsibility away from the attackers and toward the system. These rapes, she argued in the report, are motivated much more by a desire for security and respect than a need for sexual release. "In jail you're not a homosexual if you're the aggressor," one of the rapists told the reporter. "You're more of a man, if anything."[21] From these interviews the reporter did attempt to reconstruct some of the complexity of the rapists' motivations; at the same time she used the interviews to develop a central theme: these rapes were a response to the conditions of jail and especially to the conditions of this particular jail. Here is how a particularly eloquent rapist helped the reporter accomplish this task:

> Francis Harper, a convicted armed robber, decided to teach a lesson to the inmate who switched the television channel in the county jail. Harper decided to rape him. . . .
>
> "The basic thing was to keep fear in the air to keep that respect," Harper said. "I was aggressive because I was afraid. I took the fear I had and reversed it. I was afraid of getting killed."

Next in the story the reporter enumerated the systemic problems that explained, if not exactly justified, the rapist's behavior:

His belief was based on certain observations. He was in a small, crowded cell block in the "upper right" section of the jail with 10 men who were charged with or convicted of armed robbery or murder. The men, who were tense and angry about being in jail, frequently got into fights or threatened each other with rape. A guard was rarely present. . . .

Looking back on the rape, Harper believes that he was motivated not only by fear for his safety but also by feelings of anger and frustration over being in jail. And the poor conditions of the Upper Marlboro jail—including extreme overcrowding, toilets that are frequently stopped up and recreation often limited to one hour of gym a week—made those feelings even more intense, according to Harper. . . .

"I feel a lot of remorse about it," he says, referring to the rape. "I wasn't strong enough to withstand the influence of my environment. They helped me to be an animal in that jail and I submitted to it."[22]

Thus the reporter granted a degree of moral immunity to the rapist in return for his testimony against the system.

The role of the jail guards in the stories told by the rape victims and their attackers was always ambiguous. The guards did not stop the attacks, and yet it was not entirely clear that they were performing their duties improperly. The guards' reluctance to speak openly and the reporter's inability to locate the guards involved in particular cases limited her ability to narrate the guards' experiences. Nevertheless, the reporter was able to use interviews with guards to limit their culpability:

Guards say they are unable to protect inmates from rapes because the poorly designed jail makes it impossible for guards to see into most cells from their watch posts. The guards say they could minimize that by patrolling the cells more often than once every eight hours, but that there aren't enough of them to do that. . . .

The guards, who work alone, say that even when they are aware of rapes in progress they cannot protect the victims because they are afraid for their own safety.[23]

The guards too, it seemed, were victims of the system's inadequate facilities and resources.

In the second article of the series the reporter brought together the interviews with inmates and guards in a powerful indictment of the jail administration and its policies:

Interviews with about 10 guards and 60 inmates show that the jail routinely places those most likely to rape with those particularly vulnerable. . . .

In addition, those who are raped are often no better off once they've reported the rape. They are locked in a small cell with several other inmates —the same tactic jail officials use to punish unruly inmates. Sometimes, as in the mechanic's case, those other inmates are the original rapists.[24]

The jailer's explanation only adds to the outrageousness of the situation:

> During an interview two weeks ago at the jail, Gaston [the jail director] defended the jail's placement of inmates charged with misdemeanors in the same sections with those charged with violent crimes. "These people [men charged with violent crimes] are charged with, not convicted of, certain acts," Gaston said. "Under the law, they're technically innocent."

And so one last terrible irony—victims jailed with their attackers—was brought together with a display of smugly legalistic indifference on the part of the jailer. Altogether, then, this system is not merely responsible for a failure to protect jail inmates but guilty of an outrageous disregard for common decency.

In the dog attack investigation Marimow was confronted with what he called in the report "a hard core of errant K-9 officers and their dogs" that was "out of control." These police officers, unlike the guards in the jail rape investigation, were not quickly absolved of responsibility. In fact, the worst offenders were singled out for withering journalistic scrutiny. Like the guards, however, these officers were shown to be caught up in a pernicious environment that they were not strong enough to withstand. According to the report, they were part of a system that had not trained the dogs properly, that had not given the officers guidelines for use of the dogs, and that had not developed procedures for monitoring the performance of either dogs or officers.

Unlike the jail rapists, who sometimes spoke eloquently of their victimization by the system, the K-9 unit officers would not talk at all. As a result, the reporter began the process of allocating guilt to the system by using interviews with an unnamed former K-9 unit officer and with Anthony Taff, the dog trainer who had founded the K-9 unit:

> That officer, who declined to be named, says the dogs are trained to hold on indefinitely in this manner: "they have a burlap bag tied to a rope and suspended from a tree on a pulley system. The dog is taught to hang on to that bag while the trainer raises it higher and higher. . . ."
>
> Taff is appalled by such techniques. That [the pulley exercise] was positively taboo when I was in charge," he says. "The whole emphasis on this long bite and hold is entirely unnecessary. . . ."

It is the combination of "macho" police officers and unreliable dogs that leads to unwarranted attacks, says the former officer. "It's like, 'I've got the dog and I'm going to show you what he can do.' We all do that to a certain extent because we're all guy's guys."[25]

The behavior of the dogs and, more important, the behavior of the officers was, it seemed, a natural response to the failure of the police department to properly train and monitor the unit. Dogs will be dogs, after all, and guys will be guys.

Perhaps because the K-9 unit officers refused to talk, the reporter did not pursue the idea that some attacks were demonstrations of "machismo" or the allegation from at least one source that some attacks were racially motivated. The motives of the officers remained suspect but ambiguous. This ambiguity facilitated rather than hindered the point of the story, however, because it allowed the reporter to include as part of the same pattern both accidental attacks in which the dog was out of control and more ambiguous attacks in which the officer may have been out of control. The point was that, whatever the motives of individual officers may have been, the system had definitely failed.

In this investigation, as compared to the jail rape investigation, the reporter had little interview material that could be used to show a smug disregard for victims. The police department simply denied that a problem existed and would not respond further to the reporter's inquiries. But this ritual denial that journalistic convention demands be included in the story was put to strategic use as the introduction to the indictment of the system:

> For the record, the Police Department says there is no problem. John J. McKees, the department's spokesman, said the department had no way of responding to The Inquirer's request for a list of bites inflicted by K-9 dogs in each of the last three years.
>
> Many law enforcement officials strongly advocate the use of the dogs for crowd control . . . the detection of narcotics and explosives, the discovery of missing persons and the apprehension of fleeing suspects.
>
> But, The Inquirer study found, too often the dogs' use is not restricted to those purposes. Instead:
>
> ■ The police K-9 dogs have repeatedly attacked and bitten unarmed men and women with no criminal records.
> ■ Contrary to accepted standards in other K-9 units, the Philadelphia dogs are not trained to release victims quickly. . . .
> ■ The resulting dog bites have left deep and disfiguring wounds and have mangled limbs. . . .

- Police officers themselves attempting to make arrests or apprehensions have been bitten by police dogs.[26]

Here, then, was another system that was not merely responsible for a failure to protect citizens but guilty of a maddening refusal to come clean, even when confronted with the evidence.

Pam Zekman's investigation of suppressed crime reports also featured police officers whose responsibility was problematic. For this report, however, the reporter decided not to single out individual officers for blame. "The story was about a pervasive problem, a scandal, in the police department that was not necessarily the doing of one individual policeman but a systemic pressure being felt from the top," Zekman said. "To single out an individual policeman would make it look like individual policemen were guilty and [that] there were just a few rotten apples."

In this report, as in the others, the reporter used interviews to establish the systemic nature of the problem. Here, for example, was one officer's explanation of how the pressure to "kill crime" flowed down the chain of command:

PATROLMAN JERRY CRAWLEY (*taped interview*): The pressure is tremendous. You have to go along to get along.

REPORTER (*voice over*): Jerry Crawley hasn't always gone along in his 5 years on the force. He told us about the time he stood up to a sergeant who wanted him to downgrade the robbery of a newspaper boy.

CRAWLEY: He suggested that I make it a battery, and this is a quote, I was told to "make it a battery and do not mention the money." When I asked him then, "Sarge, isn't this in effect submitting a false official report?" I was physically threatened and told to get the hell out of the station because I refused to reclassify that particular incident.[27]

The interview with Officer Jerry Crawley, much like the interviews with the rapist Francis Harper and the dog trainer Anthony Taff, directed responsibility away from the individual and toward the system. Killing crime, according to Crawley and other officers, was "S.O.P.—Standard Operating Procedure" in the police department. Further, the city not only lied about its crime rate but boasted about it:

REPORTER (*voice over*): Jerry Crawley is one of a dozen policemen who told us that falsifying reports has allowed a string of police chiefs to claim Chicago's crime rate is going down, while the rest of the nation's is going up. . . . Richard Brzeczek, Mayor Byrne's appointee, has continued the tradition.

SUPT. BRZECZEK (*taped speech*): Among the 57 largest cities in the U.S., only three have a lower per capita crime rate than the city of Chicago.[28]

In this report, as in the others, the facts of system performance have been plotted as a story most akin to farce. Innocent victims are caged with their attackers, and the jailer merely says that, technically, everyone is innocent. Police dogs attack innocent citizens and sometimes even their handlers, but officials have "no way" of providing information on these attacks. Police officers are pressured to "kill crime" so that their superiors can brag about their success in controlling it. This is indeed farce but farce of a particularly cruel sort, farce that provokes righteous indignation, farce that demands a turn in the moral order. Although the conventions of journalistic objectivity discourage an explicit recognition of a turn in the moral order as the only proper conclusion to a narrative, those conventions cannot completely silence the voice of Jeremiah:

> REPORTER (*voice over*): Police Superintendent Brzeczek denied there is a policy to cover up crimes, but said he will investigate the pattern of abuses exposed in our series.
>
> SUPT. BRZECZEK (*taped interview*): If there are sufficient examples of what you are describing, and it seems to be that the problem is systemic rather than isolated, then we will have to make some systemic changes. No question about that.
>
> REPORTER: We'll be watching for those changes and reporting on the progress of Brzeczek's investigation. As to the reaction so far, dozens of policemen have called to tell us their own stories of killing crime, and the pressures they feel. But those cops are worried that an investigation will overlook the top brass, and make them a scapegoat.[29]

And, indeed, this story ended only with the fall of the wicked and a turn in the political—if not moral—order in the city of Chicago. The reporter continued to watch and report on the situation until the incumbent mayor was defeated, precipitating the resignation of the police superintendent. The reporter recalled with satisfaction the conclusion to her story:

> Brzeczek got up at his last press conference before he resigned and announced that his audit had not only confirmed our findings but more.... It was the first time in my entire career that a public official had gotten up and admitted that everything we said—and more—was true. They completely changed the whole reporting system in the police department.

Narrative as an Instrument of Understanding

The innocence of the victims in these stories was not a fiction created by the reporters, but neither was it simply *there* to begin with. Similarly, blame for the plight of the victims was not arbitrarily assigned, but neither did it simply fall into its proper place with the proper weight. Innocence and guilt had to be realized by locating the ambiguous events that had transpired on city streets and in county jails within an "order of moral existence," to use White's phrase, that could render them intellectually comprehensible and at the same time morally meaningful. In this way innocence and guilt could become the unquestioned premises for any subsequent discussion of these events.

Clearly, the realization of innocence and guilt through narrative is both a cognitive and a moral enterprise—though the reporters seemed equivocal about the nature of the enterprise. Marimow acknowledged that every story is "an effort at understanding," but he disputed the idea that reporters create coherence. Then he seemed to equivocate. "Life isn't per se organized, coherent, and lucid, but in an effort to come to grips with it, you can make it more coherent," he said. "This is really a philosophical question." In an attempt to resolve that question he eventually denied his role as narrator. "I guess, usually, I don't consider myself a storyteller," he concluded. "I consider myself a gatherer of facts."

Zekman, on the other hand, did consider herself a storyteller. "I'm creating the story," she said. "I'm putting together a series of information in a certain order that I think is understandable." For this reporter, however, the selection and sequence of information was determined by a "logical progression" and not by any moral order.

Tofani also acknowledged that storytelling technique is critical to good reporting and that it is used "to impose order" on the facts:

> There were a lot of ways to tell a story about the fact that rapes occurred in the county jail, but there were only a couple of ways to tell it in a way that would be meaningful to people. That day I first became aware of the problem, I could have written a story that day. I could have said, "This young man was raped in the jail, and the judge in the case says that rapes in the jail happen all the time. The jail warden (whom I would have called afterwards) denied the charges." And so we have "on the one hand" and "on the other hand," and people would have said, "So what?"

Though this reporter wanted to transcend the limits of conventional journalistic objectivity, to her this meant only that the story would have to be told "in a more complete way" so that readers would have more information. Even for Tofani, who seemed least certain that an immutable reality exists out there, narrative was only a cognitive instrument that could motivate readers and facilitate their understanding of the facts.

Our response to these reporters is not merely that narrative is an instrument of both cognitive and moral understanding. More than that, narrative is the instrument by which these two intellectual impulses are united. In the stories reviewed here the public can come to understand the plight of victims who are—if not entirely innocent by the standards of middle-class suburban newspaper readers—at least innocent enough to make what happened to them an outrageous injustice. Similarly, the public can come to understand the misconduct of officials who are—if not guilty of criminal malfeasance—at least guilty of indifference and hypocrisy. And so it is that these stories permit the public to "judge the moral significance of human projects," as White maintained, "even while we pretend to be merely describing them."[30]

These stories issue a compelling summons to participation in a moral universe, a summons to confront real injustice. With the Solmssens all these stories cry out for something to be done. But what? The answer is not clear because the narrative form of the summons shapes and narrows, as Schudson argued, the kinds of truths that can be told. For example, several themes of public import—the otherwise-unwarranted release of prisoners who are vulnerable to jail rape, the civil liability for injuries suffered by dog attack victims, the misallocation of police resources because of faulty crime statistics—are mentioned but not developed in much detail. Even in these stories of "systemwide problems" the individual experience is emphasized, while the social issue is marginalized.

Similarly, assessments of what exactly has gone wrong with the system are not developed in much detail. We have too little information to judge how the inaction of guards, inadequacy of jail resources, and malfeasance of jail officials each contribute to the jail rapes; to judge how police officers' racism, poor police dog training, and lax control of the unit each contribute to the dog attacks; or to judge where the pressure to kill crime actually begins. In these stories the details of individual suffering became high drama, whereas the details of how the system operates would have been anticlimactic. Finally, analyses of basic moral issues—what ought to be the responsibilities of the individual and institution, how ought we to hold them accountable—are sidestepped.

Although specific instances of civic vice and a corresponding affirmation of virtue vividly emerge from these stories, the social and political—

not to mention the moral—complexities of vice and virtue all submerge into them. The summons to participation in a moral universe issued by these stories is only that—a summons. It is neither a rigorous examination of the moral forces that uphold that universe nor a clear guide to moral action within it. These stories are, then, testament to both the powers and the limits of the moral force within narrative form.

6

The Intimate Interdependence
of Fact and Value

Philosophers long have maintained that God's own truth could never be ours. Still, we like to imagine that it could. In many domains of practical social inquiry, such as journalism, we often casually speak as if we could possess—in principle, if not fully in practice—truth in the form of the one and only account that corresponds to the things and events of a determinate world, an account free of individual interest, social value, and even language itself. We like to imagine, in other words, an account free of *us*.

Perhaps we speak of truth in this way because we find it inspirational. With this conception we seem to set ourselves a high standard for the conduct of our affairs. At the same time, however, we know very well how to cope with the impossibility of actually meeting that standard. Investigative reporters, for example, often say that they must find out what really happened in presumed instances of injustice. And yet they know well how to cope with the inaccessibility, and thus the irrelevance, of "what really happened." Moreover, they may say that first they must gather the facts, then—and only then—write the story, as if the facts are isolated scientific observations from which they will induce a theory. And yet these reporters know well how to cope with the mutual constitution of fact and narrative in which each is necessary to know the other. Finally, they may say that they must separate fact from value in their story. And yet they know well how to establish facts and tell stories that do not exist independently of values. These journalists, in other words, know how to produce reports that they are willing to call "true" *despite* their professional culture's impossible standard for the Truth.

Truth Telling as a Practical Endeavor

In this chapter we intend to provoke an argument about truth in journalism—but certainly *not* by denying that truth exists. Rather, we intend to highlight the mismatch between naive, if inspirational, conceptions of truth, on the one hand, and the actual practice of journalism on the other. Our intention is to appreciate rather than to derogate the work of those who seek to know and tell the truth about the social world. When, with that same intention, a historiographer provokes an argument by contending that what happened in the past is actually irrelevant to the work of the historian, the point turns out to be something quite appreciative and practical.[1] The past, precisely because it is past, is accessible only indirectly through its traces: records, documents, artifacts, living memory. The standard for assessing the truth of statements about the past therefore cannot be the correspondence between the statement and what really happened. The standard can be only some acceptable degree of corroboration among the traces available—and that usually demands a great deal of hard work. So it is with journalists.

To understand truth telling as a practical endeavor, the truth must be conceptualized and analyzed not merely as a condition that some statements happen to fulfill but rather as the outcome of a process for generating and defending those statements. Statements that historians and journalists are willing to call "true" emerge from hard work that begins with the location and comparison of whatever traces remain of what happened. Paul Ricoeur commented on this phase of the process:

> Grasping the past in and through its documentary traces is an observation in the strong sense of the word—for to observe never means the mere recording of a brute fact. . . . Not only does the historian's inquiry raise the trace to the dignity of a meaningful document, but it also raises the past itself to the dignity of a historical fact. The document was not a document before the historian came to ask it a question. Thus on the basis of his observation, the historian establishes a document, so to speak, behind him, and in this way establishes historical facts.[2]

But how do historians or journalists know what questions to ask? The answer is, in part, that they know the questions because they already know the story. No one has made this point more provocatively than the historiographer whose work provided much of the theoretical framework for chapter 5, Hayden White. Following R. G. Collingwood, White argued that "historians come to their evidence endowed with a sense of the *possible* forms that different kinds of recognizably human situations *can* take."[3] In turn, the form of any such situation—that is to say, the story—directs the historian's search for the facts of that situation. "It is the types of figurative discourse that dictate the fundamental forms of the data to be studied," White argued. "This means that the *shape* of the *relationships* which will appear to be inherent in the objects inhabiting the field will in reality have been imposed on the field by the investigator in the very *act of identifying and describing* the objects that he finds there."[4] In this way facts and stories are mutually constituted. For White, moreover, facts and stories can be constituted only within a system of values.

A passage from White's collection of essays entitled *The Content of the Form*, quoted in chapter 5, is worth savoring again because it will continue to sustain us as we turn from the question of how facts are organized within stories to the question of how facts and stories are known at all:

> The events that are actually recorded in the narrative appear real precisely insofar as they belong to an order of moral existence, just as they derive their meaning from the placement in this order. It is because the events described conduce to the establishment of social order or fail to do so that they find a place in the narrative attesting to their reality.[5]

And given the moral basis of narrative, facts have a moral basis as well. Values, mediated by narrative form, play a key role in knowing and describing the facts.

To argue, as we do, that

1. in practical inquiry the truth is the outcome of a process for dealing with evidence rather than with "reality"
2. facts and stories are mutually constituted in the course of that process
3. values are inherent in the process

is *not* to argue that no conditions at all are imposed upon the process. For example, some stringent conditions are imposed by what Melvin Pollner appropriately termed "mundane reason." Drawing on the phenomenology of Husserl and Merleau-Ponty, Pollner argued that practical everyday rationality makes some fundamental and unquestioned—indeed, unquestionable—assumptions about any account of the world that can be taken as true. Among these assumptions, he maintained, are the expectations that reality is always *coherent, noncontradictory,* and *determinate* (that is to say, *distinct, definite,* or *decided* and therefore conclusively ascertainable, at least in principle.)[6]

Because these assumptions are invoked before any attempt to determine, describe, or even observe reality, they are best characterized as *idealizations* of reality. These idealizations are never questioned when accounts of the purportedly real are in conflict, as so often happens in the mundane world of, say, traffic court, from whence Pollner's examples came. Mundane reason always assumes that these idealizations must hold and that differing accounts would not be in conflict had they been produced under the same circumstances (that is, the same conditions of observation and the same motivations of observers). And when accounts do come into conflict, mundane reason provides a culturally determined but vast repertoire of strategies for explaining away any potential disjunctures in reality. Thus the logic of mundane reason underlies the many socially sanctioned procedures devoted to finding, explaining, punishing, and correcting what *must be* either lies or mistakes. Following psychiatrist R. D. Laing, Pollner characterized these procedures as "the politics of experience." Journalists, like historians and traffic court judges, are accomplished politicians.

A Truth Amid Realism and Relativism

Journalists usually answer with modesty when asked whether they have found the truth in a particular story because they recognize psychological, organizational, and political constraints upon their work. However, they also speak as if there is something like God's truth that they could have found were it not for those constraints. Journalists, like most people most of the time, tend to be what the philosopher Hilary Putnam called "metaphysical realists" or "externalists." According to Putnam, externalists suppose that "the world consists of some fixed totality of mind-independent objects" and that "there is exactly one true and complete description of 'the way the world is.'" To tell the truth we must make a statement that precisely corresponds to the world as it is. And to first know the truth we must find an external perspective on the world—"a God's Eye point of view," as Putnam characterized it.[7]

Putnam's conception of truth, "internalism," posits that a question about what is true of the world can be answered only *within* a description or theory of the world. Truth, in an internalist view, is an "ideal coherence of our beliefs with each other and with our experiences *as those experiences are themselves represented in our belief system*—and not correspondence with mind-independent or discourse-independent 'states of affairs,'" he wrote. "There is no God's Eye point of view that we can know or usefully imagine; there are only the various points of view of actual persons reflecting various interests and purposes that their descriptions and theories subserve" (pp. 49–50; emphasis in original).

Putnam's internalism counters naive externalism, not by denying that there is a real world but by maintaining that the objects in it cannot exist for us independent of our conceptual systems. "We cut up the world into objects when we introduce one or another scheme of description," he argued. "Since the objects *and* the signs are alike *internal* to the scheme of description, it is possible to say what matches what" (p. 52). At the same time internalism counters facile relativism, not by insisting on a single correct conceptual system but by acknowledging that all conceptual systems are not equally adequate. "Internalism does not deny that there are experiential *inputs* to knowledge; knowledge is not a story with no constraints except *internal* coherence," Putnam maintained, "but it does deny that there are any inputs *which are not themselves to some extent shaped by our concepts*, by the vocabulary we use to report and describe them, or any inputs *which admit of only one description, independent of all conceptual choices*" (p. 54; emphasis in original).

The standard for the assessment of truth, then, is not a rigid correspondence but a realistic and flexible—a very human—coherence. For Putnam the standards for assessing the rational acceptability of a statement or system of statements (for example, a theory or a story) have largely to do with the *fit* of theoretical and/or experiential beliefs with each other. And, in turn, the standards for establishing *goodness of fit* have largely to do with human interests, values, and desires. Our conceptions of coherence and fit "depend upon our biology and our culture; they are by no means 'value free,'" Putnam maintained. "But they *are* our conceptions, and they are conceptions of something real" (p. 55).

Central to Putnam's conception of the truth is the idea that any conceptual scheme in which beliefs cohere includes values. He summarized the idea this way:

> The argument in a nutshell was that *fact* (or truth) and *rationality* are interdependent notions. A fact is something that it is rational to believe. . . . And I argued that being rational involves having criteria of *relevance* as well as criteria of rational acceptability, and that all of our values are involved in our criteria of relevance. The decision that a picture of the world is true (or

true by our present lights, or "as true as anything is") and *answers the relevant questions* (as well as we are able to answer them) rests on and reveals our total system of value commitments. A being with no values would have no fact either. (p. 201)

Put even more simply, "every fact is value loaded and every one of our values loads some fact" (p. 201).

From the internalist perspective journalists enter a world that has long been cut up into objects by schemes of description. Social institutions as well as language maintain the reality of this world. So the world presents journalists with "hard facts" along with procedures for verifying those facts. For example, that quintessential "hard news" event, a fire, presents them with such hard facts as origin, damage, and fatalities because the institutions and the language of our technical age lead them to see all fires (or, at least, any fire in which they have no personal interest) as a discrete occurrence of brief duration with scientifically defined causes and legally defined effects. Some facts (e.g., fatalities) have, in Putnam's phrase, "clear empirical test conditions" (i.e., a count of bodies recovered), and other facts (e.g., origins) have what might be called clear *bureaucratic* test conditions (i.e., the official report of arson investigators) (p. 159).

To help sustain the notion that the news, at least in principle, can always correspond quite precisely to what really happened, journalists may cite paradigmatic cases of hard facts like those of a fire. And when called upon to defend the truth of particular news stories, they may cite their careful adherence to the procedures for gathering such facts. They do not, however, typically address the question of how and why the world has been cut up into these particular facts and not others to describe "the fire." As mundane reasoners, they need never question the schemes of description in which they live and work.

Even if journalism's institutional culture adheres to a simplistic externalist conception of the truth, the work of investigative reporters provides an interesting opportunity to critique such conceptions. Because these reporters cannot always rely on the clear empirical test conditions and the socially sanctioned bureaucratic procedures that serve to maintain the credibility of daily hard news reporting, they cannot easily defend the truth of their reports with glib references to paradigmatic cases of hard fact. They can, however, defend the truth of their reports by reviewing the hard work that went into the verification of facts and stories, and as they do, they reveal, even if inadvertently, how facts and stories are mutually constituted within a value-loaded conceptual scheme that renders them both morally ordered and true. For several such reviews of journalistic practice we return to the words and work of the three distinguished reporters whose award-winning stories were featured in chapter 5. Familiarity with the texts of those stories will be useful as our focus turns in this chapter from narration to verification.

Eliciting Facts

Investigative reporters, in one way or another, affirm their commitment to the idea that they can and must find out what really happened. But like historians and judges, they must rely on documents, records, artifacts, and memories in the effort to do so. Under these conditions the process for establishing the truth cannot entail the examination of what really happened, followed by the production of the single correct account that corresponds to what really happened. Rather, the process must entail the location and examination of existing accounts and the production of still another account that can be accepted as authoritative. Any correspondence is not between the authoritative account and reality but among the various accounts. And throughout this process reporters must work to satisfy the preexisting conceptions about the form that reality *must* take: coherent, determinate, noncontradictory.

Investigative reporters are unlikely to analyze their epistemological situation in quite these terms; nonetheless, they do know how to deal effectively with the situation. Their rendering of the situation would go more like this: reporters set out to get the story, but they know that the only way to do so is to get everyone else's story first. They also know that they are likely to hear different stories from different sources. As a result, they expect to piece their story together through a painstaking process of corroboration among multiple sources and sorts of evidence. Bill Marimow, for example, understood from the beginning of his investigation into the Philadelphia K-9 unit that he would be working with police records and other documents as well as the testimony of the individuals who (in his particular, morally oriented "scheme of description") were to be the "victims" in his story. He also understood that the correspondence between these textual materials would be far from exact but that somehow he could fit them together into a single determinate account of events. Here is how he reconstructed his epistemological situation as he began his work:

> The police have to file a complaint if they arrest someone, or they have
> to file an accident report if it is an accident. That's good because it's evi-

dence independent of the victim, who may have contacted you, that something really did happen at the subway concourse at seven-thirty, that there was a K-9 officer on the scene, and that there were other officers on the scene. That report, in combination with the victim's account, will usually give you the whole range of what you can expect to hear. The police account will probably be the set of facts most unfavorable to the victim, and the victim's account will be the set of facts most unfavorable to the police.

It'll be your job to look at these and find everything else: police records, court records, interviews with victims and eyewitnesses, medical records, photographs, and physical evidence. For instance, it would be interesting to see [the victim's] pants. I'd assume that they would have been blood soaked. You could examine them, you could give them to, say, a veterinarian and ask if these holes were consistent with dog-bite wounds.

As Marimow made clear, the first task of the investigative reporter is to locate and/or elicit statements and other sorts of evidence. Loretta Tofani began her reporting of sexual assaults in the county jail by conducting detailed interviews with those sources she understood to be the victims of her story:

I collected a lot of stuff that was useless, but what I put in [the story] were things that described or corroborated the crimes; the story line in each of the cases: Where the person was when it happened. How it happened. How the rapists approached him. Where the guard was. Whether he screamed. Exactly what they did to him. Exactly what they said to him. What the names were of the people who did it to him. How long it occurred. What he did afterwards—did he go the medical room? All the essential questions of what happened when he was raped and what happened afterwards.

This was painful for the victims and so we ended up talking about a million different things during those conversations. Do you have a girlfriend? What do you do in real life? Where did you grow up? How many brothers and sisters do you have? All those things gave me a sense of the person, but most never ended up getting into the story because they were off the point. . . . I mean, I really did want a sense of the person such as occupation and position in society. That did end up getting into the story.

The victims' accounts provided much information with the potential to become the facts of what really happened, though not all the information was "on the point." From the beginning of the reporting process, however, the reporter understood that the "essential questions"—those most relevant to "the story line in each of the cases"—concerned not merely the occurrence of rape but the problems of the system (the jail was poorly designed, for example, and the guards were unable or unwilling to respond) as well as the brutalizing of innocent victims (people whose position "in real life" was not that of hardened criminal but average citizen). The facts of the attack (e.g., the screams of the victim), along with its circumstances (e.g., the location of the guards) and consequences for the victim, were all what Putnam would recognize as the "moral facts" that would endow events in this jail with moral, as well as social and political, meaning. Thus, just as Ricoeur and White would have predicted, the reporter's story line—innocent victims encountering an unjust system—identified the essential questions that the reporter had to ask. The facts and the story began to emerge simultaneously from these interviews.

Verifying Facts

Next the reporter must attempt to verify the facts that have emerged. Tofani's procedure for doing so could not have been to compare the victims' accounts to what really happened. It could only have been to compare these accounts to other accounts that she had elicited. The essence of journalistic verification, as Tofani made clear, is corroboration among accounts:

> There was still that doubt in my mind as to whether they were really telling me the truth. I carried the clause, "If, indeed, this has happened," around with me through much of the story. And so, the problem became finding out whether they were telling me the truth—whether indeed it had happened. I spent an awful lot of time documenting that.
>
> The first thing was getting the jail medical workers to talk to me, which was not an easy task. Only a couple of them did. I went to their homes at night and asked them. They were very disturbed about all the rapes they were seeing. Over time, as trust developed, they gave me the medical records of these rape victims. From those medical records, I could see that, in fact, these men had been raped. . . . There was clear evidence like semen in rectums, and there were physical injuries like bruises and broken bones.
>
> And then, I talked to the rapists themselves about what they had done. Their stories corroborated the victims' stories. It was only coming to the end of that line—really fleshing out each individual story—that I become certain that it was true.

Tofani's conviction that only by "fleshing out each individual story" could she know the truth of the rape charges is a testament to the centrality of corroboration in the practical production of the truth. Ideally, she could triangulate three sources—the victim, the medical record, the rapist—or at least she could compare two sources to flesh out each story. And yet in one case she had only the word of the victim. In discussing that case, however, the reporter honored the principle of corroboration in her acknowledgment of its breach:

> I had doubts about that one case all the way through to the end, and I'm afraid I don't have a good answer to how that one got in the story. I talked to another, more experienced reporter about it, and I said, "Look, there's no real corroboration." He asked me a lot about this guy—what he was like. I had spent a lot of time talking to this guy, and I said that he really did seem disturbed about it, and he was able to describe it in very complete detail. Even when I would talk to him about it weeks later, the details would not change, and he seemed to have it very clear in his mind that this had happened. The other reporter felt it was solid enough. I wasn't sure, but I trusted his judgment and went with it.

A social scientist might recognize the victim's consistency as a sort of test-retest reliability. There is, however, another answer to how this case got into the story. The case was that of Gary McNamara, a twenty-seven-year-old air-conditioner repairman who was raped while awaiting trial on charges of stealing some jewelry from a department store. One night, a week after his arrest, McNamara was awakened by a pillow stuffed against his face. Then he was thrown to the cold floor. Next, as Tofani reconstructed the story:

> "I felt something, I think it was a fist shoved inside of me," says McNamara. "I felt sheer terror."
>
> He had been assigned to the 3D area with about 35 other inmates, most of whom had been charged with armed robbery or murder, according to jail guards. McNamara's cell was a few feet from the guard. During the rape, however, the guard could not see into McNamara's cell because inmates had draped the entrance to the cell with black plastic trash bags, according to McNamara. . . .
>
> About a week later, McNamara visited the jail medical technician, a man who has less training than a registered nurse, but McNamara did not tell him he had been raped. "I was afraid it would get back to them," he said, referring to the men who raped him.[8]

McNamara's story, as Tofani acknowledged, was "compelling" because it caught up so many of the themes the reporter wished to develop: uncounted rapes, inadequate jail facilities, and, most important, victims who were not hardened criminals but who were subjected to a terrible punishment. The principle of multiple corroboration bent under the weight of this case's value to the larger story—but it did not break. Tofani and her colleague could allow themselves to be convinced of McNamara's story, not only by its consistency but also by its fit with the stories of other victims caught in this hellish place. The essential moral facts of this story, the facts of innocence and guilt, were corroborated by their correspondence to, and coherence within, a very particular and terrible sort of human situation—jail rape—that had become painfully recognizable to the reporter.

Pam Zekman's investigation into the "killing" of crime reports provides still more examples of the hard work that goes into journalistic verification. First, she had to get the accounts of the victims' whose crime reports had been declared by the police to be unfounded, and then she had to verify the victims' claims that the crimes had in fact occurred. Like Tofani, Zekman could sift through many cases until she found a few with the needed degree of corroboration. Nonetheless, finding corroborative accounts was a significant reporting achievement:

> We had a great deal of difficulty with the rape story, finding rape victims who would be interviewed and who were credible. . . . We wanted rape cases where it was more than just the woman's word against the cops, where there was something extra. In the case of one girl there were the hospital records. The police department had just totally dismissed the hospital records and said that she was lying. Well, the hospital records confirmed that she had been raped. There was something tangible, not one person's word against another. And in the other case there was a witness that saw the rape. I mean, not many people witness rapes so we had very high standards. We were looking for rape cases where there was some extra piece of evidence.

The work of information gathering is long and laborious, as these reporters all testified, but corroboration does not seem to be problematic in their recollections of their work. Corroboration seems simply to *be there*, among the accounts, or else it isn't. "Their stories corroborated the victims' stories," Tofani said simply of her extensive interviews with rapists, as if she had found a precise point-for-point match among the accounts. But in the journalistic setting corroboration rarely means a perfect point-for-point replication of accounts. Reporters must expect to hear, as Marimow said, "a whole range" of stories. Realistically, then, corroboration can mean only that certain facts must somehow match up to each other. But which facts and how should they match up? The answers to these questions are crucial examples of the tacit knowledge of the journalistic craft. Journalists must know the answers well enough to get on with their work, but they do not articulate those answers very clearly. Nonetheless, reporters' commentary on their work offers some insight into practical standards of corroboration in this domain of inquiry.

The question of "which facts?" is usefully addressed by beginning with Zekman's dictum: "If it's a pivotal fact, you've got to have corroboration, if not double corroboration." The notion of a "pivotal fact" neatly captures the idea that stories turn on a few key situations or events. In particular, the stories to be told by these reporters, much like the stories told in courtrooms, all turn on specific acts of wrongdoing.[9] If the victims in Tofani's and Zekman's stories were not raped and if the victims in Marimow's story were not bitten by police dogs, these reporters have no stories at all. As we have noted, however, what is "on the point" in each case is much more than merely the attack. Facts that address the essential questions of innocence and guilt are also pivotal facts. Among the first questions Tofani asked of the medical records when she finally obtained them were "What were the injuries? Do they relate to the injuries that the victim told me about?" The nature and degree of injuries are pivotal to a story that turns not merely on assaults against jail inmates but on brutalization of innocent men. In this way the emerging story line designates some facts as pivotal and sets the standard for their verification. The story determines those facts for which "you've got to have corroboration, if not double corroboration."

The question of "how facts match up" can be usefully addressed by beginning with Tofani's comment: "It was only coming to the end of that line—really fleshing out each individual story—that I became certain that it was true." The notion of "fleshing out each individual story" calls to mind Stephen Pepper's useful distinction between multiplicative and structural corroboration.[10] Multiplicative corroboration requires separate stories to provide precisely the same fact as when separate scientific experiments yield identical results. Structural corroboration, on the other hand, requires separate facts to fit precisely together in the same coherent story.

Superficially, Tofani's work seems to be a straightforward example of multiplicative corroboration. Several different sources of evidence—the testimony of the victim and the attacker as well as the medical records—all provided at least one identical fact: rape. However, the reporter's claim to have corroborated the fact of rape was supported not merely by use of the word *rape* in the various accounts of the attack. In fact, that word or its synonyms might never have been used. Rather, the claim was supported by the coherent and noncontradictory character of the various accounts and records that the reporter had so painstakingly elicited. When, for example, the victim's testimony was corroborated by the medical record, it was not because the two sorts of evidence repeated exactly the same items of information. Rather, it was because the two sorts of evidence provided distinct but related items that fit together well—that is, the description of an assault that was consistent with the record of injuries. The degree of fit among the sources of evidence in turn was sufficient to justify the use of a particular description: rape.

Therefore the corroboration needed to "flesh out" a story is likely to be more structural than multiplicative. But whether structural or multiplicative, corroboration draws upon degree-of-fit criteria that are difficult to articulate. Despite Tofani's insistence that she found cases with unequivocal corroboration, she acknowledged, if only fleetingly, that she did have to make judgments about degree of fit between items of information. "In getting the medical records you want to find out if it happened when he said it happened," she said, adding, "If it's off by a couple of days, it's not a big deal." So the corroboration of pivotal facts, seemingly so easy in principle, draws upon tacit knowledge of what constitutes a satisfactory fit. Perhaps any competent mundane reasoner would agree that a couple of days is not a big deal in this particular context. But exactly how many days would be?

Structuring Stories

Standards and procedures for structural corroboration would defy formalization in journalism, even if journalists were willing to acknowledge the mutual constitution of fact and story. The story lines essential to structural corroboration, after all, are firmly grounded in the conventional wisdom of the culture, and yet they are easily adaptable to varied applications. A reliable, yet permutable, repertoire of story lines stands ready to explain the ways of the world and to tacitly guide the location and corroboration of relevant facts about the world. Zekman illustrated the process with a hypothetical example in which she had excellent documentation of a pivotal fact. Indeed, she had what seemed to be a "smoking gun" in the form of an incriminating memo. Nonetheless, she knew that she needed to draw together facts from a variety of sources into one of those "recognizably human situations" of which Hayden White wrote:

> A memo from the head of a giant real estate company telling his salesmen that he wants them to practice "panic peddling" would not be enough for me to do the story. I would want evidence that it had been done.... I'm going to go to that neighborhood. I'm going to knock on doors, and I'm going to find some white homeowner who's gotten a call from that real estate company telling him blacks are coming and his property value is going to go down.... I would probably even put people to work as salesmen in those real estate offices to see if that's what they were trying to do.
>
> Now, it's not often that you get somebody coming in with a document. More often what you'll get is somebody coming in and telling you about it with no documents, and you have to go to those added lengths. The memo would be a wonderful thing to have. It might allow you not to have to go undercover, but I would still want the victims. Without the letter I'd probably have to go undercover because I'd want to know that it was policy in the office and not just one salesman run amok.

Much as a prosecuting attorney would seek to establish motive, means, and opportunity, the reporter would seek to include in the story any evidence of an intention or a policy of wrongdoing. She also would seek to demonstrate actual instances of wrongdoing as well as the effect of that wrongdoing on the victims. All this would be necessary for a story that corroborates and justifies the charge of "panic pedaling."

Zekman's example captures our contention that an investigative story is structured by a story line that serves to identify and corroborate the pivotal facts. These facts in turn embody—or "flesh out"—the story line. In Zekman's example, the story line is the familiar motive-action-consequence schema. In the three reports that are our primary focus here, an essential element of the story line is the brutal encounter between an innocent citizen and an unjust system—a plot that identifies as pivotal not only the facts of the actual encounter (the rape, for example) but also the many facts of the victim's innocence and the villain's guilt. And so, for example, Tofani's story required verification not only of the rapes but such facts as the background and injuries of the victim, the inadequacies of the jail, and the indifference of the jailer. In turn, all the facts came together into a credible and compelling report of a systemwide problem that attested to the reality of those facts.

Reporters often use the metaphor of piecing together a puzzle when they speak of locating facts and assembling them into a story. The notion of interlocking jigsaw puzzle pieces that fit precisely together into a picture is an attractive metaphor for structural corroboration of both fact and story. However, in this image of pieces predetermined in shape and number coming together into a picture that is also predetermined by reality, the puzzle metaphor reflects too naively the assumptions of metaphysical realism. The set of facts that seems to interlock so convincingly into the story has been shaped by that story in the first place, just as the story has been shaped by a moral order.

In sum, the story line guides the establishment of the facts; at the same time the facts must also justify the selection of the particular story line. Journalists recognize that the facts constrain their choices, but they also recognize that they do have choices to make. "There were a lot of ways to tell a story about the fact that rapes occurred in the county jail," as Tofani acknowledged, "but there were only a couple of ways to tell it in a way that would be meaningful to people." Making wise and morally defensible choices from among the meaningful ways to tell a story, however many ways may exist, is key to the search for the truth that is to be found between realism and relativism.

Resolving Disjunctures

To argue that fact and story are mutually constituted does not imply that reporters falsify facts and stories. The whole point here is to understand journalistic procedures for verifying the truth. And, as we have argued, verification in this practical setting means corroboration among multiple accounts. Although facts and stories constitute each other, they also constrain each other because the various accounts that reporters use to construct their own accounts must in fact (and in story) agree with each other in the ways we have sketched. But what if accounts do not agree?

Marimow, for example, confronted an unruly collection of story materials in his reporting on the police dog attacks. He had, as he said, a "whole range" of accounts in each case, and he readily acknowledged discrepancies among those accounts. "I believe that a story's truthful if you have done everything you can to get all sides of a story and then synthesize, analyze, and then publish that—and not disregard something because it might make your story gray instead of black," he said. Mundane reason insists, however, that only one coherent story can be the truth, and it demands that reporters resolve any discrepancies that would create a significant disjuncture in reality. Of course, reporters cannot seek resolution by testing an account against "what really happened." No such test is possible (and if it was, reporters would already know the truth and would not need to worry about discrepant accounts at all). Rather, reporters turn to their repertoire of strategies for dealing with mistakes and lies. That is to say, they invoke the various procedures of the journalistic craft for evaluating the *credibility* of accounts.[11]

Tofani, for example, judged the medical records to be highly credible based on the bureaucratically sanctioned origins of such records. "A medical record is something that you can trust, so I would go with that, even though there was no corroboration from the victim," she said. "I don't think that the medical technicians have any reason to lie in a case like that. I think they are generally pretty professional about it, and you could see by the record itself that it was all very carefully done." She relied heavily on the medical records in one case in which the victim was vague about the attack and could not identify his attackers. "There were extensive, extensive injuries, and the victim was in the hospital for a long time," she said of that case. "Because the medical records were so good, I felt like I could go with it."

Reporters often summarize their assumptions about the credibility of accounts by assigning metaphoric *weight* to them. "I would give tremendous weight to a trained observer at the scene who had no reason whatsoever to fabricate anything," said Marimow, adding, "I would put myself at the very top of the scale." He gave only a little less weight to witnesses who, though untrained, had "no axe to grind," as with the Solmssens who witnessed the attack on Joey Loftus, "the boy" who was too drunk to remember what happened:

> The independent witnesses who don't know the police and who don't know the victim, to my mind, are the likeliest tellers of the truth. In cases where there are independent witnesses like the Solmssens in the Loftus case, I would tend to rely more heavily on their accounts than the accounts of anyone else simply because they have nothing to protect at all. . . . I would give very little weight to what Joey Loftus said he remembered. I questioned him carefully about what he had to drink and about what he remembered. It was clear to me that his recollection was, as I wrote, at best hazy and imprecise.

The notion of evidentiary weight is a useful organizing principle for the journalist's repertoire of disjuncture-resolution strategies. The specific weights assigned to various accounts do, however, vary from reporter to reporter and even from story to story. Under some circumstances reporters may assign greatest weight to visual evidence such as videotape, whereas under other circumstances they may assign it to legal documents or financial records. But whatever the hierarchy of weights, reporters carefully consider the weight of the various accounts available when attempting to establish a pivotal fact, especially when those accounts provide less than satisfactory corroboration. Marimow chose to write about the attack on Joey Loftus based on an account to which he allocated greater weight than that of the victim himself—the bystanders. Similarly, Tofani chose to write about an assault for which the victim could provide limited corroboration because she had an account to which she allocated great weight—the medical records.

Implicit within the concept of weight is a set of assumptions about the conditions under which mistakes are made and lies are told. A hierarchy of weights both reflects and renders judgments about the accounts and those who offer them. For example, reporters place little evidentiary weight on the accounts offered by the targets of their investigations, who presumably have much to hide. Out of fairness, however, reporters will quote from those accounts, and they may even be so gracious (or so cautious) as to characterize those accounts as "a version of events" or "an interpretation of the facts," as Marimow did:

> To me there is a whole range of what the truth is and that in order to do a story fairly and thoroughly, you've got to talk to everyone involved, and you have to get all possible interpretations of the facts. That's why I think it's really important that you force the subject of the story to know that you're planning to write this story and that you feel very strongly that facts are subject to interpretation and that before you write this story you want to hear what his or her account is.

When confronted with alternative interpretations of the facts, reporters may invoke the traditional journalistic idea that they must tell both sides and let the public decide. "I think what I try to do is to get all possible points of view, all accounts of one incident," Marimow said. "I evaluate them so that I have a sense of what I believe really happened, and then I present them in such a way that readers will have the advantage of the information that I had in order for me to make up my mind." But as Marimow subtly acknowledged, reporters do not want to leave their beliefs about what really happened open to public doubt. When they present their readers with "the advantage of the information" that they had, reporters convey their sense of the evidentiary and moral weight to be allocated to various interpretations.

We have already seen many examples of the rhetorical and narrative strategies that reporters can use to convey their sense of the weight that should be accorded the words of villains. Pollner called these strategies "the ironicizing of experience," an appropriate if unpoetic label for a process that goes on in courtrooms, newsrooms, and just about everywhere else. "The ironicizing of experience occurs when one experience, tacitly claiming to have comprehended the world objectively, is examined from the point of view of another experience which is honored as the definitive version of the world intended by the first," Pollner wrote, offering his view of the territory covered by Muecke. "The irony resides in the subsequent appreciation that the initial experience was not the objective representation that it was originally purported or felt to be." Turning the villains' words against them in just this way is an important tactic in the journalistic "politics of experience."[12]

With this in mind, Marimow's reference to "a whole range of what the truth is" cannot be mistaken for a willingness to admit the possibility of multiple and/or indeterminate "schemes of description." Although denials and other contradictory accounts may be quoted in the report, they can never threaten the journalistic commitment to mundane reason. The "advantage" that the reporter sought to bestow on his readers was the information necessary to resolve any apparent disjuncture in reality on behalf of the one true interpretation—his. Indeed, if he had entertained any serious doubts about his interpretation, *he would not have published it*—a situation to which we return in chapter 7.

Establishing Patterns

The intimate connection between fact and value often runs through judgments of relevance. "The decision that a picture of the world is true . . . and *answers the relevant questions*," as Putnam argued, "rests on and reveals our total system of value commitments."[13] And so the connection between fact and value is revealed as these reporters seek answers to the most relevant or essential questions—the questions that summon into existence moral facts concerning innocence and guilt. The connection is further revealed as the reporters select particular cases of victimization to be portrayed in their report and assemble these cases into a coherent *pattern* of villainy. A pattern of cases is crucial to the ultimate point of any story that concerns not merely individual wrongdoing but institutional breakdown in, for example, the criminal justice system.

To demonstrate a pattern of institutional breakdown requires multiple cases, but not just any cases will do. Criteria for the selection of cases to be featured in the completed report sometimes include the representativeness of the cases. "If it's a story that affects the whole city, and you don't want people to assume that it affects only the black community, then you're going to pick a spectrum of victims to make that point," said Zekman. "You make those choices when you have them, but you don't always have them." Although considerations of representativeness may *constrain* reporters' choices, they do not *determine* the choices. Tofani, for example, decided early in the project that the selection of rape cases could not be left to chance:

> One of the biggest decisions, if not the biggest decision, I had to make with the jail rape series was which rape victims to write about. In the early stages of that story I didn't realize that a jail meant that people hadn't been convicted of crimes and were legally innocent. I mean, I didn't understand the distinction between a jail and a prison. I thought all these guys were in there for, you know, armed robbery or murder—all those really awful things. Part of the reason I thought that was because of the method I had chosen to try to collect the names of rape victims. I walked around the courthouse hour after hour, stopping lawyers in the hall and saying, "Listen, have you any clients who have been raped? Will you tell me who they are?"
>
> I did get names from the lawyers . . . but by this method I was getting all these creeps. The first victim I talked to was a guy who had raped five women. I just found people who had done really awful crimes, and it was only later that I found out that a lot of those people were in for shoplifting or drunk driving. I made the decision that the people I was going to write about were the legally innocent people or the people who were in on minor crimes: the shoplifters and the drunk drivers. I would include examples of people who were in on very serious things as well, but I was going to select the innocent ones for the bulk of my cases.

Tofani was not oblivious to the idea of representativeness, but her decisions were not guided by the social scientific logic of sampling. Her goal, after all, was not to present a cross-section of cases that represented the universe of all rape cases. Rather, her goal was to highlight cases that could summon the moral outrage of her readers—the cases of "legally innocent people or the people who were in on minor crimes." Although she did attempt to establish the frequency of assaults in the jail, she did not attempt to determine the percentage of assaults on "innocent victims" as opposed to "guilty victims." Given the ambiguity of innocence in this setting, that task would have been difficult. But more to the point, it was unnecessary because public indignation is not activated by a particular number or percentage of cases but by a few particularly compelling cases. This is not a scientific logic concerned with parameter estimates of what *does* happen but rather a moral logic concerned with stories of what *can* happen. The reporter captured the logic of her choices well. "These victims were people that readers could identify with," she said. "You know, 'That could be my son in for drunk driving.'"

Thus to show the pattern *of* the cases reporters look for a particular pattern *in* the cases selected for attention. Like Tofani, Marimow looked for cases with specific features that suggested an institutional breakdown. "When selecting K-9 cases, I had to judge, first of all, was the use of a dog appropriate in the case?" he said. "Is there enough of a pattern to suggest that there are many or few K-9 officers in Philadelphia who are unable to control their dogs? If there is a pattern, which cases illustrate the pattern?" The reporter recognized that the concept of pattern is problematic. He acknowledged that no formula exists for determining the presence of a pattern, but he was willing to defend the pattern as an empirical reality:

> It seems to me that without being mathematical about it, if you have several attacks that have been questioned by independent witnesses and the attacks have been upon people with no criminal records and no history of violence, then you have enough to start thinking about a story. To me, nine cases of people who were legally innocent or factually innocent, backed up with independent witness, was enough to start thinking, "story."
>
> If it's a real pattern, then, it's out there in the world. To me, a pattern is a recurrent mode of conduct. If time and time again an officer's dog is accidentally attacking people, that, to me, is a pattern. "Time and time again" can be three or four times, but if an officer's dog attacks three citizens or four citizens by accident over a one-year period, that to me is a pattern of questionable attacks.

Marimow offered his defense of the pattern's empirical reality within the context of his argument that he made no moral judgments, only news judgments concerning the importance of his story. Despite his care to present his judgments about the pattern as value free, the empirical reality of the pattern clearly depends upon several significant moral facts: many victims are *innocent* and the use of dogs is *unjustified*. The importance of such moral facts to the pattern became explicit as the reporter introduced the pattern in the first article of the series:

> That pattern: A few officers and a few dogs account for a disproportionate number of attacks and dog bites.[14]

A few paragraphs later the reporter presented the details of the pattern as a set of bulleted points. For example:

- The police K-9 dogs have repeatedly attacked and bitten unarmed men and women with no criminal records.
- Contrary to accepted standards in other K-9 units, the Philadelphia dogs are not trained to release victims quickly after an initial bite. . . .
- The resulting dog bites have left deep and disfiguring wounds and mangled limbs requiring expensive and extensive hospitalization.

The only conclusion that can reasonably be drawn from this pattern is another, larger moral fact: "The bottom line," as the reporter said, "is that it's *a problem*."

In the jail rape story the reporter did not explicitly refer to "a pattern," but her presentation of the connections among the cases is much the same as in the dog attack story. Her succinct bulleted points are a recurring motif of investigative reports:

According to guards and inmates, rapes and sexual assault cases in the county jail share certain characteristics:
- They occur in cells out of sight of any guard. . . .
- The rapes are particularly violent. . . .
- Many of the rapists are charged with or convicted of murder or armed robbery and are placed with those awaiting trail on nonviolent charges.[15]

The presentation of the pattern provides a compelling display of both multiple and structural corroboration for these fundamental moral facts: a public system has *failed*; *innocent* citizens can be, and have been its *victims*; and the *guilty* officials ought to be held *accountable* not only for *malfeasance* but also *indifference* and *hypocrisy*.

Knowing and Telling What's True

We do not dispute the contention that these investigative reports are true. We have argued, however, that simplistic conceptions of truth deviate not only from what philosophers typically say but also from what reporters actually do. Therefore we wish to dispute what *it means to say* that these reports are true.

First, we dispute any contention that these reports are true because the reporters have constructed them to precisely correspond to "what really happened." The reporters could not have done so because they had no access to what really happened. They had nothing to which their accounts could correspond except other accounts—those of victims, villains, witnesses, and so on. So the claims to know the truth about what happened cannot rest on a claim to have achieved a state of correspondence to reality but rather on a rigorous process of corroboration among accounts.

We also dispute any contention that these reports are true because the reporters first uncovered the facts and then pieced them together into the story. The reporters could not have done so because facts and stories do not exist independently of each other. Facts are the pieces from which stories are made, but stories are necessary to determine the relevance of potential facts and to structurally corroborate those facts. Only in the context of a coherent story can the "essential questions" be formulated and in turn the "pivotal facts" identified and corroborated. Thus the attempt to learn the truth begins and ends with stories.

Finally, we dispute any contention that these reports are true because the reporters avoided the bias that results from the intrusion of values into their work. The reporters could not have done so because the answers to the essential questions are easily recognized as the moral facts of innocence and guilt. Because facts are "pivotal" only within a story framework and in turn a moral framework, values necessarily structure the verification procedure. Knowing and telling the truth is ultimately under the control of the values that reporters share with their communities.

We do not deny that there is truth to seek. We contend, however, that those who seek a truth defined in terms of a naive metaphysical realism attempt the impossible, and therefore they attempt far too little. This paradox is easily resolved: because naive realism demands an exact correspondence between value-independent statements and a mind-independent reality, it subverts thoughtful consideration of what practical truth seekers must actually try to do. Naive realism, for example, allows journalists to assert that corroboration simply is (or isn't) there. The standards of corroboration remain embedded in the tacit knowledge of the craft. Further, naive realism allows journalists to assert that first they establish the facts and then they write the story from those facts. The story lines that help to constitute the facts remain submerged in the unexamined common sense of the culture. And finally, naive realism allows journalists to ignore the crucial connection between relevance and values. The moral forces that animate not only investigative reporting but the entire intellectual enterprise of practical social inquiry remain obscured by the contention that facts can exist without values or values without facts.

When it comes to truth, investigative journalism seems better in practice than in theory. If nothing is so practical as a good theory, this genre of journalism has little to say about truth. If, on the other hand, nothing is so theoretical as good practice, investigative journalism has some useful lessons about the role of values in the practical pursuit of truth.

7

Journalistic Judgment and the Reporter's Responsibility

Investigative journalism is an exercise in public conscience despite itself. Reporters are willing to take significant responsibility for the truth of their stories, but they are reluctant to take responsibility for the moral judgments embodied in those stories. Moreover, they are adamant in their rejection of responsibility for any political or other public consequences of their work. They would like to be responsible, as one reporter said, for simply "telling people something they don't know."[1]

Nonetheless, as compared to other genres of journalism, especially daily reporting, investigative reporting is the very model of journalistic responsibility. At least, it is one useful model. Despite investigative reporters' desire to limit their responsibility for any social and political consequences of their work, they do acknowledge the possibility of personal consequences for the individuals mentioned in their stories, especially those who stand accused of wrongdoing. And in that context, as another reporter said, journalists face an "awesome responsibility."

The confrontation with this delimited, if still awesome, responsibility provides an opportunity to consider the larger meaning of journalistic responsibility. As a key term in the rhetoric of grievance against the news media, *journalistic responsibility* is more often ritually invoked than seriously analyzed. And when taken seriously, it is more often a demand for restraint in publication of the news than an expanded definition of the news itself. Investigative reporting, however, points toward a conception of journalistic responsibility defined not as a constraint imposed on news dissemination but as a principle that can animate the news-gathering process.

Responsibility and the Justification of Knowledge Claims

In this chapter we begin by focusing on the sort of responsibility that investigative journalism unequivocally accepts. Although reporters often say that they must find out what really happened, typically they are modest about their success. They are willing to say that their stories are "true" but not necessarily "the truth." When pressed on the distinction, they turn to the notion of factual accuracy. "We tend to use the term *accuracy* more than anything else," said Jim Steele. "Have we quoted people properly? Did the individual involved in fact do this? Did that in fact happen?" According to this reporter, accuracy in the recording of such facts is often the best that journalists can do. "The truth, I suppose, is some ultimate notion of the complete story on everything," he said. "I think of 'the truth' as some ultimate thing that no one ever achieves in any endeavor."

Nonetheless, Steele saw investigative reporting as an opportunity to move beyond the limitations of daily reporting and to get somewhat closer to that complete story on everything. "I remember a lot of frustration in balancing out the coverage—these people say this and those people say that," he recalled of his days as a young reporter covering local politics. "In the end you were terribly frustrated about what might have been the actual case." Of his work as an investigative reporter, he said modestly, "At least, we test the statements that people make."

Investigative reporters can escape some frustrations faced by daily reporters because they have, in Pam Zekman's phrase, "the luxury of time." But the fact that investigative reporters are less responsible for meeting a daily deadline than other reporters does not explain how they are more responsible for their stories. A useful way to characterize how investigative reporting transcends the constrained objectivity of daily reporting draws upon the philosopher's concept of epistemic justification—the grounding of knowledge claims.

Philosophers ordinarily define knowledge as justified true belief. A justified belief offers *adequate grounds* for its acceptance as knowledge. A justified belief, in other words, is grounded by supporting evidence and by reasons for accepting that evidence. Justification and truth are conceptually distinct, however, because a true belief may not be justified (it may, for example, have been a lucky guess); conversely, a justified belief may not be true (the evidence may have been deceptive). Nonetheless, justification is a matter of whether the grounds for a belief are, in William Alston's phrase, "sufficiently indicative of the truth."[2]

No absolute or ultimate resolution exists for the question of whether grounds are sufficient. That is to say, no criteria can exist that are independent of human understanding and therefore ultimately objective. Consonant with Putnam's internalism, as reviewed in chapter 7, Alston argued that justification is *"having truth-indicative grounds within one's 'perspective on the world.'"*[3] Also consonant with Putnam's internalism, this view of justification resists an "anything goes" sort of relativism. The criteria for adequate justification may vary from one context to another, but these criteria are—or ought to be—always well anchored in the vast network of human knowledge and interest. We are forever denied certainty in the formulation of our beliefs, but we can always test and debate their adequacy.

Philosophers also ordinarily associate justification with the *existence* of adequate grounds for acceptance of a belief rather than with any actions that may be taken to establish those grounds or to defend them. That is to say, justification is a matter of merely having grounds for acceptance of a belief rather than a matter of doing something in particular with those grounds. In an excruciatingly dull example of the sort that philosophers seem to like, we may be adequately justified in believing that a pencil and pad are on the desk simply because we have them in view. Neither investigation nor discussion need be undertaken to establish the grounds for belief about the location of these particular office supplies; we simply *have* the ground. Alston does insist, however, that the idea of having sufficient grounds means that those with a claim to knowledge must, themselves, have access to those grounds. He also insists that they must in fact have based their belief on those grounds. It is not enough, in other words, for the grounds to exist somewhere in the world; those with a claim to knowledge must indeed *have* them.

For philosophers, then, justification is a condition that knowledge claims must fulfill, not a task that knowledge claimants must undertake. (As reviewed in chapter 6, the practical tasks of collecting, evaluating, and assembling evidence to establish grounds for acceptance of a belief are all included in our conception of verification.) In this chapter, however, we argue that the notion of *having* sufficient grounds, along with the requirements that they be accessible and the basis for belief, all point to an activity in practical inquiry that is distinguishable from the various tasks of verification. That is, in the real world of investigative journalism, reporters must not only work to verify the grounds for their claims, they must also consciously decide to accept those grounds. As something going on in the real world, then, the condition of *having* sufficient grounds presupposes not only the process of collecting, evaluating, and assembling those grounds but also the process of *deciding to accept*, or *choosing to believe*, that they are sufficient.

Our concern here might well be termed the phenomenology of justification—that is, the *experience* of having sufficient grounds for a knowledge claim. We acknowledge that, in speaking of justification as a mental process, we are bending the term to our purposes. Moreover, we acknowledge that, in drawing a distinction between the processes of verification and justification, we are dealing with a difference that journalists would not readily recognize in their work. Reporters sometimes do in fact talk about their belief in a story or in a key part of it, but they do so in the context of the activities that we have identified as verification. That is, they often portray their belief in the truth of the facts as a necessary and inevitable outcome of their work to verify those facts.

If they are willing to recognize justification at all, they would see it as the last phase in that long process of getting the story right. Like water turning slowly to ice, the work of verification yields the experience of justification under the proper conditions. Indeed, the notion that the story ultimately crystallizes in the mind of the reporter has a certain metaphorical elegance, but whatever trope best represents the relationship between verification and justification, our focus on the latter is motivated by two concerns. First, something in fact is going on here that is worth talking about; second, it is worth talking about because it is the moment in the news-gathering process when journalists most consciously confront their responsibility for the truth of their stories. It is the moment when these practitioners, to return to Donald Schön's conception of expertise, are the most "reflective."[4]

Contexts of Justification

Because no ultimate or absolute standards of justification exist, what counts as sufficient grounds for a knowledge claim varies from one domain of inquiry to another. A justified belief, according to rhetorician John R. Lyne, is one "that has been shown to be legitimate within a context of justification."[5] And as investigative reporters attempt to go beyond the constraints of daily reporting to find out, as Steele said, "what might have been the actual case," these reporters move from one context of justification to quite another. More accurately, we might say that they move from a context that makes fewer justificatory demands to a context that makes far more.

In the context of daily reporting, as sociologists Gaye Tuchman and Mark Fishman have shown in their landmark studies of news as social knowledge, journalists are often able to avoid responsibility for justifying their claims at all—especially when they report on government officials and bureaucracies.[6] Put another way, daily reporters often don't have to *decide* what they believe to be true in the same way that investigative reporters have to decide. Daily reporters ordinarily accept at face value— not necessarily as true but at least as news—the claims they glean from the beats they cover. "Information which is bureaucratically organized, produced, and provided is hard fact," Fishman argued, "it is the stuff that makes up straight reporting."[7] In this context, then, reporters take responsibility for the accurate transcription of official discourse but not the veracity of that discourse.

If veracity does not justify publication, what does? The answer, according to Tuchman and Fishman, is simply that daily journalism has come to define the process and products of the public bureaucracies that range from the police department to the State Department as news of public importance. This, as Fishman noted, is "a position of convenience," for as Alvin Gouldner reminded us, "it always remains easier to publish accounts consonant with those offered by the managers of social institutions—accounts which thereby reinforce conventional definitions of social reality and the existent system of stratification."[8] Beyond mere convenience, however, Fishman proposed two mutually supportive explanations for daily reporters' ready acceptance of bureaucratic accounts.

One explanation reflects what Fishman characterized as the "socially sanctioned character of the bureaucrats' competence to know."[9] Reporters not only accept bureaucrats as having a special vantage point from which they can observe events but as having social and political *authority* to know what they know. Thus within their officially sanctioned domains bureaucrats appear to daily reporters as self-evidently competent and authoritative knowledge holders. The other explanation reflects the performative character of bureaucratic proceedings and outcomes. Following the philosopher J. L. Austin, Fishman defined *performatives* as utterances that do something rather than merely say something. Performatives, it follows, cannot be true or false because they are things in themselves and not statements about things. For the daily reporter, therefore, a bureaucratic account of something *becomes* something. Much as a contract *is* an offer and an acceptance, so, for example, a police report on a crime *is* a fact of the case. Together these two reasons for the ready acceptance of bureaucratic accounts often reduce daily journalism to the coverage of mere appearances—"coverage of the performing rather than the actual government," to use another of Herbert Gans's useful phrases—but together they enable reporters to operate within a context of justification that eases their burden by demanding little independent analysis or evaluation of what passes as knowledge.[10]

In sum, knowledge claims made in daily journalism often need not be *epistemically justified* by reporters because they are *bureaucratically justified* by the context in which they arise. Even in the absence of sufficient grounds to accept those claims as *true*, sufficient grounds may still exist to accept them as *news*. Claims made in investigative journalism, however, are rarely so epistemically fortunate. In the absence of sufficient grounds to accept them as true, no grounds exist to accept them as news. This is because claims made in investigative journalism are critical of those "managers of social institutions" mentioned by Gouldner—for example, criminal justice officials. Moreover, the claims often originate with sources who have little or no standing in any social institution—for example, victims who are not so innocent. "The most difficult part of this problem," reporter and editor John Ullmann said about the difficulty of deciding what to believe under these circumstances, "is when the central people that you are writing about are disreputable to begin with." Although daily reporters can merely accept many claims as news, whatever their truth may be, investigative reporters must decide what they believe to be the truth.

Investigative reporters are able to articulate at least something of their decision making about the truth in several settings: when a *pivotal fact* is in dispute and when a set of pivotal facts reveals a larger, undeniably *moral fact*. In this chapter, then, we revisit two critical moments in journalists' struggle to find out what really happened. In chapter 6 our focus was on what reporters do to get the facts. In this chapter our focus is on how reporters come to believe those facts. Journalists may not draw this distinction, but they are able to describe situations, some quite dramatic, in which they were compelled to decide what they believed. We take these descriptions as opportunities to examine a psychological and organizational process that is deeply buried in the activities of information gathering and story writing but critical to the *responsible* production of social knowledge.

Justification of Pivotal Facts

Although reporters do not ordinarily use the vocabulary of justification to discuss their work, they might be willing to say that they do indeed have sufficient grounds for acceptance of any claims that they make in their stories. But they might also argue that, in saying this, they are really saying nothing more about their work than what they have said all along—simply that they work hard to get the story. The argument that there really isn't anything going on in the news-gathering process beyond the activities that we have identified as verification seems reasonable so long as those activities proceed, laboriously perhaps, but without significant uncertainties or contradictions. When verification proceeds in this way—when, for example, several independent sources all satisfactorily corroborate the pivotal facts—any practically useful distinction between verification and justification does seem to dissolve. The facts seem simply to speak for themselves in a believable way. In such situations the sense of direct access to the truth seems overwhelming, and the question of whether the grounds for belief are "sufficiently indicative of the truth" seems, well, just too damn philosophical.

Journalists like to claim that in the end the facts can and do speak for themselves. Nonetheless, they also recognize that they encounter many situations in which the facts do not speak very plainly—that is, when the task of verification encounters uncertainties and contradictions. And when the facts that refuse to speak with the desired clarity are essential to the story, journalists cannot avoid a decision about the sufficiency of grounds. "It's only an issue—a real issue—when there are competing claims for the truth of what happened," said Ullmann about the situations in which reporters are called upon by editors, lawyers, and their own skepticism to explicitly justify their claims. "If it's a linchpin of the story," he concluded, "you have to make a decision." He added, however, that he couldn't imagine why anyone would publish a story with unresolved claims about a linchpin element.

When asked about such situations, reporters no longer speak as if they have direct access to the plain truth. "When you reach a conclusion in an investigation where you have conflicting fact,' said Don Shelby of WCCO-TV in Minneapolis, "what you have arrived at—what you believe to be the truth—is an opinion." And faced with the thought of a conflicting fact, this reporter paused to ponder his commitment to philosophical realism. "The truth is a general thing out there," he said, sounding at first like a true-believing realist. Then he added: "I can have a view of the truth, but I'm one person. I can say, 'My investigation, my finite abilities, my limited number of questions asked, my examination of the facts indicate to me that this is the truth.' What I have just rendered [in the story] is an opinion."

Moreover, when asked about situations in which they encounter conflicting facts, reporters speak of their thought processes and the mental images that mediate their attempts to form "an opinion" about the truth. In chapter 6 and throughout this book we have encountered several important examples of such conceptions—for example, the metaphor of a puzzle in which the pieces finally click into place. One conception commonly invoked in situations in which reporters struggle with questions of sufficiency of evidence is that of the weight of evidence—a metaphor that provides a particularly interesting case study in the phenomenology of journalism because it also has currency in the philosophy of science, in the law, and in common sense.[11]

We have already seen a reporter "weighing the evidence" when, in chapter 6, Marimow evaluated the testimony of various witnesses to a particular police dog attack. When asked to generalize about the weight assigned to witnesses' testimony and other sorts of evidence, Marimow quite reasonably assigned the greatest weight to the trained observer with no axe to grind and the least weight to the drunken victim and to his friends. However, when Shelby, another reporter who spoke just as assuredly about "weighing the evidence," was asked to generalize about weight, he assigned weights quite differently, though no less reasonably:

> The heaviest evidence would be the act itself captured on videotape. The act itself. Undeniably these people met with these other people and discussed bribes, and money changed hands and went into the pocket. That's a big heavy piece of evidence. There's very little more you have to do to substantiate that the thing happened. You can put facts with it, like what time did it happen, what date did it happen, names of the participants, but the act itself happened. . . . Secondary to that kind of video document would be a paper document that outlined the suspected act which was attested to by the parties involved.

Shelby, like Marimow, began his hierarchical arrangement of evidentiary weight with a general statement about the sort of evidence with the greatest weight. However, his arrangement, like Marimow's, soon became merely an illustration of the general idea of weight rather than a rigorous articulation of principles for assessing the quality of evidence. Shelby's illustration of weight drew upon that staple of local television investigative reporting: the consumer rip-off story. Specifically, it drew on a story about a basement waterproofing scam in which a hidden camera recorded high-pressure sales tactics. In addition to the video, the story used an important "paper document" in the form of a training manual outlining the sales tactics.

Below these two crucial items of evidence Shelby placed post hoc accounts of those events captured on video. Among such accounts he cited statements by "participatory witnesses" (especially confessions) as the heavier sort of evidence and statements by "nonparticipatory witnesses" as the lighter. In the waterproofing investigation the statement of a former salesman exemplified the former sort of evidence, whereas the latter was exemplified by the statement of an expert attesting to the shoddiness of the waterproofer's work. Below those accounts Shelby placed material that could best be described as "preevidentiary," material that is not evidence but may lead to evidence. This included hunches, or "presumptions," as the reporter called them. Of the least weight, according to this reporter's hierarchy, was "the anonymous phone call—as light as you can get."

Clearly, Marimow's and Shelby's hierarchies cannot both reflect some singular fundamental dimension of evidentiary quality. Each, however, reflects the demands of the communication medium in which its creator worked. The television reporter's arrangement of the evidence was an attempt to generalize from a story well suited to the demands of televisual discourse in which videotaped images of wrongdoing are an expected feature. The print reporter's arrangement, on the other hand, was an attempt to generalize from a story in which visual images were far less likely to be obtainable, and, in any case, poignant quotes from eyewitnesses are an expected feature of the discourse.

Each hierarchy also reflects the demands of a particular investigation that yielded a particular array of evidence. Moreover, each reflects the demands of a particular pivotal fact in that investigation. Marimow focused on the provocations that culminated in an unjustified dog attack. Shelby focused on high-pressure sales tactics that culminated in a fraudulent waterproofing contract. In Shelby's illustration, videotape provided excellent evidence that the tactics had actually been used. The sales manual was lower on the hierarchy because it only suggested that the tactics might have been used. (This evidence probably would have been heavier had Shelby arranged his hierarchy with regard to other crucial facts in the story, such as whether there was a well-established pattern of such tactics.) He ranked the testimony of the "participatory witness," the former salesman, lower than the manual because, without the manual or the tape, the salesman's claim that the company used the tactics would come down to his word against others.' (This evidence also might have been heavier had the issue been the establishment of a pattern.)

Though each hierarchy was specific to a particular story and a particular pivotal fact—not to mention, enumerated on the spot in answer to an interviewer's question—each was quite clear in mind of the reporter. Indeed, both reporters precisely, if differently, specified the psychophysics of evidentiary weight. Marimow gave the drunken victim and each of his friends 1 point on a scale that ranged from 1 to 100. He gave the witnesses with no axe to grind "somewhere up in the nineties, if they'd seen the whole thing." And he would have given himself, had he seen the attack, "even higher in the nineties" because of his training and experience. Shelby assigned no specific values, yet he was no less precise. "One nonparticipatory witness, one piece of material evidence, and one document," he concluded, "weigh as much as the videotape act."

Whatever their idiosyncrasies, these hierarchies are both quite rational. Each could be defended with reference to a number of considerations such as "weigh the possible motives of the witnesses." These hierarchies, however, are not a set of formal rules or even general principles. Rather, the idea of weight is a metaphor for a vast, mostly unarticulated, "repertoire of examples, images, understandings, and actions," to return to Schön's description of how professionals think in action. The idea of weight is, in short, a metaphor for all the journalistic common sense about how to evaluate and use the testimony of drunks, scam artists, cops, innocent bystanders, and anyone else who turns up in a story.

The metaphor of evidentiary weight focuses all that common sense on the question of what is reasonable to believe. This becomes clear when at last the reporter proceeds to weigh all the evidence and come to a decision. "It's simply the scales," said Shelby:

> You take inculpatory evidence and stack it up, and you take the exculpatory evidence and stack it up. You have to be very truthful to yourself. You have to be as vigorous in seeking the exculpatory information as you are in seeking the stuff that's damning. And once gathered, you watch the way it falls. And you say the preponderance of evidence is that this thing occurs in a damning way, but sometimes there's perfect balance, and your investigation continues. You keep going and going and going.

"Going and going and going," of course, is how investigative reporters use "the luxury of time" that their news organizations grant them. Sooner or later, however, the investigation must yield decisive evidence or else, as

Ullmann suggested, it must be abandoned. "There has to be something to tip the balance," Ullmann concluded, "and what would tip the balance could be a virtually infinite number of things."

Perhaps, with the metaphor of weights and scales, reporters are a little too glib about their decision making. As we saw in chapter 6, the coherence—that is, the "fit"—of evidence is extremely important to the verification process and is likely to figure into decisions about sufficiency of grounds as well. But if the metaphor of weight helps journalists not only to justify their truth claims but to explicitly recognize the need to do so, the metaphor should command our respect and our constructive criticism. Given the highly context-specific nature of the hierarchies examined here, however, any attempt to study the psychophysics of evidentiary weight is probably less valuable than simply designating "the weighing of evidence" as a moment in the news-gathering process when responsible journalists will pause to reflect on their practice. The moment of decision about the sufficiency of grounds is yet another point in the process that demands, in Michael Schudson's phrase, "mature subjectivity aged by encounters with, and regard for, the facts of the world."[12] Such subjectivity is the product not merely of reporting experience but reflective consideration of that experience.

This moment of individual reflection may be a moment of organizational reflection as well. Shelby provided a dramatic example of newsroom introspection from his investigation into the failure of law enforcement agencies to aggressively pursue allegations of child sexual abuse. The most dramatic material to emerge from the investigation concerned well-documented cases against respected citizens, including a doctor, a scout leader, and a judge. The allegations against the judge, unlike those against the others, had never before been made public. And late in the investigation Shelby got word that the judge would kill himself should the allegations become public. "You have to be more certain of this than that the sun will rise tomorrow," Shelby recalled telling himself when he realized that a life could be at stake. "You have to be morally certain that what you're saying is true."

Thus a decision based merely on the preponderance of evidence would not do. In the attempt to achieve a sense of moral certainty Shelby decided to talk once again with the teenage boy who would be the judge's primary accuser in the story:

> Tuesday afternoon I made a phone call to one of the boys who was going to be on the air Thursday, and I said, "I'm coming out to get you."

He said, "What for?"

And I said, "I'll tell you later."

I had lie-detectored these guys. I had them ID [the judge] out of six very difficult photographs of gray-haired, heavy-weight, middle-aged men. I had them describe artifacts in the house (bronze ducks, the titles of books on the bedstead), draw maps of the house, and then compare it with people who had been in the house. . . . Now, I'm getting ready in two days to accuse the judge of some pretty bad things—or rather, these kids are going to accuse him.

I brought the kid in. It was eight at night. I drove him to the station, and then I said, "Take me to [the judge's] house."

He said, "Why?"

I said, "I just want you to drive me to [the judge's] house. Do you know where it is?" I said, "You described it, that it's on [a particular street], that it's yellow with a three-car garage. You've given me all that stuff. I want you to take me there."

He said, "Okay," and went right to the house. . . .

I said, "Thanks," and drove him home.

In addition to this final test—a test not so much of the boy's story as of the reporter's moral certainty about the story—Shelby tried to find out if the judge's suicide threats had any substance. "I started an ancillary investigation to find out if it was true that he was going to kill himself," Shelby said. "I called his attorneys. I called his friends on the bench, and I called his social friends. The reading from those people closest to him in a personal way was that he wouldn't." In these conversations Shelby volunteered little information about the focus of the investigation, but he found that he didn't have to. "They all seemed to know what it was," Shelby recalled. "They all knew he did it and covered for him."

Finally, as the reporter recalled, he took the results of this last-hour work to his superiors:

See, part of the story was that everybody knew, and nobody would say anything. Fellows on the bench knew that [the judge] did this and wouldn't say anything. Cops knew and wouldn't say anything. And all along we're talking about this crime as a crime of people who wouldn't say anything.

I looked at my boss and I said, "You've got a decision. You're one of them or you're one of us. You're the guy saying, 'God damn it! Why don't these people talk about stuff like this?' You've got to stand behind your word or change your opinion."

My boss said, "Let's go with it."

Clearly, Shelby's late-night ride to the judge's residence was not merely one more interview with a problematic source. Rather, it was a particularly dramatic example of what Schön would recognize as an on-the-spot experiment intended to yield a final affirmation of the story's linchpin. The reporter needed not merely to believe the teenager but to believe with *moral certainty*—a term that expressed well the fundamental fusion of epistemological and ethical concerns that the reporter faced in this situation. Although this example began with a question of the individual journalist's responsibility for the truth of a pivotal fact, it ultimately concerns another issue of journalistic responsibility—responsibility for the consequences of publishing the fact, even if it is true.

This is a classic dilemma in journalism ethics, and journalists typically approach that dilemma, as Shelby and his colleagues did here, by collectively weighing their judgments about the public importance (i.e., newsworthiness) of the story against their perceptions of potential harm to individuals. "It's a process," as Lucy Morgan said of newsroom decisions about sensitive stories, "of talking each other into, and out of, these things." This deliberative balancing of the ethical scale, however, must always follow a balancing of the epistemic scale. That is to say, any ethical judgment is predicated on a firm belief, if not absolute moral certainty, in the truth of key facts. Pam Zekman expressed this sense of personal conviction, as tested by colleagues, this way:

> I hope we have our facts lined up well enough so that, by the time we're done, I'm convinced personally that I have the evidence and my bosses are convinced and our lawyers are convinced to go on the air and to accuse somebody, in the simplest cases, of an action that violates the law or, in the more difficult cases, of something that violates some ethical guideline or threshold of decency or whatever. You have to be constantly aware of the fact that you are going to be affecting their livelihood, family, everything.

Justification of Moral Facts

Shelby's account of his late-night quest for moral certainty revealed a reporter who knew well that, with regard to a particular pivotal fact, he had to *decide*. Similarly, with regard to the larger moral facts (such as a pattern of institutional failure to protect the innocent) reporters know that they may confront decisions about what they believe to be true. Pam Zekman offered an elementary example in which she had to defend use of the term *exploit* in a story. Her investigation concerned pharmacies that defrauded Medicaid by selling prescription drugs to addicts:

Did those people sit down and say: "Let's exploit addicts. We can make a lot of money off of exploiting addicts, and here's how we'll do it?" I don't know. I wasn't at that meeting, but the end result of what they did was to exploit addicts. Can I go on the air and say they exploited addicts? I can say that it is fact that they submitted the bill [to Medicaid] for ten drugs but [the patient] only got two of them. I feel very confident about those facts . . . [but] the interpretation of those facts is probably subject to debate.

And after a "tug-of-war" with her colleagues, the reporter decided that the term was "subjective" but that she would use it on the air. "It's more than an interpretation," she finally concluded. "We think it's an accurate portrayal of what was happening."

With the conclusion that addicts had been exploited this journalist had decided to report in unambiguously moral terms a moral fact that she had come to accept as the truth. She would have been unlikely to characterize her conclusions as "a moral fact," even if she had known the phrase, because it would have blurred the simplistic objective-subjective distinction that has long been central to the journalistic vocabulary. Without the concept of moral fact she bridged the distinction with the argument that her conclusion was "accurate," if "subjective." Nonetheless, this was a situation in which the reporter was called upon to justify a moral fact to her colleagues. And although Zekman might have been compelled by her boss to use some other word, her tug-of-war was not merely a debate about semantics. It was a decision concerning what could legitimately be concluded about *the reality* of the situation that her investigation had uncovered.

In the presence of lingering uncertainty or disagreement about the justification of moral facts reporters may search for summary language that seems less overtly moralistic—that is, in Bill Dedman's phrase, to "push the facts and restrain the tone." (Morgan, for example, changed *lied* to *failed to tell the truth* in the story about the county sheriff because the latter phrase would be, as she said, "less of a red flag.") But if reporters cannot find acceptable summary language, they will have to work all the harder to make those facts appear to speak for themselves, using the rhetorical and narrative strategies that we saw in earlier chapters. Reporters cannot avoid conveying moral meanings in their discourse.

One situation in which investigative journalists must make a conscious decision about the sufficiency of grounds concerns the conclusion that wrongdoing is "widespread" or constitutes a "pattern." Sometimes, as Morgan said of her investigation of wrongdoing in a county sheriff's office, the pattern may "shout at you." Other times, however, the facts of the situation must be coaxed to speak of a pattern. Another of Zekman's debates with her coworkers provides an example in which the pattern shouted at the reporter but apparently not at the station's attorneys. The story concerned a number of mishandled autopsy cases in the medical examiner's office:

> How many cases is a pattern? Can you give me the number? Six? Twelve? Two dozen? There's no definition for that. It turned out not to be a legal argument. The lawyers were arguing from a subjective judgment about what makes a pattern. We had a couple of dozen examples that we could absolutely prove. In my mind it was a pattern because it involved more than one pathologist and a cross-section of types of cases. Is that a pattern to you? I don't know. I felt with that many cases we had enough to go with the story.
>
> I think it's very subjective—very subjective. . . . But if I'm going to say that there's a pattern, I want enough cases on the air that will convince you, the viewer, "Yes, she's got a pattern! Oh, she's got a cast of thousands! My God, she could keep going forever with examples!"

Here again Zekman saw the judgment to be made as "subjective," but in this instance she was concerned not only about her belief in the reality of the pattern but her audience's belief as well. Clearly, she understood that she was being held responsible for the public justification of her claim.

Situations in which reporters must decide whether the wrongdoing constitutes a pattern provide especially important examples of decisions about the sufficiency of grounds. The moral logic, as it might be called, of many investigative journalism projects is not merely that some bad things have happened but that bad things can and do happen because the system has failed. This logic does not necessarily depend on showing that many bad things have happened but only that enough bad things have happened to raise concerns about the system's failure. (For example, as Stephen Kurjian pointed out, it didn't take many instances of police officials who were giving their relatives some of the city's towing business to demonstrate a conflict of interest in the Boston police department.) However, this moral logic does depend upon a convincing demonstration of the system's culpability for the failure. Therefore reporters typically want to show that the systemic failure has produced "widespread" problems or "a pattern" of harm that ought not to have occurred and that must be addressed by appropriate authorities. In this way the fact that the wrongdoing and its consequences are widespread or patterned is important not only in establishing the reality of the problem but in allocating responsibility for it.

Even when a statement about a pattern is not made explicitly in the story, reporters still convey—and justify—such a claim by presenting enough cases to convincingly demonstrate a pattern. Marimow, for instance, maintained that using the word *pattern* in his story about police dog attacks was justified but not really necessary:

> It was a story that was written by me and edited by my editors. I tend to be very, very conservative when I write something. If I had it to do my way, this story would have said something like this: "In the course of a three-month investigation the *Inquirer* found cases in which K-9 dogs have attacked and mauled innocent civilians, cases in which the attacks have left deep puncture wounds and years of psychological trauma, cases in which civil suits have been filed and adjudicated, costing the city thousands of dollars."
>
> My preference as a reporter—and it would be as an editor too—is when you summarize your findings, to say the *Inquirer* has found cases in which bing! bing! bing! That way you only say exactly what you know, and you don't interpret it too much. The editors felt that what I had was strong enough so that I could make it much broader, and in fact I think it was strong enough.

Here, then, is a reporter whose insistence on the sanctity of the fact-value separation makes him somewhat uncomfortable with explicit references even to "pattern." His response to the rather-too-clear *moral* fact of the situation is to express a lingering wariness about overinterpretation and a desire to stick as closely as possible to what he takes to be the hard facts of the cases. Nonetheless, had he merely summarized his findings as "cases in which bing! bing! bing!" (that is, as the bulleted points quoted from his story in chapter 6), the reality of the pattern would not have been any less clear. For Marimow, just as for Zekman, the "pattern" of wrong-doing was real enough, whether the word was used in the story or not; at the same time its reality was understood to be a "judgment" or an "interpretation" that had to be defended to coworkers and, in the finished story, to the audience.

In making such judgments and interpretations journalists take into account not only the number of cases (as was the issue in Zekman's story about the medical examiner) but also the types of cases. Like Zekman, Steele maintained that figuring the number of cases needed for a story was "a subjective process." He also said that choosing the particular cases was merely a matter of "common sense." In the investigation of special tax exemptions granted by Congress to well-connected citizens, common sense always seemed to guide Steele to the exemptions that were, to use his term, "individualistic"—those most carefully tailored to the demands of one or a few individual beneficiaries and therefore the most outrageously unfair. The choice of cases, Steele concluded, "is one of the great challenges that you deal with in these series—how you write it to show the magnitude of the issue without writing some gigantic story that puts people to sleep."

More insight into how common sense guides the selection of cases comes from the *Chicago Tribune*'s investigation into conflicts of interest among members of the city council. In this story, much as in Barlett and Steele's tax exemption story, the reporters wanted to make the point that the wrongdoing did not reflect merely the behavior of a few bad apples. Rather, it was a failure of the system—in this case a failure of the council to enact ethical guidelines, or even expense-reporting guidelines, for its members. According to reporter Bill Gaines, the newspaper's interest in the story was not motivated by the number of conflicts or the number of aldermen involved. "We decided there was a problem because there was no control in the law," he said. "We were saying that what was wrong was that they were *able* to do this."

Nonetheless, the reporters needed to show that the conflicts were, in Gaines's phrase, "widespread" enough to justify concern about that lack of control. For Gaines the notion of "widespread" did seem to have something to do with scale—that is, with the number of offending aldermen. He recognized, however, that "it's a judgment somebody has to make" and that reasonable judgments could vary—some might say that corruption is widespread if a majority of the fifty aldermen were offenders, others might say so if only 10 percent were. But more important than the number of offenders was the distribution of offenders across categories relevant to Chicago politics. "I think the main thing about using the term *widespread* is that it's not just the aldermen from the Southwest Side that are doing this, or the newly elected aldermen who are doing this, or the aldermen from one party or one race or something like that," he said. "It's just aldermen."

For Gaines and his colleagues this empirical, if imprecise, test of "widespread" was necessary to justify this powerful statement of moral fact in the lead of their first article:

> The Chicago City Council, the largest and most expensive in the country, is a corrupt and inefficient body that habitually puts aldermen's personal concerns before the public good.
>
> It has squandered its chartered power to set the city's course and surrendered itself to political housekeeping and profligate spending.[13]

"Support your lead," Gaines said, citing conventional wisdom of the journalistic craft. And to do so in this article the reporters chose a number of examples that showed the conflicts of interest were indeed widespread. "We saw this picture, and we wanted to illustrate it in the story so that our illustrations were widespread," Gaines recalled. "We made sure that we didn't have all of the illustrations on one side of town or all them from one political faction." They presented these illustrations in the familiar form of bulleted points. For example:

- A North Side alderman hands out business cards for a friend's jukebox and pinball machine company to tavern owners awaiting approval of liquor license applications, urging them to employ the company's services.
- A West Side alderman, who persuaded a drugstore chain to stock a soft drink he markets, boasts that the chain also has secured his vote on the city council.[14]

And so on. "In the first day's story we named as many aldermen as we possibly could and said, 'This is what's going on,'" Gaines said of the series. "Then we indicated that we were going to write about different, particular individuals as representative of that." Subsequent articles in the series went on to provide many detailed illustrations of the aldermen's activities.

According to Gaines, the *Tribune* team never really doubted that what was going on in the council was widespread or that their lead was in fact justified. But whereas these reporters may have encountered moral facts that seemed to speak for themselves as much as such facts ever do, a *Star Tribune* team was faced with facts that required more intensive interrogation. The team, Lou Kilzer and Chris Ison, and their editor, John Ullmann, were conducting an investigation of the St. Paul, Minnesota, fire department. Their story turned on a large number of suspicious fires, many experienced by family and friends of the fire chief, that had been poorly investigated by the fire department. The story also focused on family and friends who were in occupations that could benefit from fires, such as public claims adjusters and building contractors.[15]

The *Star Tribune*'s investigation could not substantiate any instances in which the fire chief had directly benefited from arson, but it revealed many instances in which the chief had done little to hinder his close associates from benefiting financially. Ullmann compared the situation confronted by his team to that of prosecutors in arson cases. "Arson cases are always circumstantial—motive, means, opportunity—and yet they are made," he said. "People on a jury can decide without a reasonable doubt that arson has occurred." Unlike Shelby, who sought "moral certainty" in his investigation of the judge, Ullmann and his team sought only to make a case "beyond a reasonable doubt" in the investigation of the fire chief.

To make the case that the fire chief had tolerated serious improprieties the reporters set out to document a pattern of suspicious, but improperly investigated, fires in St. Paul. Unlike Gaines and his colleagues, who could use commonsense definitions of conflict of interest to assess the behavior of the city council, Ullmann and his colleagues knew that they could not rely on their readers' or their own common sense in the matter of arson. The team turned to an outside arson investigator whose detachment and expertise, according to Ullmann, were beyond question:

> We did a lot of things to try to establish that (a) he had no connections in the state, and (b) he was a reasonable witness. And then we told the readers that we had hired him and that these were his conclusions about the evidence. That's one of the ways that I operate—especially when I'm outside of the commonsense arena. I think reasonable people would agree on it—and if they don't, so what? We told them what we thought, and we told them why we came to that conclusion. If they don't agree, they don't have to.

Here once again a journalist has invoked the notion that ultimately the reader must decide. However, he also made it quite clear that, whatever the reader might decide, he and his colleagues needed to be certain about the claim that many suspicious fires had in fact been improperly investigated. The judgment of the expert, it turned out, was quite clear: many investigations had been slipshod, and the fire chief should indeed be held culpable. After working through a number of cases with the expert, the journalists came to accept his opinion. As Ullmann described the process, the reporters gradually became willing to say to themselves, "He thinks this, and we believe him because . . ." Moreover, they became willing to write what they believed. Ullmann concluded: "You don't have to put the phrase, 'We believe him because' into the story, but you do have to put what follows [that phrase] into the story. And during the course of the investigation *you* have to come to believe it."

The *Star Tribune*'s report of the investigation, which won the Pulitzer Prize for Kilzer and Ison, led with yet another powerful statement of moral fact:

> A multimillion-dollar industry profiting from arson and suspicious fires is flourishing in St. Paul with the assistance of several key firefighters. And much of the money has flowed to two men linked to Fire Chief Steve Conroy.

A yearlong *Star Tribune* investigation shows that Conroy has contributed to a culture in which arson has thrived. He has tolerated shoddy fire investigations and allowed firemen to moonlight for a firm that has represented alleged arsonists in fire insurance claims.[16]

A few paragraphs into the story the the reporters brought opinion of the expert to bear in support of these facts:

"I've never seen such a pattern of impropriety as in the St. Paul Fire Department," says Elden Boh, a fire investigation expert hired by the Star Tribune.

Much of the second article in the two-part series was devoted to Boh's analysis of past arson investigations and to allocating blame for the inadequacy of those investigations. Here, then, was an expert, called upon by journalists to objectify a moral claim, who performed his role with reassuring confidence:

Arson expert Elden Boh of Denver, Colo., said the pattern of poor investigations is too widespread and covers too many years to be attributed to only the individual failures of investigators. Much of the responsibility, he concludes, rests with the chief, who has tolerated substandard investigations and clear conflicts of interest for nearly two decades.[17]

In the familiar form of bulleted points the article went on to detail common errors and oversights that Boh attributed to the arson investigators. For example:

- They didn't interview owners or occupants of buildings that burned.
- They didn't check for a history of fires attributable to one person or one address, a fundamental step that can raise important suspicions.

And so on. Based on Boh's analysis, the article went on to review in detail a number of suspicious fires as examples of what could, and did, go wrong in arson investigations. The expert's role in the justification of key moral facts is clear. Boh gave the *Star Tribune* team what another reporter, Jack Reed, speaking of his own use of experts in a story about a public official, characterized as "knowledge of what a public official *should be.*" That is to say, he gave them knowledge of essential moral facts.

Although Ullmann was reluctant to discuss the "morality" of this story, he was willing to say that the reporters had shown that something was in fact "wrong" in the St. Paul Fire Department. Ullmann characterized the detailed review of arson investigations as "observations," but he also characterized the application of Boh's standards to those investigations as a "judgment." This sort of acknowledgment, that observations have been made within an evaluative framework, is about as far as journalists are likely to go toward explicitly acknowledging that, as Hilary Putnam said, "every fact is value loaded and every one of our values loads some fact."[18]

The Model of Responsibility

For what, finally, is journalism responsible? It is tempting to casually answer, "The truth." The truth is not always at issue in journalism, especially in daily reporting. When the truth is at issue, however, investigative journalism points the way toward a more precise and practical answer to the question than simply "the truth." We can reasonably ask all genres of journalism to be responsible for truth claims, whether pivotal and moral, that the reporters have come to believe as a result of their best effort to establish the grounds for those claims and after a judicious decision that those grounds are sufficient. Journalism is not, then, responsible for simply knowing the truth, but we can ask individual journalists and their news organizations to be *responsible for placing themselves in the best possible positions to know and for consciously deciding that they do know.*

To whom is journalism responsible? The temptation here is to casually answer, "The public." Investigative journalism, however, suggests a personalized, practitioner-centered conception of journalistic responsibility. If, as a society, we agree that we must stop demanding a specious objectivity on the part of journalism and acknowledge that we must accept a "mature subjectivity" on the part of individual journalists, we should ask all journalists and their organizations to decide for themselves—and in all honesty with themselves—what they believe to be true. We must ask them, first and foremost, to be *responsible to themselves.*

But what, then, does journalism owe the public? The idea of justification (as embodied in the work of the best investigative reporters) suggests that all journalists owe the public an articulate presentation not only of their claims but of the grounds for accepting them. Ullmann seemed to be saying exactly this when he insisted that reporters must always include in their story whatever follows the phrase "we believe him because." This would constitute yet another meaning of public accountability in journalism—an account of the grounds for accepting claims. Perhaps, however, that is the casual answer that should not be accepted uncritically.

Why don't journalists owe the public what we demand of them: not only the grounds for belief but belief itself—or at least their best effort to persuade us of the truth? It is easy to imagine that journalists would denounce any such demand as outrageous, but these investigative reporters turn out to be more ambiguous on the point than might be imagined. In response to questions about the morality of their enterprise, as we have seen, they frequently invoke the idea that their audience, not they, must decide such questions. Indeed, they sometimes even invoke that idea not only with regard to moral facts but with regard to those supposedly incontrovertible pivotal facts. Zekman, for example, argued the virtue of television in this regard:

> One of the things I like about television more than newspapers is that you can let people reach their own conclusions. I'm not asking them to accept my judgments about, say, the credibility of a witness as much as a newspaper reporter does. I put them on, and the viewer can make up their own minds as to whether, for example, the rape victim was really raped.

Here again a reporter seems to suggest that the audience is left to decide what to believe; but of course, this is the same reporter who said, "I want enough cases on the air that will convince you, the viewer, 'Yes, she's got a pattern! Oh, she's got a cast of thousands! My God, she could keep going forever with examples!'"

In the same vein Zekman, like all the others, insisted that, if possible, statements made by those implicated in the wrongdoing be included in story. And in this setting too reporters invoke the idea that the audience must be allowed to decide the veracity of those who stand accused. But reporters also realize that such statements, as mandated by the conventions of journalistic objectivity, have become a ritualized display of journalistic fairmindedness. Such statements are, then, a "credibility tactic" intended to say more about the veracity of the reporter than the accused.[19] "I want people focused in on what we're reporting and not focused in on criticizing the quality of the investigation," said Zekman. "One of the things you want to avoid is people saying, 'Yeah, she presented her story, and she never gave the guy a chance to tell his side of the story.' So we put the guy on TV, and we let you decide if you believe our facts or if you believe him." But, of course, the reporter expects the audience to believe her and to see the statement of the accused for exactly what it is, whether an evasion, excuse, rationalization, or an outright lie. "Sometimes, I've found that reporting the other person's side of it—doing those final interviews with people—enhances the story because the arguments that they have to defend are not believable, sometimes laughable, sometimes incredible," Zekman said. "It only enhances the facts that we have."

In light of such pragmatic concerns about the management of credibility any insistence that the audience is left to decide important issues of fact seems disingenuous or, more charitably, unreflective. What exactly the public is supposed to decide is yet another aspect of journalism in which the institutional rhetoric is at odds with actual practice. Journalists may insist that the facts must speak for themselves to a public that must decide for itself about those facts, but as we have seen, journalists are skilled at making the facts speak eloquently concerning the public decisions that must be made. To gauge the gap between how practitioners *talk* about their responsibility in regard to public decision making and how they actually *participate* in that decision making, we return once more to several masterworks of investigative journalism and to the commentary of their authors.

Marimow was among the most adamant of the reporters that we interviewed about the notion that the public must decide and that, to serve this end, the journalist must faithfully seek and present "all possible points of view." Returning again to the K-9 cases, he offered an example of how "getting the other side of the story makes an interesting story even more interesting." When piecing together the stories of the various dog attacks, Marimow had made what he considered to be "assiduous efforts" to get the police officers' versions of events. These efforts included certified letters sent to officer's homes that went unanswered and requests through the police department for interviews, which were denied. Because some of the attack victims had sued the city, however, transcripts of legal proceedings were available. From these the reporter pieced together accounts of several attacks.

One such attack was that by officer Daniel Bechtell and his dog, Ace Number 8, on Mark Sadler outside a bar late one Philadelphia night. "By really endeavoring to get the whole truth—the whole perimeter of the truth—from victim Mark Sadler's view of the truth to officer Daniel Bechtell's view of the truth," Marimow said, "I was able to present conflicting accounts and let the public decide." In his story's reconstruction of the attack the reporter did indeed include both Bechtell's and Sadler's accounts as obtained from transcripts. More important, however, the story interspersed those accounts with the accounts of several witnesses who offered the most detailed and frightening versions of the attack. From Officer Bechtell's account, for example, the story quoted the officer as telling Sadler that he was "under arrest for disorderly conduct." From a witness's account, however, the story quoted the officer as saying to Sadler, just before releasing the dog, "Come here, you motherf—."[20]

The reporter's reconstruction of the confrontation concluded with a comment from the lawyer who chaired the panel appointed to arbitrate Sadler's civil suit against the city after his acquittal on a disorderly conduct change:

> Zell, who presided over the trial-type procedure, said in an interview that "my feeling was that Bechtell was out of control. There's absolutely no question about it: That boy was not doing anything wrong. He was found not guilty by a court, and the civilian witnesses—God!—they took time out from their jobs to come down here and testify for him. I believe them."[21]

In his story the reporter skillfully indicated that he had put substantial journalistic legwork into the verification of the account and that he had been dispassionately open to disconfirmation—that is, to "the other side." However, he had also shown that the officer's side was not, in either sense of the term, the *right* side. Thus the officer's version of events had little value in the verification or justification of the reporter's claims about the facts of the attack. Rather, its value in the story was to affirm the authority of the reporter and in turn the credibility of his claim that wrongdoing had occurred. What, then, ought the public decide about the facts of this case or about the pattern of which this case is a part? Thanks to the reporter's hard work, the answer is clear.

Steele was another reporter who was adamant in his insistence that the public must decide. Returning again to "The Great Tax Giveaway," he argued that the profiles of those who received the special tax exemptions were entirely accurate descriptions on a fact-by-fact basis. "Look to see what the paragraphs are and what the statements are," he said. "You've got documentation across the board." He maintained that the point of the profiles was simply to document that certain individuals and companies received benefits from the tax code not available to all citizens. "Take the Fort Worth widow," Steele said, referring to the lead profile in the series. "They [the widow's agents] had a bill in Congress that exempts the estate of her late husband from paying the estate taxes that other estates in similar positions would have to pay." Steele acknowledged that readers might form a negative impression of the widow, but he maintained that he and his partner had not set out to convey any particular impression of her. "All we wrote about was that they were seeking this special provision," he said. "The fact that they were seeking that special provision might create the impression in the minds of readers that she is greedy. I think somebody could naturally come to that conclusion about her, but we're not sitting down saying, 'We're going to make this gal look greedy by putting this in.'"

Steele argued that the facts themselves, not his paragraphs and statements about them, were the source of any impression that readers might form about the widow and the others who received the special tax exemptions. "What creates the impression is what they've done, not what we've done, not what we've written, unless we have misconstrued the facts on something," he said. "They are the ones who sought this unusual treatment in contrast to other people in the same situation." According to Steele, the reporters could not be held responsible for impressions. "We basically ignore the concept of impression, feeling, or image because once you get into that, it's open season," he said. "Every person's impression can be different because we are all such individuals."

If this reporter suddenly sounds like a contemporary literary critic who holds that all meaning resides in the reader and none in the text, his work provides an excellent opportunity to consider the construction of moral meaning within a journalistic text. A rhetorical strategy of "The Great Tax Giveaway," as detailed in chapter 4, was to juxtapose the language of the federal tax code with the profiles of the individuals and companies that benefited from the special exemptions. And in the case of the Fort Worth widow, the code said:

> For purposes of section 2656(b)(8) of the Internal Revenue Code of 1986, an individual who receives an interest in a charitable remainder unitrust shall be deemed to be the only noncharitable beneficiary of such trust if the interest in the trust passed to the individual under the will of a decedent who resided in Tarrant County, Texas, and died on October 28, 1983 at the age of 75, with a gross estate not exceeding $12.5 million, and the individual is the decedent's surviving spouse.[22]

The "decedent's surviving spouse" turned out to be Geraldine Ballard, wife of the late Joseph J. Ballard Jr., an heir to a fortune made in part from the 7-Eleven convenience store chain. When asked about the exemption, Ballard was quoted as saying, not greedily but demurely, "I really just can't explain it because I don't understand it myself." She referred the reporters to the bank that was handling her husband's estate, but then she added, "I presume you are referring to the bill that Jim Wright was putting through."[23] As the next paragraph in the story explained, "Jim Wright," also a citizen of Fort Worth, was the Speaker of the U.S. House of Representatives at the time. And in the paragraph after that, another member of the House was quoted as saying that the new tax code (which had saved the Ballard estate $4 million) "reaches deep into our national sense of justice—and gives us back a trust in government that has slipped away in the maze of tax preferences for the rich and powerful."

A sidebar to the story provided, if not an "impression" of the Ballards, then at least more "paragraphs and statements" about them. "Joseph J. Ballard Jr.," it began, "was fond of fine wines, animals, golf and Texas history."[24] Next came a eulogistic overview of the Ballards' charitable work and the sources of their wealth. But then came more details of the tangled estate. In his will Joseph Ballard had created a trust to maintain the historic family estate, including, according to the sidebar, "all salaries of domestic servants and employees." He had created another trust to provide income for Geraldine Ballard and also for his brother. No sooner had Geraldine Ballard filed a suit against her brother-in-law over this trust than the IRS presented her with a bill for an additional $4 million in estate taxes. The sidebar went on to explain the relevant tax law and concluded by quoting a spokesman for the bank handling the estate. "When you put money in a trust, you have to follow these very defined rules as to whether you get a tax deduction," said the banker. "[The IRS is] just saying we didn't totally follow all the rules. And we're saying they're being too picky."

Well? Might any impression have been conveyed in this story? Might any reader resentment have been triggered against someone who can claim so demurely to know so little about her personal financial affairs because, it turns out, she is confident that the Speaker of the House will take care of her; someone whose mansion and servants are already maintained by a trust fund; someone who is heir to a fortune but has sued her family for more; someone whose tax advisers whine that their mistakes ought to be fixed by a special exemption in the federal tax code? And might any reader wrath have been directed at the "reformers" who granted the special exemption even as they promised to do away with the maze of tax preferences for the rich and powerful—those hypocrites who did the same for hundreds of other rich and powerful constituents even as they spoke of renewing public trust in government? Well?

Despite the protestations of investigative reporters about facts speaking for themselves and readers or viewers deciding for themselves, this story shows that the actual work of investigative reporting is to compel the facts to speak—and, what's more, to speak in a way that urges a public decision about right and wrong. Investigative journalism is indeed an exercise in public conscience despite itself. And because of this reluctance to come to terms with itself as a form of moral discourse, its vision of journalistic responsibility blurs somewhat. Does investigative journalism really have no responsibility for impressions? And what of all the other sorts of moral meanings that investigative reporters work so hard to reveal? Some reportorial reflection beyond worries about an "open season" would be reassuring.

Such ambiguities not withstanding, investigative journalism offers a model, quite different from daily journalism, of what journalists can be held to owe the public. Investigative reporters accept responsibility for a process of verification that culminates in their decision to accept certain facts as true (or at least as accurate). Investigative journalism suggests that, even if journalism cannot, or should not, be held responsible for what the public believes, it can be held responsible for an account of the facts—both pivotal and moral—that the investigators believe to be true. Even the responsibility for simply "telling people something they don't know" ought to be regarded as "awesome."

8

The Value(s) of News

At the turn of the millennium the news remains an essential form of knowledge about the social world—though a form met with deepening distrust within that world. In response journalists are joining their critics in earnest reflection upon the intellectual means and the social ends of news work. If, as Donald Schön maintained, more reflective practitioners are more actively committed to meeting the needs of their world, we might expect some new, more socially engaged forms of news to emerge from this historic time of reflection.[1]

Although a fully realized and widely accepted alternative to conventional journalistic practice—what critic Jay Rosen insightfully called a new "theory of credibility"—has yet to emerge, many intellectual resources are available to sustain journalistic reflection and renewal.[2] Investigative reporting is one such resource. This particular form of news as knowledge points toward a revised and expanded set of news values—values *for* the news more than merely *in* the news—that might establish new terms for journalists' engagement with the world. Because these values already tacitly guide some of the best journalistic practice, they might find a place in a new theory of credibility that is at once reflective and practical.

Journalism's Lingering Glassy Essence

Even if "almost nobody talks about objective reporting anymore," as Jack Fuller maintained in *News Values: Ideas for an Information Age*, we should not suppose that anybody has articulated a clear and compelling alternative to it.[3] Although Fuller questioned the "independence between the observer and the phenomenon observed," he nonetheless insisted that "journalism's duty to the truth requires it to present a full depiction of reality—good and bad."[4] He understood that in "pure narrative, value is expressed solely through the selection of fact," but he argued that "there are still good reasons for generally withholding ultimate value judgments in news reporting."[5] As Fuller worked his erudite and carefully nuanced way through many intellectual issues in journalism, he revealed that, even if the term *objectivity* is out of vogue, its legacy endures.

What, specifically, endures is an allegiance to the *ideal* of language as strictly denotative and purely referential—language as the medium for "a clear picture," "an undistorted image," or—in Fuller's terms—"a full depiction" of all the mind- and language-independent objects that presumably constitute social reality. Allegiance to this ideal explains why, despite the recent fuss about objectivity, both practitioners and the public are still drawn to the virtue of *glass* as a metaphor for the role and responsibility of journalism: the news is to be a *window* on the world, a *mirror* of society, a *lens* that brings the personalities, problems, and policies of the day into focus.

Metaphors of glass—journalism's "glassy essence" (to appropriate the line from Richard Rorty that he appropriated from William Shakespeare)—quietly convey important normative claims about the news, especially when journalistic practice comes under hostile public scrutiny.[6] Indeed, these metaphors establish the premises for any scrutiny at all.[7] When, for example, an editor at the *San Jose Mercury News* was asked to explain why nearly 75 percent of the newspaper's editors and reporters said they would publish a photograph of a woman in agony, legs shattered, being pulled from earthquake rubble, he replied: "The earthquake was a horrible event, and no matter how unpleasant the image, they say the newspaper must mirror reality."[8] Even when acknowledging the inevitability of some distortion in any narrative, journalists turn to metaphors of glass to defend the authenticity of news. "All storytelling involves some distortion," wrote a *New York Times* editorialist in critique of a television docudrama. "But the difference between news and fiction is the difference between a mirror and a painting."[9] Journalistic metaphors of glass illustrate Mark Johnson's argument about the "irreducibly metaphoric character" of conventional morality.[10] In such metaphors an entire conception of what journalism ought to be is conveyed in a simple figure of speech that can encompass no moral imperative other than the accurate reflection of facts.

Metaphors of glass, as Rorty explained without reference to journalism, are the legacy of the seventeenth-century concept of the mind as a mirror to the world and knowledge as the quality of its reflection. "To know is to represent accurately what is outside the mind," Rorty wrote, describing the seventeenth-century concept. "Without the notion of mind as mirror, the notion of knowledge as accuracy would not have suggested itself."[11] What undermines knowledge, it follows, is whatever interferes with the mind's images, whatever causes the mind to *re-present* the world in inaccurate or distorted ways. One such cause is the character of language—often ambiguous and always value laden. And so it was that John Locke came to advocate the purification of language. As John Durham Peters summarized Locke's quintessential Enlightenment project: "Once language was purged of its imperfections and organized on sound principles, ideas would flow from mind to mind with all the ease that a lodestone 'communicates' with a piece of iron."[12]

To produce news that shines with a glassy essence journalists must try to reflect the world in language undistorted by human interest and value. Throughout this book, however, we have shown that within investigative reporting—a journalistic tradition deeply committed to pursuit of the truth—fact and value are always intimately interconnected by language that is never strictly denotative or purely referential. Investigative journalism removes some constraints of daily reporting to more fully report the facts, but it does so in an effort to report the profoundly moral facts (or better, we should say, the immoral facts) of suffering and injustice in the world. Moreover, it uses certain stylistic features of journalistic objectivity, but it does so in an effort to amplify the call for public indignation at the facts. To be sure, investigative journalism does not stand as the final arbiter of moral standards, but it does locate, select, interpret, and apply standards for assessing the performance of officials and institutions. In these ways it contributes to the crafting of the moral order.

But even as investigative reporting shows us how journalism can both respect truth and engage value, it tries to deny this, its greatest virtue. Investigative reporters expend significant intellectual effort reconciling their craft's stated norm of moral disengagement with their all-too-apparent moral craftwork. They struggle to conceptualize their work in strictly empirical terms—as nothing other than an accurate report of unambiguous facts. And in doing so they deny themselves a powerful moral vocabulary with which to respond openly and explicitly to questions of human interest. The moral craft of the investigative reporter becomes an exercise in the use of irony to establish an implicit frame of moral reference and in the casting of story characters to illustrate conceptions of innocence and guilt. As a result, the moral craftwork is accomplished unreflectively (if not entirely unself-consciously) and without any acknowledgment that journalism might be held accountable for the moral order that it helps to fashion.

We contend nonetheless that investigative reporting displays facets that could be polished to shine with more than a mere glassy essence. As discourse that fuses hard fact and human value, it points toward forms of journalism that can more actively engage the social world while respecting the truth, forms that can embrace an enlarged sense of social responsibility while setting realistic standards for its practitioners. In this way, so we argue, investigative reporting exemplifies for all other genres of journalism a set of news values that is appropriate not merely to an information age but to an age of renewed commitment and purpose, both for the news and for the public.

Journalists' Engagement with the World

As journalists rethink the nature of their engagement with the social world, they might pause to consider a key contention of their critics—that their engagement does not cease upon publication of the story. Journalism is a force in the world that it purports merely to portray. And in the case of investigative journalism, with its proud lineage to the muckrakers in the era of progressive reform, critics have long recognized a special potential for political influence: the ability to bring social problems to public attention as well as to push particular reforms higher on the policy agenda.[13]

A good example from among the investigations studied in this book is the *Philadelphia Inquirer*'s report on federal tax reform, which affected the public and policy makers far beyond Philadelphia. "Outrage over the selling of tax breaks to relatively high-income, favored constituents was also voiced in other cities in which all or parts of the series appeared, especially those with representatives on congressional tax-writing committees," reported the *Washington Tax Letter* (a publication of the Arthur Anderson & Co. accounting firm for readers with more than a passing interest in the federal tax code).[14] Soon that outrage became audible on Capitol Hill. "Regardless of what one might think of their accuracy or slant, those articles appear to have had a permanent effect on the legislative tax-writing process," the *Tax Letter* grudgingly acknowledged. "Already, as part of the technical corrections legislation, tax committee staffs were directed to carefully investigate each requested amendment to ensure that the proposal had general application, rather than benefiting only one taxpayer." So it seems the American people are not yet so cynical that reformist appeals fail to move them to outrage—though such appeals may move them most easily when both social equality and taxpayer self-interest are clearly at stake.

Not all investigations create an uproar that reverberates through the corridors of power. Often, as one reporter said, they "sink without a trace." If the social role of investigative journalism is conceptualized entirely in terms of its engagement in the process of policy making, any investigation that gains the attention of policy makers but yields no particular policy change would be dismissed as merely "symbolic," or at best "deliberative," rather than truly "substantive."[15] (Policy makers may have talked about the problem, but they didn't seem to *do* anything about it.) Moreover, any investigation that goes entirely unacknowledged by policy makers would be dismissed as failing to accomplish any public outcome at all. If, on the other hand, investigative journalism is conceptualized more broadly, as moral discourse, those investigations with a deliberative outcome, or with no apparent outcome at all, cannot be so casually dismissed.

If investigative journalism is understood to engage the world not only as a political force but as a cultural form, *every* investigation must be understood as a call to the conscience of the community—a call to affirm, whether by policy change or popular condemnation, that a particular situation on Capitol Hill or in city hall constitutes an instance of civic vice, or else to confirm by inaction or indifference that the situation does not. Every investigation is a test of what one reporter described as "the community consensus on values and how they apply in particular instances." Stories that summon public outrage and/or official action reward the journalists' selection of situations for public attention as well as their application of standards to those situations. Such stories may simply reinforce the prevailing conceptions of civic virtue and vice, or they may instead facilitate the further development of those conceptions through their application to new and different situations. On the other hand, stories that meet with public indifference and official inaction may not be told again, and the prevailing conceptions of virtue and vice may begin to wither away. Whether an investigation evokes public outrage or elicits no response at all, it is a process by which the virtues of "the system" are always tested and sometimes contested.[16]

If journalists have been reluctant to acknowledge responsibility for anything other than the factual accuracy of their reports, perhaps it is because they have assumed that responsibility must entail blame for what citizens and policy makers do (or fail to do) with the facts that presumably have been transmitted to them. "I don't think you can be responsible because you really have no control over the process," said Steele of public and policy-maker response to his reporting. "Though, I suppose, you would feel very bad if you brought something to light, and there was this completely crazy reaction to it." So, although this reporter might feel bad about crazy reactions, he does not want to be held accountable for the thoughts or actions of either citizens or policy makers. "The only other option," he concluded, "is not to write about these issues."

For this reporter journalistic responsibility comes down to an either/or deal. Either journalists must be absolved of responsibility for anything other than factual accuracy, or they will fall silent. Steele acknowledged that journalists sometimes do encounter situations in which they must assess the potential harm to individuals or organizations. And in such situations (which he maintained are more likely to be encountered in ethics seminars than actual newsrooms), journalists must weigh the potential for harm against the "obligation to bring that story to the public's attention." But when it comes to stories about the breakdown of social systems, Steele argued, journalists rarely err on the side of overzealousness. "The fact of the matter is that the reverse happens in American journalism ninety-five percent of the time," he said. "Many stories are not printed because they are extremely controversial and will produce a reaction that editors do not want to deal with. They would like to go home that night at seven o'clock and not have their phone ring off the wall." According to this reporter, if journalists are to be held responsible for any impact of their stories, their phones will ring even less than they do now because they will print even fewer controversial stories.

A new conception of news values might help to expand this constrained either-or understanding of journalistic responsibility. To be sure, the term *news values* remains remarkably ambiguous. Sometimes it refers to criteria for selection of news stories: prominence, proximity, oddity, conflict, and so on. Sometimes, as in Fuller's usage, it refers to standards of professional practice as they are manifested in the news: balance, accuracy, fairness. And sometimes it refers to political or cultural norms, such as individualism, that are thought to be promoted by the news.[17] In the best investigative reporting, however, we have found still another meaning of the term—a conception of value that extends well beyond traditional news values to encompass basic ideals of public communication. What we have found are examples of journalism that underscore the value of community dialogue over objective detachment and public deliberation over official pronouncement. With this in mind, our conception of journalistic responsibility emphasizes less policy-maker *action* than sustained public *interaction*.[18]

Three values or ideals best explain the overall value of investigative reporting. We shall refer to these values in a vocabulary that resonates more with the scholarship on public communication—a tradition of learning going back to the Enlightenment and beyond to the classical world—than with the conventions of contemporary news reporting. With this vocabulary we mean to problematize the usual terms of journalistic practice but at the same time to appreciate the lasting accomplishments of that practice.

We take the accomplishments of investigative reporting to be:

- Publicity—bringing to public attention serious instances of systemic breakdown and institutional disorder that have been mostly unnoticed or intentionally concealed
- Accountability—demanding an account of the situation from those who are responsible
- Solidarity—establishing an empathetic link between those who have suffered in the situation and the rest of us.

These values both prescribe and describe the practice of investigative journalism. In turn, these values can help to enlarge our expectations for journalism and yet ground those expectations in the realities of news work. To illustrate each of them we shall return to the investigative report that, arguably, is the best of all those examined: "The Color of Money" by Bill Dedman. The guidance that the best investigative journalism has to offer, after all, is to be found less in some theoretical system than in the example set by the best stories from the best reporters. "The Color of Money" is especially worthy of a last look because its limitations, no less than its virtues, highlight the lessons that the best investigative journalism has to offer those who seek to renew journalism's intellectual foundations.

The Priority of Publicity

To recognize the value of publicity in the enterprise of investigative journalism is not to confuse news with public relations. The public now may associate the term *publicity* with efforts to gain "prestige for a person or issue" and render them "ready for acclamatory assent," as Jürgen Habermas described the "transmuted function" of publicity that characterizes the practice of public relations today. Here, however, we intend to honor the idea of publicity that is associated with the origins of the concept of public opinion in eighteenth-century Europe.[19] We understand the idea of publicity to entail not only the transmission of public information but the construction of the place and the occasion for the conduct of public affairs. Indeed, we understand the idea to entail not only the enlightenment of the public but its creation. As a democratic principle, publicity underscores the idea that the news can set an agenda—both political and moral—independent of, and even contrary to, whatever officials and policy makers might prefer to set. Publicity as a value of investigative journalism contradicts publicity as a value in public relations: it represents an opportunity to avoid, not foster, what Alvin Gouldner described as the "*fusion* of media accounts with manager accounts of social reality."[20]

The venerable ideal of publicity points to an important but often neglected power of the press, namely, the power to bring about, in Peters's phrase, a "symbolically changed public sphere."[21] Investigative reports may or may not influence individual citizens in a scientifically measurable way. But even in the absence of a detectable shift in "public opinion" on specific issues, as Peters reminded us, investigative reporting can engender significant and enduring change in the way public affairs are perceived, understood, and debated. By publicizing conduct deemed to be a violation of the moral order, investigative reporters can create a "dazzling spectacle"—a "media event" that can have an impact "by rearranging the symbolic order of social life."[22] A reframed public sphere poses a challenge to officials and policy makers because they must concern themselves not only with an outraged public but with the *image* of an outraged public. Put a little differently, judgments made in response to the public and its opinions may turn out to be judgments made in response to a *perceived* public and its opinions—the "public as a robust fiction," as Peters called it.[23] In this way a "symbolic" public can be real enough to matter. Publicity therefore needs to be understood broadly enough to include the role it plays in creating a symbolic realm in which few really participate but from which participation gains, properly or improperly, its authority and legitimacy.

With the idea of publicity, then, we celebrate the moral energy that investigative journalism contributes to the creation of a symbolically charged public sphere. "My job was to find the stories that *were* stories but that we were not covering," said Dedman of his assignment to charge the public sphere of his city. Thus, when asked why "The Color of Money," a series about racially biased mortgage lending in Atlanta, was worth five months of his life, he said that even though the story fit "some traditional criteria of significance and interest," it otherwise would have gone unreported. "I was given only one direction about what kind of stories to pursue, and that direction was to figure out what the sacred cows were and to hold public barbecues." A dazzling spectacle, indeed.

Work on "The Color of Money" began when a community organizer, the sort of source that other reporters might ignore, told Dedman about his experiences with racial bias in mortgage lending. The reporter found no recent stories about mortgage lending in his paper and realized this was one of those stories that *was* a story but that the paper was not covering. Sometime later, when he talked to the paper's banking reporter, Dedman learned that members of a community group had come to the paper on that very day with a petition challenging the merger of two banks. The group maintained that one of the banks had failed to lend in accordance with the terms of the Community Reinvestment Act. And as it turned out, the community group was one in which Dedman's source was active. When the banking reporter said that he wasn't planning to write about this issue, Dedman asked to take it over. "This wasn't something even on the scope of a banking reporter in Atlanta," Dedman said. "It was, as he told me later, a no-win situation for a banking reporter because it would make everybody on his beat mad if he wrote it—which is a source of tension for beat reporters."

As Dedman recalled, he felt compelled to take on the story because it fit his self-conception as an investigative reporter. Though he did not say that he was *morally* compelled or *ethically* compelled, he was compelled nonetheless:

> So, first of all, it was a story because we hadn't been covering it. It was a story because it dealt with powerful interests that the paper had historically been cozy with but that we didn't intend to be cozy with anymore. It also dealt with race, which interested me. I was persuaded that this was one of the few really significant issues going on.
>
> I don't think it was an accident that [this was] during a period on the Atlanta paper when, from my point of view, there was a flowering of investigative reporting. A couple of reporters did a story about resegregation of public schools in the country, and a couple of other reporters did stories about farms in south Georgia which were essentially slave farms: if you got in trouble with the county, the court would assign you to a farmer to work; and if you didn't work, you went to jail. Those were the three significant reporting projects we did that year.

Dedman understood his reporting on these "powerful interests" to be not only newsworthy but right. "I want to look back and see that I have written things that wouldn't have gotten in the paper if I hadn't done them," he said. "Maybe that's just ego, but it's one of my measures of whether I was doing the right thing or not." For this reporter, however, doing the right thing turned out not to be easy. That "brief flowering" of investigative reporting at the *Atlanta Journal & Constitution* ended for Dedman when the editor, Bill Kovach, and the owner, Cox Enterprises, had "a falling out," as Dedman described it. "They [Cox] certainly didn't want us doing that kind of story," Dedman said. "It was part of a larger dispute about whether they got to run the paper because they owned it, or he got to run the paper because he was the editor of it. When he left, I left."[24]

In a craft in which practitioners still must claim to separate fact from value, this reporter's measure of his work is as close to a moral vision as we are likely to find. Another reporter might simply have said that stories ought to fit "some traditional criteria of significance and interest" and have left it at that. And even Dedman did not hasten to elaborate on the system of moral principles that might define the topics worthy of the reporter's time and energy. Of course, no such system of principles exists within the craft to elaborate. Investigative journalism has only the basic commonsense values of the larger culture—fairness, honesty, and so on— to define what is of "significance and interest." That is the most fundamental limit within which journalism must operate.

But if investigative reporters begin their work with only unelaborated moral common sense, they conclude their work by producing a report that articulates specific standards for the evaluation of public conduct. Reporters select, interpret, and apply these standards (indeed, as discussed in chapter 3, this is a key aspect of investigative journalism as moral discourse), but the process always begins with a search for usable standards that can be presented as "objective." And most often these standards are, as one reporter said, "borrowed" from other social institutions. Thus Dedman's knowledge of right and wrong depended heavily on two federal statutes: the Community Reinvestment Act 1977 and the Equal Credit Opportunity Act of 1974. These laws defined the way that, in Dedman's phrase, "the system is supposed to work."

To those seeking journalistic renewal "The Color of Money" is a reminder that journalism cannot be more morally insightful or wise than its evaluative resources, such as the law, equip it to be. Like most investigative reporting, the series evaluated conduct against standards that could be taken as objective because they were consensual (or, at least, legally sanctioned). Clearly, the series was a test of "the community *consensus* on values and how they apply in particular instances," and it could not stray very far from that consensus. Although "The Color of Money" offers assurance that journalism still can comfort the afflicted and afflict the comfortable, it is also a reminder that journalism is conservative morally and intellectually, even if not always in narrowly partisan, Republican-versus-Democrat, terms.

Nonetheless, within the general limits set by the current consensus, "The Color of Money" highlights an important value. If journalists are expected to *publicize* fundamental community concerns, they would do well to consider how the investigative reporter's fundamental concern in this story—the way the system is *supposed* to work—transcends the daily reporter's shallow concern with the way system has worked in the last twenty-four hours. Investigative journalists may try to evade responsibility for their knowledge of how the system is supposed to work, but at least they offer that knowledge to the public in the form of accessible evaluative standards. They may submerge much of their moral and conceptual framework beneath the drama of victims and villains, but at least they are more forthcoming than most other reporters about the principles they use to construct their representations of reality. Here, then, is a model journalism that is guided, if not by an internal moral compass or some new theory of credibility, then at least by a set of operating procedures more compelling than the objectivity of daily reporting. If journalism is to initiate dialogue and sustain deliberation, investigative journalism offers some ideas for deciding what's worth thinking and talking about.

A Call to Accountability

Public attention to concerns that might otherwise go unheeded implies attention to voices that might otherwise go unheard. And in investigative journalism this means much more than merely a quote or two from some atypical source. At their very best the accounts of victims and villains that are the staple of this genre of journalism can give voice not only to those who suffer injustice but to those who work injustice. That is, the call to accountability registered by investigative journalism not only *allows* the victims to speak but *demands* that the villains speak as well. In this way the value of publicity implies the value of public accountability.

Carefully crafted accounts of villainy require carefully crafted opportunities for villains to explain or disclaim or try to deny responsibility for the vices attributed to them. This is in part a matter of journalistic protocol, a way of honoring the traditional news values of fairness and balance; it anticipates critics who might otherwise complain that the story was biased or one sided. But it is also a matter of accountability, a demand by journalists that violators of the moral order account openly and candidly for their violations. It serves notice that the press, much like the courts, can compel testimony.[25] Individuals who decline a journalist's call for accountability can be held in contempt of the public, a fate often worse than being held in contempt of court. "No comment" becomes evidence of guilt, and no judge can intervene in the court of public opinion to recognize and explain the constitutional protections against self-incrimination.

Although every investigative reporter offers the right of reply, Dedman was determined to call the mortgage lenders to account, as he said, "by rebutting their rebuttals of the findings." Invoking the investigative reporter's commitment to getting to the bottom of things, Dedman said, "I was persuaded, at this point in my career, that I didn't have to write stories in which he-said-she-said and that I could independently arrive at the facts." With this in mind he offered the representatives of the financial institutions the chance to meet with him to explain why they had been making many more loans in white middle-class neighborhoods than in comparable black neighborhoods:

> The way we approached it was that we got the numbers, and we scheduled a meeting with every one of the big banks and savings and loans. They all agreed to a meeting that included the highest official available at the bank, like the executive vice president or somebody at the top, the head of mortgage lending, the Community Reinvestment Act compliance officer, and, of course, the PR person. So they would always have four people on their side, with me and the photographer on our side. I would bring my tape recorder, and they would bring theirs.

In these meetings the reporter was asking questions on behalf of every citizen of Atlanta who had ever been denied a loan because of race, or rather he was asking questions on behalf of every citizen of Atlanta . . . period. Here is the reporter's impression of a typical encounter:

> They would all sit back in their chairs in a defensive crouch. I would ask them questions, and they would look at me like I was some alien. When one of them would come up with an explanation, they would all come forward

in their chairs. All this was conducted very delicately because race was on the table. There was usually one black person in the room—the company's minority community affairs person.

One rebuttal was, "Well, it's income."

I said, "No, the white and black neighborhoods have similar income levels."

Then somebody said, "There is a lot of bad houses in some neighborhoods, you know, substandard housing." (At a couple of institutions somebody went so far as to say, "You know, those people don't keep up their houses." But generally, it was put much more delicately than that.)

I said, "Well, I thought that might be the case, so we got some figures from the city. Remember, we only looked at comparable middle-income white and black areas, and the rate of substandard housing, according to the city's planning department, is higher in the white neighborhoods than in the black neighborhoods."

So they all sat back in their chairs again. There was a long silence, and then someone suggested very delicately that maybe these people didn't pay back their loans.

I said, "You have data on that. Could you give me some data to back up that theory?"

They said, "Oh, no, we couldn't divulge any of that information."

I said, "Well, the only thing I could look at was the performance of the large black-owned bank that historically has been the lender of last resort in black neighborhoods. . . . It has one of the lowest percentages of defaults on single-family mortgages of any bank of its size in the country."

So they sat back in their chairs again. On it went. As a reporter, it was fun.

Dedman said that if he could write the story again, he would include even more of the financial institutions' attempts to rebut the results of his reporting. In that way he could more completely and convincingly demonstrate that all their rebuttals could be, in his words, "knocked down." Moreover, since he completed the project, new regulations requiring financial institutions to publicly report more information have been enacted, and he would use these new sources of data to more fully rebut the rebuttals. Here, then, is one more irony in a field of discourse that is rich with irony: investigative reporters must often work hardest to give voice not to the oppressed and dispossessed who might otherwise be *forced* to remain silent but to the powerful and privileged who might otherwise *chose* to remain silent.

Just as the second communication value, accountability, is implied by the first, publicity, so are the limits of investigative journalism with regard to each. If powerful interests are to be called most fully to account, journalists must draw other social institutions, especially government, into a dialogue—particularly if they are to engage in any discussion of either punishment or policy reform. The initial investigative report must generate enough of a charge to compel officials to respond; when officials do respond, subsequent news reports can publicize, and thereby reward, their contribution to the ongoing discussion. In all of this "The Color of Money" was very successful. Dedman's initial report expanded the dialogue beyond the pages of his newspaper, and his subsequent reports recounted those discussions. "You need to keep up the momentum," an editor urged Dedman. "Nobody has fixed anything yet."

Among the follow-up stories was one that led with this: "Georgia legislators should approve a law requiring banks and savings and loans to lend in all segments of their communities, the state banking commissioner said Friday." Another with this: "The Atlanta chapter of the NAACP called Monday for a boycott and federal investigation of white-owned Atlanta banks and savings and loans." And still another with this: "Atlanta's largest banks say they will lend $65 million—at interest rates as low as prime rate—for home purchases and home improvements, particularly on the metro area's black Southside."[26]

Dedman fondly recalled one follow-up story precisely because of its dialogic quality. Thinking about this story long after its publication, he could not help being drawn once again into the discussion of which his work had been a part. As he recalled:

> William Proxmire [then the chairman of the Senate Banking, Housing and Urban Affairs Committee] wrote the federal regulators a letter asking if our story was true. We ended up publishing a twenty-column-inch piece on their rebuttal, which was basically, "Yes, the numbers are all true. Yes, there is this disparity; but that doesn't mean that anybody is intentionally discriminating."
>
> Well, we hadn't said that anybody was *intentionally* discriminating, though that's where the argument got debated. The financial institutions said, "We don't discriminate." But we said, "*In effect* you do. The law says that discrimination in effect is the same as discrimination by intent. That's the Equal Credit Opportunity law."

Of these stories, Dedman said, "It was just old-fashioned newspaper crusading." But then he appended this important afterthought: "We just kept the heat on, not really saying what anybody ought to do." In this offhanded way the reporter provided an important reminder that journalism cannot be more morally efficacious than the social institutions, most often government, to which it looks in expectation of reform. Like most other old-fashioned newspaper crusading, "The Color of Money" and the stories that followed were a discussion more of problems than solutions, perhaps because the reporting of problems seems to engage only the facts, whereas deliberation on solutions obviously invokes values as well. The latter are most easily left to other institutions, not only to enact but to conceive, articulate, and debate.

Within the limitations set by this tradition of problem-oriented discourse, however, "The Color of Money" offers a model of virtue that transcends not only daily reporting but many other examples of investigative reporting as well. This story did not merely indict the system for its failure (though the computer analysis of lending patterns did so convincingly). Drawing on the reporter's discussions with the representatives of the financial institutions, as well as with others in the community (real estate brokers in African American neighborhoods, for example), the story went on to explain the context and causes of the system's failure. If the bankers did not discriminate *by intention*, how did the lending system discriminate *in effect*? Among all the remarkable elements that went into this story, the reporter was most proud of his success in answering that question. Here, then, is a model of journalism with the intellectual resources to make a far larger contribution to public deliberation on solutions.

A Sense of Solidarity

At its best investigative reporting engages our conscience by inviting us to identify with the plight of the less fortunate. It accomplishes this not by reciting facts but by crafting stories with this premise: some of us are being treated unjustly and the rest of us must know. In this way it promotes "imaginative identification with the details of others' lives," as Rorty put it, and thus helps to build the only foundation for life together: an awareness of our "common susceptibility to humiliation" and in turn "a sense of human solidarity."[27] This is a human bond, Rorty insisted, without philosophical pretense. "Solidarity is not thought of as recognition of a core self, the human essence, in all human beings," he argued. "Rather, it is thought of as the ability to see more and more traditional differences (of tribe, religion, race, customs, and the like) as unimportant

when compared with similarities with respect to pain and humiliation—
the ability to think of people wildly different from ourselves as included
in the range of 'us.'"[28]

More than simply putting a human face on the numbers, as daily
reporters might do in a story about, say, the unemployment rate, investigative reporters tell stories of victims who are deserving of our concern
because they are not so very different from us. And sometimes reporters
must work very hard to create the conditions for empathy with victims
who do not at first seem deserving—for example, jail inmates who have
been sexually assaulted or drunken teenagers who have been attacked by
police dogs—but whose victimization nonetheless ought to be seen as a
moral outrage. In "The Color of Money" the victims were middle-
income, credit-worthy citizens of Atlanta, but the reporter knew well that
"race was on the table" and that he needed to tell stories that could evoke
concern across the deep American divide of color. The computer analysis
of mortgage lending patterns allowed him to "get away from the anecdotes," as Dedman characterized his accounts of victims and villains, but
he knew all along that these accounts would remain an essential feature
of his report. "The anecdotes were no longer what proved the story," he
said, "but the anecdotes were what persuaded people that it was true or
that got them to read it." Whatever the evidence, it is the "anecdotes"
that created the conditions for empathy and in turn solidarity.

"I had several fits and starts getting people to tell me their stories,"
Dedman recalled. "Nobody wanted to be on the front page of the newspaper saying they had been turned down for a loan." But then he "lucked
into a story" that came to symbolize the point of the series. "I went to city
hall, talked to some affluent, upper-middle-level bureaucrats, and asked
them what their experience had been," Dedman said of his early attempts
to begin a conversation with his community. "When I asked them if they
knew of people who had applied to the big banks, they all said, 'You
should talk to Lomax.'" And so the reporter sought out Michael Lomax,
a faculty member of Spelman College and the chair of the Fulton County
Commission, who once had been denied a home improvement loan on his
house in a primarily African American neighborhood:

> Getting that story in the paper was tricky. He told me about his experi-
> ence, but I wanted to confirm that he was qualified for the loan. He would-
> n't give me his credit report, and he wouldn't share with me details that I
> wanted about his personal finances. So we ended up in this dance in which
> the editor, Bill Kovach, interviewed him before we published the story. He

agreed to tell Kovach anything that Kovach wanted to know about his personal finances. He wouldn't tell me because I was just a reporter, but he would tell the editor of the newspaper. So before we published that one, Kovach satisfied himself that there was no hidden problem in that anecdote. I was amused by the way that worked.

Bill Dedman is journalist with no illusions about the realities of the source-reporter transaction. He knew that Lomax expected to take something home from his "dance" with the *Atlanta Journal & Constitution*. "Lomax was clearly known as a member of the elite, someone who fit in with white society," he said. "I think his motivation was that the story made him appear more like a typical black person: someone who could get turned down for a loan." Nor is Dedman a journalist with any illusions about the need for "anecdotes" that make the point—he will take the opportunity to build a little solidarity wherever he finds it. "The same reason that gave Lomax an incentive to participate, you see, made him a perfect example," Dedman acknowledged. And, indeed, the irony of the example *is* perfect. Here was a member of Atlanta's intellectual and political elite who, because of race, could not get a loan to fix his house. "If I can't get a loan," said county commissioner Lomax, proving himself to be the perfect dance partner, "what black person can?"

In several previous chapters we said a good deal about how narrative shapes and narrows the truths that can be told and how irony is potentially perilous for public moral discourse. Ironic narratives of villains and victims can summon moral outrage, but reliance on such narratives equips journalism with a moral vocabulary of little more than the most rudimentary conceptions of guilt and innocence. This limited vocabulary reduces the possibility that outrage will eventually lead to a thoughtful discussion of the underlying moral issues. We are mindful, then, that journalism cannot be more morally engaged than its narrative and rhetorical strategies equip it to be.

These constraints of investigative storytelling notwithstanding, "The Color of Money" continues to offer a model of great virtue. With its quantitative documentation of bias and its explanation of how that bias is built into the system, this story is far more than a collection of anecdotes. Nonetheless, ironic narrative is an essential feature of all investigative reporting. If "The Color of Money" has the effect of building solidarity across the divide of race (rather than the effect of prompting cynicism about the possibility of justice), we can credit the story with just the right ironic tone. But if indeed that is its effect on its audience, we must acknowledge that there is virtue in both the story and its audience. Investigative journalism can summon empathy only if the audience is willing to give it and can build solidarity only if the audience is willing to work at it. And so "The Color of Money" reminds us of one more limitation of journalism: it can be no more moral or wise than the citizens who sustain it.

News Values and Moral Purpose

Investigative journalism, as we have insisted throughout this book, is an exercise in public conscience despite itself. Nevertheless, the authentic—even if deeply conflicted—commitment by the best investigative reporters to the ideals of publicity, accountability, and solidarity signals a new set of values to all others who practice the reporter's craft. The patient yet relentless drive to get to the bottom of things—not merely to expose but to fully publicize instances of suffering and injustice that others might want the public to disregard—anticipates a commitment to "a journalism of conversation," in James Carey's apt metaphor, that will transcend reportage of governmental functioning and political maneuvering.[29] And in the same way, the investigative reporter's adversarial instinct—a deep desire to see that those who work suffering and injustice are held publicly accountable—promises forms of public deliberation in which the powerless are empowered to speak and the powerful compelled to do so.

Among the three ideals, solidarity may seem most alien to the values of contemporary journalistic practice. But now, at the turn of the millennium, this value seems most urgent. The investigative reporter's dramatic narratives about victims and villains—stories about lives that may be far from ours and yet disconcertingly near—point directly, even if unsteadily, toward forms of journalism that can help satisfy the most basic needs of social life in an ever more complex and conflicted world. As "partisans of solidarity," to invoke a phrase from Rorty that challenges journalists' comfortable self-conception of nonpartisanship, investigative reporters write stories that can remind us of our shared vulnerability to suffering and injustice and thereby enhance our tolerance for differences of race, religion, and so on.[30] But more than that, the very best investigative reporting can help us envision forms of journalism that not only accept such differences but more fully and effectively confront them in an attempt to establish common ground. And this, to extrapolate from the work of Habermas, would position journalism as an agent of reform and reconciliation.

In Habermas's strong conception, solidarity demands intersubjectivity, which in practical terms means "reciprocal perspective taking."[31] Whereas for Rorty, conversation promotes *tolerance of difference* and, in turn, a greater reluctance to inflict cruelty, for Habermas it promotes *insight into difference* and, in turn, a bond of reciprocity and mutual understanding.[32] Solidarity, as Habermas conceived it, emerges from— and subsequently strengthens—the kind of genuinely dialogic conversation Charles Taylor had in mind when he wrote about how communication can take us over a certain threshold and into a universe of discourse where commonality is not simply shared but established.[33] Such conversation promotes a sense of "ours" that is something greater than a mere aggregation of "yours" and "mine." An authentic "journalism of conversation" therefore would regard solidarity as a regulative ideal, a standard of performance intended to guide journalists by insisting on insight into others as a goal of good reporting.

In Habermas's understanding of solidarity we find an explicitly moral purpose for the news media—an opportunity for journalists to participate in the crafting of a moral order worthy of their open and candid support. At the same time, this understanding of solidarity poses a challenge for journalists that is commensurate with the needs of a culturally plural society like the United States and a global order in which nations and national identities compete for recognition, legitimacy, and authority. Understood as a call for insight into difference—whether among neighbors or nations—and a search for common ground, the ideal of solidarity is not so alien to contemporary journalism as it may have seemed.

Even so, we do not suppose that either reporters or the corporate executives who pay them will easily accept solidarity as key to a set of values that can transcend objectivity. For reporters, objectivity is a well-rehearsed routine for the production of news, whereas solidarity offers no ready formulas for the discussion of public affairs. And for media managers objectivity has long been the basis of news as a commercial product, whereas solidarity and the other values are of uncertain economic advantage. However, we do suppose that, at the very least, the education of future journalists can encourage more socially engaged and morally meaningful forms of news. The judgment of history, after all, is likely to fall more gently on those who teach the journalists—and all citizens—of the future that, as members of the media or other powerful social institutions and simply as human beings, they must seek the wisdom to know what is right and the courage to speak the truth about it.

In the future we may all come to see the search for common ground as natural and necessary in any conversation about the social world. Perhaps we will be allowed to learn in peace and safety that our everyday political differences could be eased by an ongoing public discourse of human solidarity. But perhaps we will be *compelled* to learn from greater suffering and injustice in a dangerously discordant world that we have no other choice than to become more careful keepers of this and other essential human values. Whatever awaits, journalism could help each of us be a better custodian of conscience.

Notes

Preface

1. Clifford Geertz, *The Interpretation of Cultures* (New York: Basic, 1973), p. 9.

2. This book incorporates material from three previously published articles: James S. Ettema and Theodore L. Glasser, "Narrative Form and Moral Force: The Realization of Innocence and Guilt Through Investigative Journalism," *Journal of Communication* 38, no. 3 (1988): 8–26; Theodore L. Glasser and James S. Ettema, "Investigative Journalism and the Moral Order," *Critical Studies in Mass Communication* 6 (1989): 1–20; James S. Ettema and Theodore L. Glasser, "The Irony in—and of—Journalism: A Case Study in the Language of Liberal Democracy," *Journal of Communication* 44, no. 2 (1994): 5–28.

1. Introduction: The Reporter's Craft as Moral Discourse

1. Pam Zekman, "Elevator Rip-Off: An Open and Shut Case," WBBM-TV, Chicago, August 23–26, 1983. Quotations from this story and other television news stories used in this book are taken from the reporter's transcript of the series.

2. Pam Zekman, "Killing Crime: A Police Cop-Out," WBBM-TV, Chicago, November 7–9, 1982.

3. We do not claim to have originated the phrase "custodians of conscience" in the context of investigative journalism. but neither do we have a citation for it. We would gladly acknowledge whomever ought to be credited with the phrase.

4. Loretta Tofani, "Terror Behind Bars," *Washington Post*, part 1 of the series Rape in the County Jail: Prince George's Hidden Horror, September 26, 1982, p. A18.

5. Jonathan Kaufman, "At Boston's Top Levels, Few of the Faces Are Black," *Boston Sunday Globe*, lead story for the series Boston Jobs: The Race Factor, April 23, 1983, p. 22.

6. Jack Fuller, *News Values: Ideas for an Information Age* (Chicago: University of Chicago Press, 1996), p. 14.

7. Celeste Michelle Condit, "Crafting Virtue: The Rhetorical Construction of Public Morality," *Quarterly Journal of Speech* 73 (1987): 79.

8. Richard Rorty, *Contingency, Irony, and Solidarity* (New York: Cambridge University Press, 1989).

9. Hayden White, *The Content of the Form: Narrative Discourse and Historical Representation* (Baltimore: Johns Hopkins University Press, 1987), p. 21.

10. Hilary Putnam, *Reason, Truth, and History* (New York: Cambridge University Press, 1981), p. 201.

11. This is a note in which we might have cited Michel Foucault (and every other major contributor to the analysis of knowledge and representation in the last half century). However, we were once warned by a reviewer—unknown to us by name but clearly a veteran reporter—that "neither academia nor journalism needs any more Frenchified deconstructivists." With this in mind we shall cite here a single book in which a highly respected scholar comes to terms with the uncertainties of knowledge and representation in yet another field of inquiry that aspires to speak the truth: Clifford Geertz, *Works and Lives: The Anthropologist as Author* (Stanford, Calif.: Stanford University Press, 1988).

12. We acknowledge, however, that ours is a study of investigative journalism as practiced in the United States in the late twentieth century. We claim no universal understanding of news and morality—a point usefully illustrated by Silvio R. Waisbord's study of investigative journalism as practiced in Colombia, Uruguay, Argentina, Chile, Peru, and Brazil, where journalists do not understand their role in the same way American journalists understand theirs. See Waisbord, "Investigative Journalism and Political Accountability in South American Democracies," *Critical Studies in Mass Communication* 13 (1996): 343–63.

12. Donald A. Schön, *The Reflective Practitioner: How Professionals Think in Action* (New York: Basic, 1983), p. 18.

2. In Search of Skills Not Taught in Textbooks

1. Jeffey Marx and Michael York, "Boosters' Cash, Gifts Lined Pockets of UK Players," *Lexington Herald-Leader*, part 1 of the series Playing Above the Rules, October 27, 1985, p. 1.

2. Ibid., p. 1.

3. Donald Schön, *The Reflective Practitioner: How Professionals Think in Action* (New York: Basic, 1983), pp. 18, 19.

4. Michael Schudson, *Discovering the News* (New York: Basic, 1978), pp. 192, 194.

5. Lucy Morgan, "Successful Fisherman or Dixie's Drug 'Godfather'?" *St. Petersburg Times*, part 2 of the series Dixie County: Smuggler's Haven, April 15, 1982, p. 1B.

6. Lucy Morgan, "State Agents Question Role of Dixie Sheriff," *St. Petersburg Times*, part 3 of the series Dixie County: Smuggler's Haven, April 16, 1981, pp. 1B, 6B.
7. Lucy Morgan, " 'Most Corrupt County in the U.S.'" *St. Petersburg Times*, part 1 of the series Dixie County: Smuggler's Haven, April 14, 1981, p. 1B.
8. Lucy Morgan, "Sheriff Short Made List of Secret Targets," *St. Petersburg Times*, Inside the Pasco County Sheriff's Department: A Special Report, December 3, 1983, p. 1.
9. Ibid., p. 10.
10. Some important examples of the extensive research literature on news "frames" include Todd Gitlin, *The Whole World Is Watching: The Role of News Media in the Making and Unmaking of the New Left* (Berkeley: University of California Press, 1980); William A. Gamson and Andre Modigliani, "Media Discourse and Public Opinion on Nuclear Power: A Constructionist Approach," *American Journal of Sociology* 95(1989): 1–37; Robert M. Entman, "Framing U.S. Coverage of International News: Contrasts in Narratives of the KAL and Iran Air Incidents," *Journal of Communication* 41, no. 4 (1991): 6–27; Robert M. Entman, "Framing: Toward Clarification of a Fractured Paradigm," *Journal of Communication* 43, no 4 (1993): 6–27; W. Lance Bennett and Regina G. Lawrence, "News Icons and the Mainstreaming of Social Change," *Journal of Communication* 45, no. 3 (1995): 20–39.
11. Jonathan Kaufman, "At Boston's Top Levels, Few of the Faces Are Black" *Boston Sunday Globe*, lead story for Boston Jobs: The Race Factor series, April 24, 1983, p. 1.
12. Ibid., p. 22.
13. Bill Dedman, "Atlanta Blacks Losing in Home Loans Scramble," *Atlanta Journal& Atlanta Constitution*, part 1 of the series The Color of Money, May 1, 1988, p. 1A.
14. Pam Zekman, Jay Branegan, William Crawford, and William Gaines, "Filth and Neglect Bared at Von Solbrig Hospital," *Chicago Tribune*, September 7, 1975, p. 1.
15. William Gaines, "Lives Are Held in Grimy Hands," *Chicago Tribune*, September 7, 1975, p. 10.
16. Donald L. Barlett and James B. Steele, "A Millionaire Businessman and His Island Tax Shelter," *Philadelphia Inquirer*, part 2 of the series The Great Tax Giveaway, April 11, 1988, p. 6. (All page cites to *Inquirer* series refer to the pages in the paper's reprints of the series.)
17. Ibid., p. 9.
18. Bill Dedman, "Southside Treated Like Banks' Stepchild?" *Atlanta Constitution*, part 2 of the series The Color of Money, May 2, 1988, p. 4A.
19. Loretta Tofani, "The Strong Inmates Exploit the Weak," *Washington Post*, part 3 of the series Rape in the County Jail: Prince George's Hidden Horror, September 28, 1982, p. A1.
20. John Ullmann, *Investigative Reporting: Advanced Methods and Techniques* (New York: St. Martin's, 1995). See also John Ullmann and Steve Honey-

206   2. In Search of Skills Not Taught in Textbooks

man, eds., *The Reporter's Handbook: An Investigator's Guide to Documents and Techniques* (New York: St. Martin's, 1983).

21. William Freivogel and Jon Sawyer, "Inquiry Sought in General Dynamics Tapes," *St.Louis Post-Dispatch*, September 26, 1984, p. 1.

22. William Gaines and Ann Marie Lipinski, "Ward Offices Mix Private, City Business" *Chicago Tribune*, part 3 of the series City Council: The Spoils of Power, October 6, 1987, p. 8.

23. Carlin Romano, "WHAT? The Grisly Truth About Bare Facts," in Robert C. Manoff and Michael Schudson, eds., *Reading the News* (New York: Pantheon, 1986), p. 38.

24. Schön, *Reflective Practitioner*, p. 295.

3. The Paradox of the Disengaged Conscience

1. Herbert J. Gans, *Deciding What's News: A Study of CBS Evening News, NBC Nightly News, Newsweek, and Time* New York: Vintage, 1980), pp. 185–86. News of moral disorder, as Gans defined it, reveals "instances of legal or moral transgressions, particularly by public officials and other prestigious individuals who, by reason or virtue of their power and prestige, are not expected to misbehave" (p. 56). In contrast to news of social disorder, which "monitors the respect of citizens for authority," news of moral disorder evaluates "whether authority figures respect the rules of the citizenry" (p. 60).

2. Ibid., pp. 183, 293.

3. Daniel C. Hallin, *We Keep America on Top of the World: Television Journalism and the Public Sphere* (London: Routledge, 1994), p. 53.

4. Celeste Michelle Condit, "Crafting Virtue: The Rhetorical Construction of Public Morality," *Quarterly Journal of Speech* 73 (1987): 79.

5. John C. Behrens, *The Typewriter Guerrillas: Closeups of Twenty Top Investigative Reporters* (Chicago: Nelson-Hall, 1977); the quote is from p. xxiv of Behrens. David Weir and Dan Noyes, *Raising Hell* (Reading, Mass.: Addison-Wesley, 1983).

6. Clark R. Mollenhoff, *Investigative Reporting: From Court House to White House* (New York: Macmillan, 1981), p. 345.

7. In regard to constitutional duty, see Vincent Blasi, "The Checking Value in First Amendment Theory," *American Bar Foundation Research Journal*, no. 3 (1977): 520–642. In regard to psychic baggage, see S. Robert Lichter, Stanley Rothman, and Linda S. Lichter, *The Media Elite: America's New Powerbrokers* (Bethesda, Md: Adler & Adler, 1986).

8. David H. Weaver and G. Cleveland Wilhoit, *The American Journalist: A Portrait of U.S. News People and Their Work* (Bloomington: Indiana University Press, 1986); David H. Weaver and G. Cleveland Wilhoit, *The American Journalist in the 1990s: U.S. News People at the End of an Era* (Mahwah, N.J.: Erlbaum, 1996). Weaver and Wilhoit found in the 1980s and again in the 1990s that only about 20 percent of the journalists surveyed rated "adversary of government" as an "extremely important" role. At the same time, roughly two-thirds of the journalists rated the investigation of government claims as an extremely important

journalistic function. Roya Akhavan-Majid suggested a plausible explanation for this apparent discrepancy in her study of the effect of questionnaire wording on the expression of professional attitudes. Although most journalists are reluctant to endorse adversarialism as a defining characteristic of their role, they are willing to endorse what Akhavan-Majid described as the more specific and less affect-laden functional dimensions of that role (e.g., investigation of government claims) when those dimensions are posed as separate questions. See Roya Akhavan-Majid, "Questionnaire Wording and Editor Perceptions," *Mass Comm Review* 21 (1994): 250–58.

9. Michael J. O'Neill, "The Power of the Press: A Problem for the Republic—and a Challenge for Editors," *ASNE—1982: Proceedings of the 1982 Convention of the American Society of Newspaper Editors* (Easton, Pa.: American Society of Newspaper Editors, 1982), p. 14.

10. Mollenhoff, *Investigative Reporting*, p. 354.

11. James Melvin Lee, *History of American Journalism* (Cambridge, Mass.: Riverside, 1923), p. 95.

12. Lee, *History of American Journalism*, p. 195; Dan Schiller, *Objectivity and the News: The Public and the Rise of Commercial Journalism* (Philadelphia: University of Pennsylvania Press, 1981), p. 47.

13. Louis Filler, *The Muckerakers* (University Park: Pennsylvania State University Press, 1976), pp. 9–10.

14. Hallin, *We Keep America on Top*, pp. 20, 24; James W. Carey, "The Communications Revolution and the Professional Communicator," *Sociological Review* 13 (January 1969): 33, 36.

15. Bernard Weisberger, *The American Newspaperman* (Chicago: University of Chicago Press, 1961), p. 160.

16. Stuart Hall, "The Rediscovery of 'Ideology': Return of the Repressed in Media Studies," in Michael Gurevitch, Tony Bennett, James Curran, and Janet Woollacott, eds., *Culture, Society and the Media*, pp. 56–90 (London: Methuen, 1982).

17. Gans, *Deciding What's News*, p. 69.

18. Daniel P. Moynihan, "The Presidency and the Press," *Commentary*, March 1971, pp. 50, 52.

19. O'Neill, "The Power of the Press," pp. 14, 18.

20. See David L. Eason, "On Journalistic Authority: The Janet Cooke Scandal," *Critical Studies in Mass Communication* 3 (1986): 429–47.

21. See Stanley Fish, *Is There a Text in This Class? The Authority of Interpretive Communities* (Cambridge, Mass.: Harvard University Press, 1980).

22. Gans, *Deciding What's News*, p. 196.

23. William Gaines and Ann Marie Lipinski, "Ward Offices Mix Private, City Business," *Chicago Tribune*, part 3 of the series City Council: The Spoils of Power, October 6, 1987, pp. 1, 8.

24. Ibid., p. 8.

25. Of all the improprieties that public officials might commit, it is probably hypocrisy that most outrages Kurkjian's "common man." Thus the peccadilloes

of the powerful may become stories if they suggest hypocrisy. Use of marijuana by a public official, for example, may or may not be a story, according to Marimow. "I don't think anybody knows where, on the hierarchical scale of values, the usage of marijuana is in contemporary society," he said, "but I would say that it is definitely a story if the guy is an outspoken critic of marijuana usage." If mere impropriety combined with hypocrisy seems too ineffectual a basis for a powerful investigative story, recall the fall of presidential aspirant Gary Hart.

26. William K. Marimow, "A City Roughed Up: The K-9 Cases," *Philadelphia Inquirer*, April 15, 1984, reprint, pp. 3, 4.

27. Jack Reed and Lucy Morgan, "Doing Business with the Boss in Pasco," *St. Petersburg Times*, Inside the Pasco County Sheriff's Department: A Special Report, December 11, 1983, p. 1B.

28. Pam Zekman, "Killing Crime: A Police Copout," WBBM-TV, Chicago, 1982.

29. Loretta Tofani, "Terror Behind Bars" *Washington Post*, part 1 of the series Rape in the County Jail: Prince George's Hidden Horror, September 26, 1982, p. A18.

30. Loretta Tofani, "Justice May Not Be Served," *Washington Post*, part 2 of the series Rape in the County Jail, September 27, 1982, p. A8.

31. Max Horkheimer and Theodor W. Adorno, *The Dialectic of Enlightenment* (New York: Herder and Herder, 1972); Herbert Marcuse, *One-Dimensional Man: Studies in the Ideology of Advanced Industrial Societies* (Boston: Beacon, 1964).

32. Hallin, *We Keep America on Top*. See esp. chap. 2, "The American News Media: A Critical Theory Perspective." Hallin draws upon writings by Jürgen Habermas in *Knowledge and Human Interests*, trans. Jeremy J. Shapiro (Boston: Beacon, 1971); *Legitimation Crisis*, trans. Thomas McCarthy (Boston: Beacon, 1975); and *The Structural Transformation of the Public Sphere: An Inquiry Into a Category of Bourgeois Society*, trans. Thomas Burger and Frederick Lawrence (Cambridge, Mass.: MIT Press, 1989).

33. Richard Rorty, "Method and Morality," in Norma Haan, Robert N. Bellah, Paul Rabinow, and William Sullivan, eds., *Social Science as Moral Inquiry* (New York: Columbia University Press, 1983), p. 171. See also Iris Murdoch, *The Sovereignty of Good* (New York: Shocken, 1971).

34. Daniel Callahan, William Green, Bruce Jennings, and Martin Linsky, *Congress and the Media: The Ethical Connection* (Hastings-on-Hudson, N.Y.: Hastings Center, 1985), p. 19.

35. The devaluation of values, Alvin Gouldner contends, is one of the distinguishing characteristics of modern news: "News is defined against the tacit background of the unspoken premises of everyday life, and by the bench marks these provide. But with the spread of news these seen-but-unnoticed bench marks in time become *devalued, precisely because they are not given notice in the value-constructing news reports*" (emphasis in the original). See Alvin W. Gouldner, *The Dialectic of Ideology and Technology: The Origins, Grammar, and Future of Ideology* (New York: Seabury Press, 1976), p. 111.

4. The Irony of Irony-in-Journalism

1. Max Horkheimer and Theodor W. Adorno, *Dialectic of Enlightenment* (New York: Herder & Herder, 1972); Edward S. Herman and Noam Chomsky, *Manufacturing Consent: The Political Economy of the Mass Media* (New York: Pantheon, 1988).

2. Richard Rorty, *Contingency, Irony, and Solidarity* (New York: Cambridge University Press, 1989), p. 63.

3. Ibid., p. 7.

4. James W. Carey, "Journalism and Criticism: The Case of an Undeveloped Profession," *Review of Politics* 36 (1974): 245–46.

5. Rorty, *Contingency*, p. 84.

6. Ibid.

7. Thomas Rosteck, "Irony, Argument, and Reportage in Television Documentary: *See It Now* Versus Senator McCarthy," *Quarterly Journal of Speech* 75 (1989): 295.

8. Rorty, *Contingency*, p. 87.

9. Hayden White, *Metahistory: The Historical Imagination in Nineteenth-Century Europe* (Baltimore, Md.: Johns Hopkins University Press, 1973), p. 37.

10. For a discussion of irony in the language game of daily political reporting, see Theodore L. Glasser and James S. Ettema, "When Facts Don't Speak for Themselves: A Study of the Use of Irony in Daily Journalism," *Critical Studies in Mass Communication* 10 (1993): 322–38.

11. D. C. Muecke, *The Compass of Irony* (London: Methuen, 1969) p. 19, emphasis in original.

12. Ibid., p. 20.

13. Paul Fussell, *The Great War and Modern Memory* (New York: Oxford University Press, 1975), p. 7.

14. Ibid., p. 16.

15. Ibid., p. 35.

16. Muecke, *Compass*, p. 82.

17. Ibid., p. 30.

18. Fussell, *The Great War*, p. 18.

19. Muecke, *Compass*, p. 23.

20. Wayne C. Booth, *The Rhetoric of Irony* (Chicago: University of Chicago Press, 1974), p. 6.

21. Muecke, *Compass*, p. 119.

22. Reinhold Niebuhr, *The Irony of American History* (New York: Scribner's, 1952), p. 153.

23. Quoted in Muecke, *Compass*, p. 47.

24. Northrop Frye, *The Anatomy of Criticism* (Princeton, N.J.: Princeton University Press, 1957), p. 40.

25. Gaye Tuchman, *Making News: A Study in the Construction of Reality* (New York: Free Press, 1978), p. 105.

26. Robert K. Manoff, "Writing the News (By Telling the 'Story')," in Robert

K. Manoff and Michael Schudson, eds., *Reading the News* (New York: Pantheon, 1987), p. 227.

27. Donald L. Barlett and James B. Steele, "How the Influential Win Billions in Special Tax Breaks" *Philadelphia Inquirer*, part 1 of the series The Great Tax Giveaway, April 10, 1988, p. 2.

28. Muecke, *Compass*, p. 102.

29. Donald L. Barlett and James B. Steele, "How Businesses Influence Tax-Writing" *Philadelphia Inquirer*, part 3 of the series The Great Tax Giveaway, April 12, 1988, p. 14.

30. Donald L. Barlett and James B. Steele, "Disguising Those Who Get Tax Breaks" *Philadelphia Inquirer*, part 4 of the series The Great Tax Giveaway, April 13, 1988, p. 17.

31. Bill Dedman, "Atlanta Blacks Losing in Home Loans Scramble," *Atlanta Journal & Constitution*, part 1 of the series The Color of Money, May 1, 1988, p. 15A.

32. Ibid., p. 15A.

33. Muecke, *Compass*, p. 19.

34. Bill Dedman, "A Test That Few Banks Fail—In Federal Eyes" *Atlanta Constitution*, part 3 of the series The Color of Money, May 3, 1988, p. 1.

35. Ann Marie Lipinski and Dean Baquet, "Committees Work a Little and Spend a Lot" *Chicago Tribune*, part 2 of the series City Council: The Spoils of Power, October 5, 1987, p. 1.

36. Ibid.

37. Ibid., p. 8.

38. Ann Marie Lipinski and William Gaines, "An Alderman Who Earned While He Learned" *Chicago Tribune*, part 4 of the series City Council: Spoils of Power, October 7, 1987, p. 14.

39. Ibid., p. 1.

40. Muecke, *Compass*, p. 102.

41. Ibid., pp. 1, 14.

42. Dedman, "Atlanta Blacks Losing," p. 15A.

43. Bill Dedman, "Fulton's Michael Lomax: 'If I Can't Get a Loan, What Black Person Can?'" *Atlanta Journal & Constitution*, part 1 of the series The Color of Money, May 1, 1988, p. 1.

44. Barlett and Steele, "How Businesses Influence Tax-Writing," p. 14.

45. Ibid., p. 16.

46. Barlett and Steele, "How the Influential Win," p. 4.

47. Donald L. Barlett and James B. Steele, "A Millionaire Businessman and His Island Tax Shelter" *Philadelphia Inquirer*, part 2 of the series The Great Tax Giveaway, April 11, 1988, p. 8.

48. Jean Baudrillard, *Selected Writings*, ed. Mark Poster (Stanford, Calif.: Stanford University Press, 1988), pp. 210, 212.

49. Ibid., pp. 213–14.

50. In strikingly similar terms American television critic Mark Crispin Miller expressed dismay at the decline of public discourse with the argument that those

in the public-turned-audience have become "spectators of their own annihilation," and their response is nothing more than "a nervous sneer." The attitude of these spectators, according to Miller, is a relentless irony that has long since degenerated into cynicism: "pure irony denudes the world of every value, devastating—just with a little smile or deft repetition—whatever person, concept, feeling, belief, or tradition it encounters, until there is nothing left but the urge to ironize" [Mark Crispin Miller, *Boxed In: The Culture of TV* (Evanston, Ill.: Northwestern University Press, 1988), p. 321].

51. Nina Eliasoph, "Political Culture and the Presentation of a Political Self: A Study of the Public Sphere in the Spirit of Erving Goffman," *Theory and Society* 19 (1990): 473.

52. Ibid., p. 474.

53. If indeed Baudrillard's prose exhibits rather too much of that Gallic flamboyance, consult the following works (among many others) from the good old U.S. of A.: E. J. Dionne Jr., *Why Americans Hate Politics* (New York: Simon & Schuster, 1991); James M. Fallows, *Breaking the News: How the Media Undermine American Democracy* (New York: Pantheon, 1996); Jeffrey C. Goldfarb, *The Cynical Society: The Culture of Politics and the Politics of Culture in American Life* (Chicago: University of Chicago Press, 1991); Kathleen Hall Jamieson, *Dirty Politics: Deception, Distraction, and Democracy* (New York: Oxford University Press, 1992).

54. Thomas C. Leonard, *The Power of the Press: The Birth of American Political Reporting* (New York: Oxford University Press, 1986), p. 198.

55. Ibid., p. 194.

5. The Morality of Narrative Form

1. Michael Schudson, *The Power of News* (Cambridge, Mass.: Harvard University Press, 1995), p. 54.

2. Ibid., pp. 61, 71.

3. Ibid., p. 55.

4. Hayden White, *The Content of the Form: Narrative Discourse and Historical Representation* (Baltimore, Md.: Johns Hopkins University Press, 1987), pp. 42, 43.

5. Hayden White, *The Tropics of Discourse: Essays in Cultural Criticism* (Baltimore, Md.: Johns Hopkins University Press, 1978), p. 84, emphasis in original.

6. Louis O. Mink, "Narrative Form as a Cognitive Instrument," in Robert H. Canary and Henry Kozicki, eds., *The Writing of History: Literary Form and Historical Understanding* (Madison: University of Wisconsin Press, 1978), p. 147.

7. White, *The Content of the Form*, p. 23.

8. Ibid., p. 21.

9. Ibid., p. 23.

10. See Walter Fisher, "Narration as a Human Communication Paradigm: The Case of Public Moral Argument," *Communication Monographs* 51 (1984): 1–22; and Walter Fisher, "The Narrative Paradigm: An Elaboration," *Communication Monographs* 52 (1985): 347–67.

11. White, *Tropics of Discourse*, p. 91, emphasis in original.

12. Hayden White, "The Narrativization of Real Events," in W. J. T. Mitchell, ed., *On Narrative* (Chicago: University of Chicago Press, 1981), p. 253.

13. John G. Cawelti, *Adventure, Mystery, Romance* (Chicago: University of Chicago Press, 1976), p. 262.

14. Loretta Tofani, "Terror Behind Bars," *Washington Post*, part 1 of the series Rape in the County Jail: Prince George's Hidden Horror, September 26, 1982, p. A1.

15. Ibid., p. A18.

16. Ibid., p. A18.

17. William K. Marimow, "A City Roughed Up: The K-9 Cases," *Philadelphia Inquirer*, April 15, 1984, p.3.

18. Ibid., p. 5.

19. Ibid., p. 6.

20. Pam Zekman, "Killing Crime: A Police Copout," WBBM-TV, Chicago, 1982.

21. Loretta Tofani, "The Strong Inmates Exploit the Weak," *Washington Post*, part 3 of the series Rape in the County Jail: Prince George's Hidden Horror, September 28, 1982, p. A8.

22. Ibid.

23. Tofani, "Terror Behind Bars," p. A18.

24. Loretta Tofani, "The Arrests That Can Lead to Terror and Humiliation," *Washington Post*, part 2 of the series Rape in the County Jail: Prince George's Hidden Horror, September 27, 1982, p. A8.

25. Marimow, "A City Roughed Up," p. 4.

26. Ibid., p. 3.

27. Zekman, "Killing Crime."

28. Ibid.

29. Ibid.

30. White, "The Narrativization of Real Events," p. 253.

6. The Intimate Interdependence of Fact and Value

1. Leon J. Goldstein, *Historical Knowing* (Austin: University of Texas Press, 1976).

2. Paul Ricouer, *History and Truth* (Evanston, Ill.: Northwestern University Press, 1965), p. 23.

3. Hayden White, *The Tropics of Discourse: Essays in Cultural Criticism* (Baltimore, Md.: Johns Hopkins University Press, 1978), p. 83, emphasis in original.

4. Ibid., p. 95.

5. Hayden White, *The Content of the Form: Narrative Discourse and Historical Representation* (Baltimore, Md.: Johns Hopkins University Press, 1987), p. 23.

6. Melvin Pollner, *Mundane Reason: Reality in Everyday and Sociological Discourse* (New York: Cambridge University Press, 1987), p. 26.

7. Hilary Putnam, *Reason, Truth, and History* (New York: Cambridge University Press, 1981), p. 49.

8. Loretta Tofani, "The Repairman," *Washington Post*, part 1 of the series Rape in the County Jail: Prince George's Hidden Horror, September 26, 1982, p. A18.

9. See Lance Bennett, "Rhetorical Transformation of Evidence in Criminal Trials: Creating Grounds for Legal Judgment," *Quarterly Journal of Speech* 65 (1979): 311–23. Bennett's analysis of the courtroom setting shows that a "story strategy underlying a case is executed through an ongoing series of tactical moves that index evidence within the developing story structure" (p. 312). One sort of tactic is the definition of items of evidence or testimony in a way that is consistent with, and adds to, the story the lawyer wishes to tell. Of course, the prosecutor works to limit the definitions of evidence or events to terms that fall within the legal definition of a particular crime, whereas the defense seeks broader or alternative definitions. What Bennett calls "the central action" of the story may require one or more definitions that are likely to be crucial to the case.

10. Stephen C. Pepper, *World Hypotheses: A Study in Evidence* (Berkeley: University of California Press, 1942).

11. To speak of procedures for *evaluating* the credibility of accounts conforms most closely to how journalists would speak of these procedures, but to speak of procedures for *constructing* credibility conforms more closely to what journalists actually do.

12. Pollner, *Mundane Reason*, p. 71.

13. Putnam, *Reason, Truth, and History*, p. 201.

14. William K. Marimow, "A City Roughed Up: The K-9 Cases," *Philadelphia Inquirer*, April 15, 1984, p. 3.

15. Loretta Tofani, "Terror Behind Bars," *Washington Post*, part 1 of the series Rape in the County Jail: Prince George's Hidden Horror, September 26, 1982, p. A18.

7. Journalistic Judgment and the Reporter's Responsibility

1. Although journalists are reluctant to accept responsibility for the consequences of their reporting, they are willing to acknowledge any positive outcomes that seem to certify the public importance of their stories. It is telling that the Pulitzer Prize board cites winners not only for story content but for outcome. Among the winners examined in this book, for example, Marimow's investigation of unwarranted police dog attacks in Philadelphia was cited for leading to an official investigation of the K-9 unit and the removal of a dozen officers from it; Dedman's investigation of racial discrimination practiced by lending institutions in Atlanta was cited for significant reforms in lending policies; and Morgan and Reed's reporting on the Pasco County sheriff was cited for leading to his removal from office by voters.

2. William P. Alston, *Epistemic Justification: Essays in the Theory of Knowledge* (Ithaca, N.Y.: Cornell University Press, 1989), p. 99.

3. Hilary Putnam, *Reason, Truth, and History* (New York: Cambridge

214 7. Journalistic Judgment and the Reporter's Responsibility

University Press, 1981); Alston, *Epistemic Justification*, p. 101, emphasis in original.

4. Donald A. Schön, *The Reflective Practitioner: How Professionals Think in Action* (New York: Basic, 1983).

5. John R. Lyne, "Rhetoric and Everyday Knowledge," *Central States Speech Journal* 32 (1981): 148.

6. Gaye Tuchman, *Making News: A Study in the Social Construction of Reality* (New York: Free Press, 1978); Mark Fishman, *Manufacturing the News* (Austin: University of Texas Press, 1980).

7. Fishman, *Manufacturing the News*, p. 92.

8. Ibid., p. 96; Alvin W. Gouldner, *The Dialectic of Ideology and Technology: The Origins, Grammar, and Future of Ideology* (New York: Seabury, 1976), pp. 122–23.

9. Fishman, *Manufacturing the News*, pp. 94–95.

10. Herbert J. Gans, *The Levittowners: Ways of Life and Politics in a New Suburban Community* (New York: Pantheon, 1967), p. 323.

11. Ronald N. Giere, "Testing Theoretical Hypotheses," in John Earman, ed., *Testing Scientific Theories: Minnesota Studies in the Philosophy of Science*, vol. 10 (Minneapolis: University of Minnesota Press, 1983).

12. Michael Schudson, *Discovering the News* (New York: Basic, 1978), p. 192.

13. Dean Baquet and Ann Marie Lipinski, "Politics, Pettiness, Profiteering," *Chicago Tribune*, part 1 of the series City Council: Spoils of Power, October 4, 1987, p. 1.

14. Ibid., p. 12.

15. As the story explained, public claims adjusters help fire victims collect as much as possible from their insurance companies in return for a commission.

16. Lou Kilzer and Chris Ison, "A Culture of Arson" *Star Tribune*, part 1 of the series Fire in St. Paul, October 29, 1989, p. A1.

17. Lou Kilzer and Chris Ison, "Investigations Often Fall Short," *Star Tribune*, part 2 of the series Fire in St. Paul, October 30, 1989, p. A8.

18. Putnam, *Reason, Truth, and History*, p. 201.

19. Lance Bennett, "Rhetorical Transformation of Evidence in Criminal Trials: Creating Grounds for Legal Judgment," *Quarterly Journal of Speech* 65 (1979): 311–23.

20. William K. Marimow, "A City Roughed Up: The K-9 Cases," *Philadelphia Inquirer*, April 15, 1984, p. 8.

21. Ibid., p. 9.

22. Donald L. Barlett and James B. Steele, "How the Influential Win Billions in Special Tax Breaks," *Philadelphia Inquirer*, part 1 of the series The Great Tax Giveaway, April 10, 1988, p. 2.

23. Ibid., p. 2.

24. Donald L. Barlett and James B. Steele, "$4 Million Saving Sought for Widow," *Philadelphia Inquirer*, part 1 of the series The Great Tax Giveaway, April 10, 1988, p. 5.

8. The Value(s) of News

1. Donald Schön, *The Reflective Practitioner: How Professionals Think in Action* (New York: Basic, 1983).

2. Jay Rosen, "Beyond Objectivity," *Nieman Reports* 47 (Winter 1993): 53. Rosen is joined in his call for "public" or "civic" journalism by a number of practitioners and critics. Among many examples see Arthur Charity, *Doing Public Journalism* (New York: Guilford, 1995); James Fallows, *Breaking the News: How the Media Undermine American Democracy* (New York: Pantheon, 1996); Theodore L. Glasser (ed.), *The Idea of Public Journalism* (New York: Guilford, 1998); Davis Merritt, *Public Journalism and Public Life: Why Telling the News Is Not Enough* (Hillside, N.J.: Lawrence Erlbaum, 1995).

3. Jack Fuller, *News Values: Ideas for an Information Age* (Chicago: University of Chicago Press, 1996), p. 14

4. Ibid., pp. 19, 91.

5. Ibid., pp. 35, 88.

6. Richard Rorty, *Philosophy and the Mirror of Nature* (Princeton, N.J.: Princeton University Press, 1979), p. 42. See also Theodore L. Glasser, "Journalism's Glassy Essence," *Journalism and Mass Communication Quarterly* 73 (1996): 784–86.

7. Metaphors of glass also shape conceptions of media marketing. "To survive," Fuller wrote, "a newspaper must reflect a specific audience, usually by holding a mirror up to particular place" (*News Values*, p. 69). Such metaphors have even generated would-be theories of mass communication. Broadcasting, in the muddled metaphor of a former Federal Communications Commission member, "is an electronic mirror that reflects a vague and ambiguous image of what is behind it, as well as what is in front of it" (Lee Loevinger, "The Ambiguous Mirror: The Reflective-Projective Theory of Broadcasting and Mass Communications," *Journal of Broadcasting*, 12 [Spring 1968]: 108).

8. Quoted in Fred Fedler, John R. Bender, Lucinda Davenport, and Paul E. Kostyu, *Reporting for the Media*, 6th ed. (New York: Harcourt Brace, 1997), p. 534.

9. "Docudrama Strikes Again," Editorial, *New York Times*, February 10, 1985, p. 20E. Carlin Romano uses this and other examples as the basis for his conclusion that, "in the absence of authoritative standards for journalistic concepts, the old-fashioned view that 'news' is simply a mirror placed before reality still lives." See Carlin Romano, "The Grisly Truth About Bare Facts," in Robert Karl Manoff and Michael Schudson, eds., *Reading the News* (New York: Pantheon, 1987), p. 39.

10. Mark Johnson, *Moral Imagination: Implications of Cognitive Science for Ethics* (Chicago: University of Chicago Press, 1993), p. 35. Johnson's argument that metaphors, as opposed to abstract principles, serve "as the basis for our self-critical reflections on our values, ideals and institutions" (p. 35) parallels Rorty's observation that "pictures rather than propositions, metaphors rather that statements . . . determine most of our philosophical convictions" (*Philosophy and the Mirror of Nature*, p. 12).

11. Rorty, *Philosophy and the Mirror of Nature*, pp. 3, 12.

12. John Durham Peters, "John Locke, the Individual, and the Origin of Communication," *Quarterly Journal of Speech* 75 (1989): 394.

13. For an examination of the role of investigative journalism in the process of political agenda setting see David L. Protess et al., *The Journalism of Outrage: Investigative Reporting and Agenda Building in America* (New York: Guilford, 1991).

14. Arthur Anderson & Co., "Philadelphia Inquirer Series on Special Tax Breaks May Have Lasting Impact," *Washington Tax Letter*, September 1988, p. 2.

15. Protess et al., *Journalism of Outrage*, pp. 231–57.

16. Don Shelby's story (see chapter 7) about a judge and other locally prominent men accused of sexually abusing children—all of them boys—provides an interesting example of contestation. Gay rights groups found the story—particularly the segment about the judge, whose reported abuse of children was patronage of adolescent prostitutes—to be less an exposé of child abuse than an exercise in gay bashing. Shelby responded that the story was intended to reveal a pattern of protection for the prominent—a pattern that had nothing to do with sexual orientation. Whatever the reporter's intent, his story raised interesting questions about the choice of specific cases to illustrate a pattern of wrongdoing.

17. Individualism, responsible capitalism, and small-town pastoralism are among the "enduring values" of news identified by Herbert Gans in *Deciding What's News: A Study of CBS Evening News, NBC Nightly News, Newsweek, and Time* (New York: Vintage, 1980), pp. 39–69.

18. For other conversational conceptions of journalism see Rob Anderson, Robert Dardenne, and George M. Killenberg, *The Conversation of Journalism: Communication, Community, and News* (Westport, Conn.: Praeger, 1994). James W. Carey, "The Press and Public Discourse," *Center Magazine*, March—April 1987, pp. 4–16; James W. Carey, "The Press, Public Opinion, and Public Discourse," in Theodore L. Glasser and Charles T. Salmon (eds.), *Public Opinion and the Communication of Consent*, pp. 373–402 (New York: Guilford, 1995); Clifford G. Christians, John P. Ferre, and P. Mark Fackler, *Good News: Social Ethics and the Press* (New York: Oxford University Press, 1993); Theodore L. Glasser (ed.), *The Idea of Public Journalism* (New York: Guilford, 1998). For a recent examination of the role of the news media in public deliberation see Benjamin I. Page, *Who Deliberates: Mass Media in Modern Democracy* (Chicago: University of Chicago Press, 1996). Some other important books on public deliberation include Benjamin Barber, *Strong Democracy: Participatory Politics for a New Age* (Berkeley: University of California Press, 1984); and James S. Fishkin, *Democracy and Deliberation: New Directions for Democratic Reform* (New Haven, Conn.: Yale University Press, 1991). For a critique of the role of conversation in public affairs that also develops the ideal of "public-ness" see: Michael Schudson, "Why Conversation Is Not the Soul of Democracy," *Critical Studies in Mass Communication* 14 (1997): 297-309.

19. Jürgen Habermas, *The Structural Transformation of the Public Sphere: An Inquiry Into a Category of Bourgeois Society*, trans. Thomas Burger and Frederick Lawrence (Cambridge, Mass.: MIT Press, 1989), p. 201. For a discussion of

the history of the idea of public opinion and the related concept of publicity, see Habermas, *Structural Transformation*, pp. 89–140. See also Keith Michael Baker, "Defining the Public Sphere in Eighteenth-Century France: Variations on a Theme by Habermas," in Craig Calhoun, ed., *Habermas and the Public Sphere*, pp. 181–211 (Cambridge, Mass.: MIT Press, 1992); John Durham Peters, "Historical Tensions in the Concept of Public Opinion," in Theodore L. Glasser and Charles T. Salmon, eds., *Public Opinion and the Communication of Consent*, pp. 3–32 (New York: Guilford, 1995).

20. Alvin W. Gouldner, *The Dialectic of Ideology and Technology: The Origins, Grammar, and Future of Ideology* (New York: Seabury, 1796), p. 158.

21. Peters, "Historical Tensions," p. 25. This argument about the role of investigative journalism is documented in Protess et al., *Journalism of Outrage*. See also James S. Ettema et al., "Agenda Setting as Politics: A Case Study of the Press-Public-Policy Connection," *Communication* 12 (1991): 75–98.

22. Peters, "Historical Tensions," p. 26. Here Peters develops an argument formulated by Daniel Dyan and Elihu Katz in *Media Events: The Live Broadcasting of History* (Cambridge, Mass.: Harvard University Press, 1992).

23. Peters, "Historical Tensions," p. 25.

24. Throughout this book our goal has been to critique the intellectual, rather than the economic, foundations of American journalism. However, Dedman's comments about his departure from the *Atlanta Journal & Constitution* are a useful reminder that intellectual and economic constraints are closely connected. See, for example, John H. McManus, *Market-Driven Journalism: Let the Citizen Beware?* (Thousand Oaks, Calif.: Sage, 1994) and Doug Underwood, *When MBAs Rule the Newsroom: How the Marketers and Managers are Reshaping Today's Media* (New York: Columbia University Press, 1993).

25. Journalists may genuinely want the villain's version of events, both as an assurance of fairness and as a response to the call for accountability. However, the villain must always remain a villain. It makes sense, then, that the investigative reporters at *60 Minutes* retain tight control of their narratives by insisting on *taped* interviews with the villains. See Richard Campbell, *60 Minutes and the News: A Mythology for Middle America* (Urbana: University of Illinois Press, 1991), p. 65.

26. Bill Dedman, "State Banking Chief Urges Lending Law," *Atlanta Constitution*, May 7, 1988, p. 1; Bill Dedman, "Atlanta NAACP Calls for Boycott, Federal Probe of Banks," *Atlanta Constitution*, May 10, 1988, p. 1; Bill Dedman, "Banks Plan to Lend $65 Million at Low Interest," *Atlanta Constitution*, May 13, 1988, p. 1.

27. Richard Rorty, *Contingency, Irony, and Solidarity* (New York: Cambridge University Press, 1989), p. 190. For an application of Rorty's ideas about solidarity to another genre of journalism, war reporting, see James S. Ettema, "Discourse That Is Closer to Silence Than to Talk: The Politics and the Possibilities of Reporting on Victims of War," *Critical Studies in Mass Communication* 11 (1994): 1–21. See also Martha C. Nussbaum, *Poetic Justice: The Literary Imagination and Public Life* (Boston: Beacon, 1995).

28. Rorty, *Contingency, Irony, and Solidarity*, p. 192.

29. James W. Carey, "The Press and Public Discourse," *Center Magazine*, March–April 1987, p. 14.

30. Richard Rorty, *Objectivism, Relativism, and Truth: Philosophical Papers*, vol. 1 (New York: Cambridge University Press, 1991), p. 29.

31. Jürgen Habermas, *Justification and Application: Remarks on Discourse Ethics*, trans. Ciaran P. Cronin (Cambridge, Mass.: MIT Press, 1993), p. 154.

32. See, for example, Rorty, *Contingency, Irony, and Solidarity* and *Objectivism, Relativism, and Truth*; Habermas, *Justification and Application*, and *Moral Consciousness and Communicative Action*, trans. Christian Lenhardt and Shierry Weber Nicholsen (Cambridge, Mass: MIT Press, 1990); William Rehg, *Insight and Solidarity: A Study in the Discourse Ethics of Jürgen Habermas* (Berkeley: University of California Press, 1994). Clearly, Rorty rejects Charles Taylor's pleas for a truly common understanding. When dealing with "different" people, according to Rorty, the "only common ground on which we can get together is that defined by the overlap between their communal beliefs and desires and our own" (*Objectivism, Relativism, and Truth*, pp. 212–13).

33. Charles Taylor, "Cross Purposes: The Liberal-Communitarian Debate," in N. L. Rosenblum, ed., *Liberalism and the Moral Life* (Cambridge, Mass.: Harvard University Press, 1989), pp. 167–78.

Bibliography

Akhavan-Majid, Roya. "Questionnaire Wording and Editor Perceptions." *Mass Comm Review*, 21 (1994): 250–58.

Alston, William P. *Epistemic Justification: Essays in the Theory of Knowledge*. Ithaca, N.Y.: Cornell University Press, 1989.

Anderson, Rob, Robert Dardene, and George M. Killenberg. *The Conversation of Journalism: Communication, Community, and News*. Westport, Conn.: Praeger, 1994.

Baker, Keith Michael. "Defining the Public Sphere in Eighteenth-Century France: Variations on a Theme by Habermas." In Craig Calhoun, ed., *Habermas and the Public Sphere*, pp. 181–211. Cambridge, Mass.: MIT Press, 1992.

Barber, Benjamin. *Strong Democracy: Participatory Politics for a New Age*. Berkeley: University of California Press, 1984.

Baudrillard, Jean. *Selected Writings*. Edited by Mark Poster. Stanford, Calif.: Stanford University Press, 1988.

Behrens, John C. *The Typewriter Guerrillas: Closeups of Twenty Top Investigative Reporters*. Chicago: Nelson-Hall, 1977.

Bennett, W. Lance. "Rhetorical Transformation of Evidence in Criminal Trials: Creating Grounds for Legal Judgment." *Quarterly Journal of Speech* 65 (1979): 311–23.

Bennett, Lance W. and Regina G. Lawrence. "News Icons and the Mainstreaming of Social Change." *Journal of Communication* 45 (1995): 20–39.

Blasi, Vincent. "The Checking Value in First Amendment Theory." *American Bar Foundation Research Journal*, no. 3 (1977): 520–642.

Booth, Wayne C. *The Rhetoric of Irony*. Chicago: University of Chicago Press, 1974.

Callahan, Daniel, William Green, Bruce Jennings, and Martin Linsky. *Congress and the Media: The Ethical Connection.* Hastings-on-Hudson, N.Y.: Hastings Center, 1985.

Campbell, Richard. *60 Minutes and the News: A Mythology for Middle America.* Urbana: University of Illinois Press, 1991.

Carey, James W. "The Communications Revolution and the Professional Communicator." *Sociological Review Monograph* 13 (January 1969): 23–38.

——. "Journalism and Criticism: The Case of an Undeveloped Profession." *Review of Politics* 36 (1974): 227–49.

——. "The Press and Public Discourse." *Center Magazine,* March–April 1987, pp. 4–16.

——. "The Press, Public Opinion, and Public Discourse." In Theodore L. Glasser and Charles T. Salmon, eds., *Public Opinion and the Communication of Consent,* pp. 373–402. New York: Guilford, 1995.

Cawelti, John G. *Adventure, Mystery, Romance.* Chicago: University of Chicago Press, 1976.

Charity, Arthur. *Doing Public Journalism.* New York: Guilford, 1995.

Christians, Clifford G., John P. Ferre, and P. Mark Fackler. *Good News: Social Ethics and the Press.* New York: Oxford University Press, 1993.

Condit, Celeste Michelle. "Crafting Virtue: The Rhetorical Construction of Public Morality." *Quarterly Journal of Speech* 73 (1987): 79–97.

Dionne, E. J. Jr. *Why Americans Hate Politics.* New York: Simon & Schuster, 1991.

Dyan, Daniel, and Elihu Katz. *Media Events: The Live Broadcasting of History.* Cambridge, Mass.: Harvard University Press, 1992.

Eason, David L. "On Journalistic Authority: The Janet Cooke Scandal." *Critical Studies in Mass Communication* 3 (1986): 429–47.

Eliasoph, Nina. "Political Culture and the Presentation of a Political Self: A Study of the Public Sphere in the Spirit of Erving Goffman." *Theory and Society* 19 (1990): 465–94.

Entman, Robert M. "Framing: Toward Clarification of a Fractured Paradigm," *Journal of Communication* 43, no 4 (1993): 6–27.

——. "Framing U.S. Coverage of International News: Contrasts in Narratives of the KAL and Iran Air Incidents." *Journal of Communication* 41, no. 4 (1991): 6–27.

Ettema, James S. "Discourse That Is Closer to Silence Than to Talk: The Politics and the Possibilities of Reporting on Victims of War." *Critical Studies in Mass Communication* 11 (1994): 1–21.

Ettema, James S. and Theodore L. Glasser. "Narrative Form and Moral Force: The Realization of Innocence and Guilt Through Investigative Journalism." *Journal of Communication* 38, no. 3 (1988): 8–26.

——. "The Irony in—and of—Journalism: A Case Study in the Language of Liberal Democracy." *Journal of Communication* 44, no. 2 (1994): 5–28.

Ettema, James S., David L. Protess, Donna R. Leff, Peter V. Miller, Jack Doppelt, and Fay Lomax Cook. "Agenda Setting as Politics: A Case Study of the Press-Public-Policy Connection." *Communication* 12 (1991): 75–98.

Fallows, James. *Breaking the News: How the Media Undermine American Democracy.* New York: Pantheon, 1996.

Fedler, Fred, John R. Bender, Lucinda Davenport, and Paul E. Kostyu. *Reporting for the Media,* 6th ed. New York: Harcourt Brace, 1997.

Filler, Louis. *The Muckrakers.* University Park: Pennsylvania State University Press, 1976.

Fish, Stanley. *Is There a Text in This Class? The Authority of Interpretive Communities.* Cambridge, Mass.: Harvard University Press, 1980.

Fisher, Walter. "Narration as a Human Communication Paradigm: The Case of Public Moral Argument." *Communication Monographs* 51 (1984): 1–22.

———. "The Narrative Paradigm: An Elaboration." *Communication Monographs* 52 (1985): 347–67.

Fishkin, James S. *Democracy and Deliberation: New Directions for Democratic Reform.* New Haven, Conn.: Yale University Press, 1991.

Fishman, Mark. *Manufacturing the News.* Austin: University of Texas Press, 1980.

Frye, Northrop. *The Anatomy of Criticism.* Princeton, N.J.: Princeton University Press, 1957.

Fuller, Jack. *News Values: Ideas for an Information Age.* Chicago: University of Chicago Press, 1996.

Fussell, Paul. *The Great War and Modern Memory.* New York: Oxford University Press, 1975.

Gamson, William A. and Andre Modigliani. "Media Discourse and Public Opinion on Nuclear Power: A Constructionist Approach." *American Journal of Sociology* 95 (1989): 1–37.

Gans, Herbert. *The Levittowners: Ways of Life and Politics in a New Suburban Community.* New York: Pantheon, 1967.

———. *Deciding What's News: A Study of CBS Evening News, NBC Nightly News, Newsweek, and Time.* New York: Vintage, 1980.

Geertz, Clifford. *The Interpretation of Cultures.* New York: Basic, 1973.

———. *Works and Lives: The Anthropologist as Author.* Stanford, Calif.: Stanford University Press, 1988.

Giere, Ronald N. "Testing Theoretical Hypotheses." In *Testing Scientific Theories: Minnesota Studies in the Philosophy of Science,* vol. 10. Minneapolis: University of Minnesota Press, 1983.

Gitlin, Todd. *The Whole World Is Watching: The Role of the News Media in the Making and Unmaking of the New Left.* Berkeley: University of California Press, 1980.

Glasser, Theodore L. and James S. Ettema, "Investigative Journalism and the Moral Order." *Critical Studies in Mass Communication* 6 (1989): 1–20.

———. "When the Facts Don't Speak for Themselves: A Study of the Use of Irony in Daily Journalism." *Critical Studies in Mass Communication* 10 (1993): 322–38.

Glasser, Theodore L., ed. *The Idea of Public Journalism.* New York: Guilford, 1998.

———. "Journalism's Glassy Essence." *Journalism and Mass Communication Quarterly* 73 (1996): 784–86.

Goldfarb, Jeffrey C. *The Cynical Society: The Culture of Politics and the Politics of Culture in American Life.* Chicago: University of Chicago Press, 1991.

Goldstein, Leon J. *Historical Knowing.* Austin: University of Texas Press, 1976.

Gouldner, Alvin W. *The Dialectic of Ideology and Technology: The Origins, Grammar, and Future of Ideology.* New York: Seabury, 1976.

Habermas, Jürgen. *Knowledge and Human Interests.* Translated by Jeremy J. Shapiro. Boston: Beacon, 1971.

———. *Legitimation Crisis.* Translated by Thomas McCarthy. Boston: Beacon, 1975.

———. *The Structural Transformation of the Public Sphere: An Inquiry into a Category of Bourgeois Society.* Translated by Thomas Burger and Frederick Lawrence. Cambridge, Mass.: MIT Press, 1989.

———. *Moral Consciousness and Communicative Action.* Translated by Christian Lenhardt and Shierry Weber Nicholsen. Cambridge, Mass: MIT Press, 1990.

———. *Justification and Application: Remarks on Discourse Ethics.* Translated by Ciaran P. Cronin. Cambridge, Mass: MIT Press, 1993.

Hall, Stuart. "The Rediscovery of 'Ideology': Return of the Repressed in Media Studies." In Michael Gurevitch, Tony Bennett, James Curran, and Janet Woollacott, eds., *Culture, Society, and the Media,* , pp. 56–90. London: Methuen, 1982.

Hallin, Daniel C. *Keeping America on Top of the World: Television Journalism and the Public Sphere.* New York: Routledge, 1994.

Herman, Edward S. and Noam Chomsky. *Manufacturing Consent: The Political Economy of the Mass Media.* New York: Pantheon, 1988.

Horkheimer, Max and Theodor W. Adorno. *The Dialectic of Enlightenment.* New York: Herder & Herder, 1972.

Jamieson, Kathleen Hall. *Dirty Politics: Deception, Distraction, and Democracy.* New York: Oxford University Press, 1992.

Johnson, Mark. *Moral Imagination: Implications of Cognitive Science for Ethics.* Chicago: University of Chicago Press, 1993.

Lee, James Melvin. *History of American Journalism.* Cambridge, Mass.: Riverside, 1923.

Leonard, Thomas C. *The Power of the Press.* New York: Oxford University Press, 1986.

Lichter, S. Robert, Stanley Rothman, and Linda S. Lichter. *The Media Elite: America's New Powerbrokers.* Bethesda, Md.: Adler & Adler, 1986.

Loevinger, Lee. "The Ambiguous Mirror: The Reflective-Projective Theory of Broadcasting." *Journal of Broadcasting* 12 (Spring 1968): 97–116.

Lyne, John R. "Rhetoric and Everyday Knowledge." *Central States Speech Journal* 32 (1981): 145–52.

Manoff, Robert K. "Writing the News (By Telling the 'Story')." In Robert K. Manoff and Michael Schudson, eds., *Reading the News,* pp. 197–229. New York: Pantheon, 1987.

Marcuse, Herbert. *One-Dimensional Man: Studies in the Ideology of Advanced Industrial Societies.* Boston: Beacon, 1964.

McManus, John H., *Market-Driven Journalism: Let the Citizen Beware?* Thousand Oaks, Calif.: Sage, 1994.

Merritt, Davis. *Public Journalism and Public Life: Why Telling the News Is Not Enough.* Hillside, N.J.: Lawrence Erlbaum, 1995.

Miller, Mark Crispin. *Boxed In: The Culture of TV.* Evanston, Ill.: Northwestern University Press, 1988.

Mink, Louis O. "Narrative Form as a Cognitive Instrument. In Robert H. Canary and Henry Kozicki, eds., *The Writing of History: Literary Form and Historical Understanding*, pp. 129–49. Madison: University of Wisconsin Press, 1978.

Mollenhoff, Clark R. *Investigative Reporting: From Court House to White House.* New York: Macmillan, 1981.

Moynihan, Daniel P. "The Presidency and the Press." *Commentary*, March 1971, pp. 41–52.

Muecke, D. C. *The Compass of Irony.* London: Methuen, 1969.

———. *Irony and the Ironic.* London: Methuen, 1982.

Murdoch, Iris. *The Sovereignty of Good.* New York: Shocken, 1971.

Niebuhr, Reinhold. *The Irony of American History.* New York: Scribner's, 1952.

Nussbaum, Martha C. *Poetic Justice: The Literary Imagination and Public Life.* Boston: Beacon, 1995.

O'Neill, Michael J. "The Power of the Press: A Problem for the Republic—and a Challenge for Editors." In *ASNE—1982: Proceedings of the 1982 Convention of the American Society of Newspaper Editors*, pp. 11–19. Easton, Pa.: American Society of Newspaper Editors, 1982.

Page, Benjamin I. *Who Deliberates: Mass Media in Modern Democracy.* Chicago: University of Chicago Press, 1996.

Pepper, Stephen C. *World Hypotheses: A Study in Evidence.* Berkeley: University of California Press, 1942.

Peters, John Durham. "John Locke, the Individual, and the Origin of Communication." *Quarterly Journal of Speech* 75 (1989): 387–99.

———. "Historical Tensions in the Concept of Public Opinion." In Theodore L. Glasser and Charles T. Salmon, eds., *Public Opinion and the Communication of Consent*, pp. 3–32. New York: Guilford, 1995.

Protess, David L., Fay Lomax Cook, Jack C. Doppelt, James S. Ettema, Margaret T. Gordon, Donna R. Leff, and Peter Miller. *The Journalism of Outrage Investigative Reporting and Agenda Building in America.* New York: Guilford, 1991.

Pollner, Melvin. *Mundane Reason: Reality in Everyday and Sociological Discourse.* New York: Cambridge University Press, 1987.

Putnam, Hilary. *Reason, Truth, and History.* New York: Cambridge University Press, 1981.

Rehg, William. *Insight and Solidarity: A Study in the Discourse Ethics of Jürgen Habermas.* Berkeley: University of California Press, 1994.

Ricoeur, Paul. *History and Truth*. Evanston, Ill.: Northwestern University Press, 1965.

Romano, Carlin. "The Grisly Truth About Bare Facts." In Robert Karl Manoff and Michael Schudson, eds., *Reading the News*, pp. 38–78. New York: Pantheon, 1987.

Rorty, Richard. *Philosophy and the Mirror of Nature*. Princeton, N.J.: Princeton University Press, 1979.

——. "Method and Morality." In Norma Haan, Robert N. Bellah, Paul Rabinow, and William Sullivan, eds., *Social Sciences as Moral Inquiry*, pp. 155–70. New York: Columbia University Press, 1983.

——. *Contingency, Irony, and Solidarity*. New York: Cambridge University Press, 1989.

——. *Objectivism, Relativism, and Truth: Philosophical Papers*, vol. 1. New York: Cambridge University Press, 1991.

Rosen, Jay. "Beyond Objectivity." *Nieman Reports* 47 (Winter 1993): 48–53.

Rosteck, Thomas. "Irony, Argument, and Reportage in Television Documentary: *See It Now* Versus Senator McCarthy," *Quarterly Journal of Speech* 75 (1989): 277–98.

Schiller, Dan. *Objectivity and the News: The Public and the Rise of Commercial Journalism*. Philadelphia: University of Pennsylvania Press, 1981.

Schön, Donald. *The Reflective Practitioner: How Professionals Think in Action*. New York: Basic, 1983.

Schudson, Michael. *Discovering the News*. New York: Basic, 1978.

——. *The Power of News*. Cambridge, Mass.: Harvard University Press, 1995.

——. "Why Conversation Is Not the Soul of Democracy." *Critical Studies in Mass Communication* 14 (1997): 297–309.

Taylor, Charles. "Cross Purposes: The Liberal-Communitarian Debate." In N. L. Rosenblum, ed., *Liberalism and the Moral Life*, pp. 159–82. Cambridge, Mass.: Harvard University Press, 1989.

Tuchman, Gaye. *Making News: A Study in the Construction of Reality*. New York: Free Press, 1978.

Ullmann, John. *Investigative Reporting: Advanced Methods and Techniques*. New York: St. Martin's, 1995.

Ullmann, John and Steve Honeyman, eds. *The Reporter's Handbook: An Investigator's Guide to Documents and Records*. New York: St. Martin's, 1983.

Underwood, Doug. *When MBAs Rule the Newsroom: How the Marketers and Managers Are Reshaping Today's Media*. New York: Columbia University Press, 1993.

Waisbord, Silvio R. "Investigative Journalism and Political Accountability in South American Democracies." *Critical Studies in Mass Communication* 13 (1996): 343–63.

Weaver, David H. and G. Cleveland Wilhoit. *The American Journalist: A Portrait of U.S. News People and Their Work*. Bloomington: Indiana University Press, 1986.

——. *The American Journalist in the 1990s: U.S. News People at the End of an Era*. Mahwah, N.J.: Lawrence Erlbaum, 1996.

Weir, David and Dan Noyes. *Raising Hell*. Reading, Mass.: Addison-Wesley, 1983.

Weisberger, Bernard. *The American Newspaperman*. Chicago: University of Chicago Press, 1961.

White, Hayden. *Metahistory: The Historical Imagination in Nineteenth-Century Europe*. Baltimore, Md.: Johns Hopkins University Press, 1973.

——. *The Tropics of Discourse: Essays on Cultural Criticism*. Baltimore, Md.: Johns Hopkins University Press, 1978.

——. "The Narrativization of Real Events," in W. J. T. Mitchell, ed., *On Narrative*, pp. 249–54. Chicago: University of Chicago Press, 1981

——. *The Content of the Form: Narrative Discourse and Historical Representation*. Baltimore, Md.: Johns Hopkins University Press, 1987.

Index